Danny J. Hubbard

Apocalypse Alive

Cover Artwork by Chris Lewis
www.clewiscreative.com
clewiscreative@hotmail.com

Reveal Publishing
4 Heritage Way
Oxford, Al 36203
http://www.revealpublishing.com

Unattributed quotations are by Danny J. Hubbard
All scripture references are from the King James Version.

Edition ISBNs
Softcover   978-0-9797005-1-4

First Edition 2008.
Printed in the United States

Contents

Introduction

Hollywood has spent billions of dollars producing movies depicting the Battle of Armageddon, Judgment Day, Battle of Holy Angels versus Evil Angels, Nuclear Holocaust, mega tsunamis, super earthquakes, catastrophic hurricanes, pestilence such as the bird flu and other viral disasters, the End of the World, along with other end-time related subjects. Everyone today seems to be enamored with natural disasters and the end of the world events. Many live in fear that they are living in the age where they might see the world come to a cataclysmic end.

Will there be a battle known as Armageddon? Will there be a Judgment Day? Will there be a battle of Holy Angels versus Evil Angels? Will there be a Nuclear Holocaust, earthquakes, erupting volcanoes and other disasters? Will this world, as we know it today, come to an end? You may be surprised at the answers found in this book. "*Apocalypse Alive*" will use the scriptures of the Bible to prove that the answers found within this book are supported by the Bible itself. As you will see, scripture will interpret scripture to provide you with the answers.

To the non-Christian, fear of the future is a very valid emotion and should not be discounted. To the true Christian, concern for the future is an emotion we all should experience. Concern for those non-Christians so they will come to know the truth found in God's word. So many people say they do not understand the Book of Revelation. Maybe you fall into this category. Some say they understand some of the Book of Revelation, but become confused about the order of events. If you want to know the answers to the questions posed above, then this book is for you. This book will use the Book of Revelation as an outline to determine what the future holds. I have organized the Book of Revelation chronologically, so you can see the order of events as they unfold. I will fill in between the lines of Revelation with other Bible scriptures to show how God wonderfully designed and planned all the details.

When you finish reading this book, you will have found the answers to the questions above. You will see that the time in which we live, are exciting to say the least. You will see and understand end-time prophecies like you have never understood them before. This book will bring hope to everyone who reads it and heeds its message. Fasten you spiritual seat belts and hang on for a spiritual ride into the future. A ride that will exercise every emotion you could possibly muster. Come with us as we embark on a journey into *"Apocalypse Alive!"*

Acknowledgments

I have not attempted to make Apocalypse Alive an exhaustive study of the end-time events. It was written to help anyone who wants to understand what the future will bring, based on the scriptures of the Bible.

The burden came to me three years ago to begin the writing of Apocalypse Alive, after having an end-time events discussion with my uncle, Donald Hubbard. He had spent time in the first Persian Gulf War back in the early 1990's and came out of the war excited with what the Bible had to say about Iraq and other end-time events. During our discussions it became apparent that even though there are many books written about these events, there seemed to be a lack of writings on the actual chronology of the events, along with supporting scripture to further solidify the timing of the events.

As a result, God placed on my heart the overwhelming desire to write and explain in a "simple and easy to understand" language the chronological order of the events as they occur, using the Book of Revelation as the outline to my book.

I could not have begun to write such a book without the help of many who were instrumental in my Christian growth. I give credit to my late Dad and Mom, Calvin "Cowboy" and Virginia Hubbard for their consistent prayers and knowledge of the Bible. Dad was a scholar when it came to the Bible and end-time events and he taught it where and whenever he could. Mom was the silent Godly prayer warrior that showed the sweet spirit of God within her every breath. They are at home with the Lord today and will be the first to begin the Rapture they so excitingly taught about.

I also want to thank Dr. Don Richards of Loganville, Georgia who was pastor to me and my family for over sixteen years and who preached the Bible and the Second Coming of Christ in truth and with zeal. He was our Bible mentor for so many years and we thank him for his steadfast preaching and adherence to the truths of the Bible.

There were several who helped with editing and supplying photographs and ideas and I am extremely grateful for their contributions as well. These are Rev. Jerry Johnston, Eloise Burgess, John and Jana Nowell, Shari Vickers, JoAnn Vickers, Dr. Don Richards and Donald Hubbard.

I want to thank Mrs. Marsha Johnson for her grammatical editing skills. A special thanks goes to Chris Lewis for his artistic talents and producing the locust demons and background scenery seen on the cover of this book. This eye-catching art brings visual effects to the Locust Demons described in Revelation 9 and Chris has a wonderful talent for creating this scene. His contact information is located in the front of the book.

Most of all there are two people in my life who gave me constant encouragement and love. I want to thank my wife Charlotte for all the hours she spent editing, correcting, supplying input, encouraging and praying for me and for the production of this book. She spent many hours in prayer and patience while I was sitting at my computer penning my thoughts and ideas for over three years. I also want to thank my daughter, Natalie Hubbard, for her excitement and encouragement. She directed me in completing the layout of the book and organizing it for printing. In addition, she taught me how to format the pictures that are contained in the book so they would print correctly. Her ability to visualize in 3D was instrumental in creating the idea for the book cover and her suggestions were used in the cover design. Charlotte and Natalie are my biggest promoters and I love them both more than words can describe.

Lastly, yet truly first, I want to thank my Lord and Savior Jesus Christ for salvation and placing the desire on my heart to undertake such an awesome project. I would never have viewed myself writing a book of any kind, but God knows the hearts of man and uses those who are willing to do what He desires. I am not worthy to produce such a book, but with

God's help I was able to accomplish what I could have never done alone.

May this book bring you blessings and understanding that only the Holy Spirit can bring to those who have the desire to understand. I pray the same blessings on the reader of this book as is stated in Revelation 1:3, "Blessed *is* he that readeth, and they that hear the words of this prophecy, and keep those things which are written therein: for the time *is* at hand;" Amen!

1

Letters to the Seven Churches

As we begin our study, these letters to the seven churches will depict church history from the beginning to the end of the church age.

Rev. 1:1
The Revelation of Jesus Christ, which God gave unto him, to show unto his servants things which must shortly come to pass; and he sent and signified *it* by his angel unto his servant John:
Rev. 1:2
Who bare record of the word of God, and of the testimony of Jesus Christ, and of all things that he saw.
Rev. 1:3
Blessed *is* he that readeth, and they that hear the words of this prophecy, and keep those things which are written therein: for the time *is* at hand.

This is the Revelation of Jesus Christ given to John the Apostle, showing John what will happen in the last days. The key statement for the entire Book of The Revelation is found in Chapter 1 Verse 3. "Keep" in the Greek means to "guard from loss or injury by keeping the eye upon." It is in the present participle, which expresses continual or repeated action. As we keep, or guard God's Word from escaping from our hearts, by keeping it in our hearts, then we will obey God. Now let us embark on our study to answer the questions presented in the Introduction.

Rev. 1:4
John to the seven churches which are in Asia: Grace *be* unto you,
and peace, from him which is, and which was, and which is to
come; and from the seven Spirits which are before his throne;
Rev. 1:5
And from Jesus Christ, *who is* the faithful witness, *and* the first
begotten of the dead, and the prince of the kings of the earth. Unto
him that loved us, and washed us from our sins in his own blood,
Rev. 1:6
And hath made us kings and priests unto God and his Father; to him
be glory and dominion for ever and ever. Amen.

These letters describe church history past, present and
future. They are the "calm before the storm." In most of the
letters we find both blessings and warnings to each type of
church found throughout history.

The messages to the seven churches have a two-fold
meaning. First, they were seven actual churches during the
time of the apostle John. Of all the churches that were in
existence during that time, God chose these seven because
they represented different truths that He wanted His church to
remember down through the ages, including today. That is
why He says at the end of each message to these churches "He
that hath an ear, let him hear what the Spirit saith unto the
churches...." Second, we can look at these seven churches
prophetically. Of all the churches in existence at this time,
God chose these seven churches to show the attitudes and
types of churches that would exist from John's time and into
the future. I will attempt to show the prophetic view of these
churches.

Let me explain. In Stage 1 the church at Ephesus
prophetically describes a period of time between
approximately A.D. 30-100. There were also churches during
this period of time that fell into the attitudes described in the
letters to all seven churches. Co-Authors Tim LaHaye and
Thomas Ice give a brief, yet clear, chart of these approximate
time periods in their book, "Charting the End Times"

(Charting the End Times, Harvest House Publishers, page 45):

Ephesus - Apostolic Church (A.D. 30-100)
Smyrna - Persecuted Church (A.D. 100-313)
Pergamos - State Church (A.D. 313-590)
Thyatira - Papal Church (A.D. 590-1517)
Sardis - Reformed Church (A.D. 1517-1730)
Philadelphia - Missionary Church (A.D. 1730-1900)
Laodicea - Apostate Church (A.D. 1900-?)

Also notice that all seven letters contain one or more of the following:
- A characteristic or description of our risen Savior, Jesus Christ.
- A promise to all Christians ("he that overcometh").
- That God knows everything that transpires within every church, whether good or bad.
- That God knows whether the individuals within each church are sincere in their hearts and works.
- God knows whether the pastor is pleasing God or pleasing man.

Rev. 1:7
Behold, he cometh with clouds; and every eye shall see him, and they *also* which pierced him: and all kindreds of the earth shall wail because of him. Even so, Amen.

John, in verse 7, does not "beat around the bush" as he tells the churches "straight out of the gate" that Jesus is coming again. Jesus coming with the clouds will happen in Revelation Chapter 19. To me, John's boldness is great! In business, when possible, I wanted to know what my target or goal was before trying to reach it or hit it. Once I had the vision of the target or goal I could begin my efforts and work to accomplish it. John gives the churches the target of the primary message behind his vision. Jesus is coming! He tells them, from the very beginning, this is what this book is all about. To those who are saved, this should bring excitement and joy, wanting to hear more about what he has to say. To those who are not saved or not in fellowship with God, this would bring fear and anxiousness, wondering what else they were about to be told. Either way, he gets their attention and he wants our attention focused on the Second Coming.

Rev. 1:8
I am Alpha and Omega, the beginning and the ending, saith the Lord, which is, and which was, and which is to come, the Almighty.
Rev. 1:9
I John, who also am your brother, and companion in tribulation, and in the kingdom and patience of Jesus Christ, was in the isle that is called Patmos, for the word of God, and for the testimony of Jesus Christ.
Rev. 1:10
I was in the Spirit on the Lord's day, and heard behind me a great voice, as of a trumpet,

If you have any doubts who Jesus is, verse 8 should clear them up. He is God! If you still have doubts as to whether Jesus is God after reading verse 8, then you need to ask Jesus to forgive you of your sin of unbelief and ask him to save you right now, right where you are. By the way, if you do believe Jesus is God, but have never asked Him to forgive you and save you from an eternal hell, then this would be a good time to do that.

To understand this book upon which you have embarked, you have to be a child of God as a result of trusting Christ as your personal Savior.

I Cor. 2:14
[14]But the natural man receiveth not the things of the Spirit of God: for they are foolishness unto him: neither can he know them, because they are spiritually discerned."

What does that mean? "Natural man" is a person who has not accepted Jesus as their personal Savior. They have not been regenerated by Jesus Christ and therefore do not have the Spirit of God living within them. They are not "saved."

Therefore the scriptures seem meaningless to them and they truly will be meaningless. To understand scripture, you must be saved. It does not take a priest or preacher to give you the meaning of scripture, as some have taught. The meaning of scripture is reserved for those who have truly trusted Jesus Christ as their personal Savior. After you trust Jesus Christ and are saved, the Holy Spirit takes up abode in your body to direct you in understanding scripture. He then makes you a regenerated person and you no longer view the scriptures in your old "natural" way. I hope you have done this, so let's continue with this study in a new exciting light.

Rev. 1:11
Saying, I am Alpha and Omega, the first and the last: and, What thou seest, write in a book, and send *it* unto the seven churches which are in Asia; unto Ephesus, and unto Smyrna, and unto Pergamos, and unto Thyatira, and unto Sardis, and unto Philadelphia, and unto Laodicea.

> Ex. 3:14
> [14]And God said unto Moses, I AM THAT I AM: and he said, Thus shalt thou say unto the children of Israel, I AM hath sent me unto you.

Once again, Jesus states "I am," which means that He is God, true deity.

Rev. 1:12
And I turned to see the voice that spake with me. And being turned, I saw seven golden candlesticks;
Rev. 1:13
And in the midst of the seven candlesticks *one* like unto the Son of man, clothed with a garment down to the foot, and girt about the paps with a golden girdle.
Rev. 1:14
His head and *his* hairs *were* white like wool, as white as snow; and his eyes *were* as a flame of fire;
Rev. 1:15
And his feet like unto fine brass, as if they burned in a furnace; and his voice as the sound of many waters.

Rev. 1:16
And he had in his right hand seven stars: and out of his mouth went a sharp twoedged sword: and his countenance *was* as the sun shineth in his strength.

Heb 4:12
[12]For the word of God *is* quick, and powerful, and sharper than any twoedged sword, piercing even to the dividing asunder of soul and spirit, and of the joints and marrow, and *is* a discerner of the thoughts and intents of the heart.

The "sharp twoedged sword" is the Word of God.

Rev. 1:17
And when I saw him, I fell at his feet as dead. And he laid his right hand upon me, saying unto me, Fear not; I am the first and the last:
Rev. 1:18
I *am* he that liveth, and was dead; and, behold, I am alive for evermore, Amen; and have the keys of hell and of death.

Verses 13-18 describe none other than our risen Savior, Jesus Christ. The seven candlesticks will be described later. The Pope of Rome claims he has these two keys, yet verse 18 completely refutes this claim. I will not discuss the two keys the Pope claims to have, but it is certainly an interesting study. They are certainly not the keys to "hell and of death." Muslims believe that someone else died in Jesus' place and therefore they do not believe He was resurrected, since He never died. Verse 18 refutes their claim both about His death and resurrection.

Rev. 1:19
Write the things which thou hast seen, and the things which are, and the things which shall be hereafter;

Here is John's charge directly from Jesus. Therefore, the Book of Revelation contains a combination of things John has seen, things that are presently occurring and things which will happen in the future. This is what the Book of Revelation is all about. This verse tells us how Revelation is to be interpreted and understood. "Hast seen" represents the past and is found in Chapter 1. "Which are" represents the present or the seven churches found in Chapters 2-3. "Be hereafter" represents the future or prophetic found in Chapters 4-22.

Rev. 1:20
The mystery of the seven stars which thou sawest in my right hand, and the seven golden candlesticks. The seven stars are the angels of the seven churches: and the seven candlesticks which thou sawest are the seven churches.

You will see that in virtually all the letters to the churches, either one or more of these future events are mentioned: the Tribulation, the Second Coming, the Millennial Reign or the New Jerusalem. Now let us see what Christ said to the seven churches.

Letter to the Church of Ephesus – Apostolic Church
A.D. 30-100

The New Testament was completed during this church era. When you think about the famous theologians who occupied this era, you can see that this church was evangelistic, bold, stood strong for their faith and very orthodox in their beliefs. However, they became too busy in works that they forgot their first love, Jesus. Some great Christians that lived during this period were the Stephen, Peter, Paul, Luke, James, etc.

Rev. 2:1
Unto the angel of the church of Ephesus write; These things saith he that holdeth the seven stars in his right hand, who walketh in the midst of the seven golden candlesticks;

All of Christianity lies in the hand of Christ and He is ever present in all the churches observing what is happening within each church.

Rev. 2:2
I know thy works, and thy labour, and thy patience, and how thou

canst not bear them which are evil: and thou hast tried them which say they are apostles, and are not, and hast found them liars:
Rev. 2:3
And hast borne, and hast patience, and for my name's sake hast laboured, and hast not fainted.
Rev. 2:4
Nevertheless I have *somewhat* against thee, because thou hast left thy first love.
Rev. 2:5
Remember therefore from whence thou art fallen, and repent, and do the first works; or else I will come unto thee quickly, and will remove thy candlestick out of his place, except thou repent.
Rev. 2:6
But this thou hast, that thou hatest the deeds of the Nicolaitanes, which I also hate.

During this era, virtually the whole world was entranced by Paganism and idol worship. These Ephesian Christians were praised for their hatred of evil, their patience and their labor for God that came after their salvation. When these people trust Christ as Savior and become "saved" out of this paganism, they know the perversion and evil that exists in such idol worship. They did not just accept someone stating that he was an apostle. They watched the lives of these people to see if they proved worthy of Christianity. Some evidently became discouraged and started to mingle their old ways with Christianity and therefore the rebuke of "thou has left thy first love," Jesus. When a church turns away from preaching the gospel, I believe God will remove His Holy Spirit influence (candlestick) from that church and it will spiritually die and go into spiritual darkness.

Verse 6 refers to a group of people called the "Nicolaitanes." Very little is known of this group, but the Greek meaning of its name may give some clue as to their "deeds." The name is taken from two Greek words: "nicao" which means to conquer, control or dominate and "laos" which means the people or laity. Therefore, their deeds, which were to be hated, were evidently their desire to control the people or laity. This means they must have been leaders in the church and wanted the status of control. The priests of the pagan worshippers were also ones who had control over the people so they could continue to deceive them with their false beliefs and make the people subject to their every whim. The life of a Christian leader is to be one of humility and service to the people and the laity and not one of control. When you find so-called religious leaders who try to control and dominate you, run away from this religion and do not have a part of their deeds.

Rev. 2:7
He that hath an ear, let him hear what the Spirit saith unto the churches; To him that overcometh will I give to eat of the tree of life, which is in the midst of the paradise of God.

You will see that each letter will contain one or more promises to those who "overcometh." This means those who repent of their sin of unbelief and put their trust in Jesus as their Lord and Savior. In other words, all of these promises will be granted to all Christians. I encourage you to commit each promise to memory for future encouragement.

We are told in Verse 7 the "tree of life" that used to be in the Garden of Eden when Adam and Eve were alive, is now in "the paradise of God," which we will see later is the New Jerusalem. The New Jerusalem is currently in heaven.

Letter to the Church of Smyrna – Persecuted Church
A.D. 100-313

Thousands of Christians were murdered for their faith during this church era. It was a time of tremendous persecution of Christians. Some giant theologians who lived during this period and lost their lives for their faith were Ignatius, Polycarp, Justin Martyr and a countless number of others.

Rev. 2:8
And unto the angel of the church in Smyrna write; These things

saith the first and the last, which was dead, and is alive;
Rev. 2:9
I know thy works, and tribulation, and poverty, (but thou art rich)
and *I know* the blasphemy of them which say they are Jews, and are
not, but *are* the synagogue of Satan.
Rev. 2:10
Fear none of those things which thou shalt suffer: behold, the devil
shall cast *some* of you into prison, that ye may be tried; and ye shall
have tribulation ten days: be thou faithful unto death, and I will give
thee a crown of life.
Rev. 2:11
He that hath an ear, let him hear what the Spirit saith unto the
churches; He that overcometh shall not be hurt of the second death.

Only two of the seven letters did not contain a rebuke to the
church. These two churches were the church at Smyrna and
the church at Philadelphia. The church at Smyrna and this time
era witnessed murder and martyrdom of Christians. Jesus must
have decided that they needed encouragement and did not
deserve any rebuke because they have stood true to Him even
unto death. He reassures them that physical death is only a
promotion to heaven for Christians and the resurrection to
come. Their resurrection will be unto life and not to the
"second death" which is the "lake of fire."

Obviously, much of the persecution is coming from pious
Jews who have no clue of who God really is. Many of these
high-ranking Jewish officials such as the Pharisees, Sanhedrin
and Sadducees worshipped their own power and control of
others instead of God himself. Jesus called them "vipers" and
hypocrites.

Mt. 3:7
[7]But when he saw many of the Pharisees and Sadducees come to
his baptism, he said unto them, O generation of vipers, who hath
warned you to flee from the wrath to come?

Therefore, they were considered worshippers of Satan,
even though they cloaked their worship in a Jewish
synagogue. Just because someone looks religious on the
outside, does not mean he is speaking truth. True Christianity

comes from the heart of love for Jesus and others. Those Christians who were at Smyrna or those during this church era, were considered "true Christians" and many lost their lives for their love of Christ.

**Letter to the Church of Pergamos – State Church
A.D. 313-590**

Constantine came to power in Rome during this church era and made Christianity the state religion. He promised white robes and gold to all who would convert to Christianity. Of course, convincing people to join your movement through bribes does not create a Christian, but does entice some to join purely for monetary reasons. As a result, there were so many pagans and idol worshippers who joined the churches that it became a worldly church. The church started to become more secular than Christian. Some great theologians during this period were Jerome and Augustine.

Rev. 2:12
And to the angel of the church in Pergamos write; These things saith he which hath the sharp sword with two edges;

This "sharp sword with two edges" is the Word of God. The Word of God cuts asunder the heart and soul to reveal truth.

Rev. 2:13
I know thy works, and where thou dwellest, *even* where Satan's seat *is*: and thou holdest fast my name, and hast not denied my faith, even in those days wherein Antipas *was* my faithful martyr, who was slain among you, where Satan dwelleth.

After the flood until the time of Belshazzar and before the Medes and Persians took over Babylon, Babylon was the center of idol and Satan worship. Satan worship and the beginning of the "gods" started with Nimrod and the building of the tower of Babel. Nimrod's wife, Semerimus, and Nimrod himself became the center of worship to the godless portion of the world of that time. After Nimrod was killed, Semerimus developed the Mother/Son cult idol worship, stating that Nimrod was resurrected to become her son, Tammuz. She then became known as the "queen of heaven."

Jer. 7:18

[18]The children gather wood, and the fathers kindle the fire, and the women knead *their* dough, to make cakes to the queen of heaven, and to pour out drink offerings unto other gods, that they may provoke me to anger.

Ez. 8:14

[14]Then he brought me to the door of the gate of the LORD'S house which *was* toward the north; and, behold, there sat women weeping for Tammuz.

Tammuz was known as the husband of goddess Ishtar. Ishtar is the Babylonian/Chaldean name given to Semerimus. Virtually all the mythological gods found in every society on earth are derived from the cult worship of the Semerimus (Mother/Child cult) and Nimrod. This "weeping" time in Ezekiel was celebrated as a holiday between our months of June and July. Around the time of the Medes and Persians, Cyrus rejected this Satan worship, and the idol/Satan worship of the "queen of heaven" moved to Phoenicia and then to Pergamos where it flourished once again. Later, this pagan worship was adopted by pagan Romanism as part of the Roman Empire. The center of this idol worship was Rome. Much of this pagan idol worship and rituals crept into the Church of Rome after Constantine became the head of the Roman Empire and "made Christianity" the accepted religion of the Roman Empire.

The Roman Catholic Papacy is known as the "Holy See." This means the holy seat for the supreme pastor of the church. As we know from history, many of the Popes were not characters whom anyone would describe as "Holy." As a matter of fact, many of them would be described as very unholy, cruel and ruthless murderers. Therefore, we can understand more the phrase "even where Satan's seat is."

Rev. 2:14
But I have a few things against thee, because thou hast there them that hold the doctrine of Balaam, who taught Balac to cast a stumblingblock before the children of Israel, to eat things sacrificed unto idols, and to commit fornication.

The doctrine of Balaam was the teaching that God's people need not be separated from the evils of the world. The children of Israel accepted this teaching and God judged them.

Rev. 2:15
So hast thou also them that hold the doctrine of the Nicolaitanes, which thing I hate.
Rev. 2:16
Repent; or else I will come unto thee quickly, and will fight against them with the sword of my mouth.
Rev. 2:17
He that hath an ear, let him hear what the Spirit saith unto the churches; To him that overcometh will I give to eat of the hidden manna, and will give him a white stone, and in the stone a new name written, which no man knoweth saving he that receiveth *it*.

Letter to the Church of Thyatira – Papal Church
A.D. 590-1517

The state church begins to control individuals and dominate them through threats and suppression. According to Dr. H. A. Willmington, "the name Thyatira means continual sacrifice and may refer in general to the Roman Catholic Church." *(Willmington's Guide to the Bible, Tyndale House Publishers Inc., page 544)*. Some of the great theologians of this period were John Wycliffe, John Huss, William Tyndale and Erasmus.

Rev. 2:18
And unto the angel of the church in Thyatira write; These things saith the Son of God, who hath his eyes like unto a flame of fire, and his feet *are* like fine brass;

Jesus is God, the all-seeing judge and His Word is unmovable. Fine brass relates to how He judges your works and tries them by fire to see if they are true works of Godly love or strictly for self-gratification and advancement.

Rev. 2:19
I know thy works, and charity, and service, and faith, and thy patience, and thy works; and the last *to be* more than the first.
Rev. 2:20
Notwithstanding I have a few things against thee, because thou sufferest that woman Jezebel, which calleth herself a prophetess, to teach and to seduce my servants to commit fornication, and to eat things sacrificed unto idols.
Rev. 2:21
And I gave her space to repent of her fornication; and she repented not.
Rev. 2:22
Behold, I will cast her into a bed, and them that commit adultery with her into great tribulation, except they repent of their deeds.
Rev. 2:23
And I will kill her children with death; and all the churches shall know that I am he which searcheth the reins and hearts: and I will give unto every one of you according to your works.

This "woman Jezebel" could relate to Semerimus and idol worship. It is well understood that the Papal Church has incorporated much of pagan idolatry into its liturgy. It has caused its members and followers to center on works for salvation and forgiveness, rather than faith in Christ. It has caused its people to worship idols and be controlled by the priests, instead of realizing that they should only answer to God and not man for their sins and forgiveness. God knows the heart of all and you cannot fool Him. He knows that much of the doctrines taught by the Papacy was derived from Babylonian Paganism or an outcrop of such. Notice Verse 19 speaks of "works" twice and that this church and church era seem to rely on its works instead of faith.

Rev. 2:24
But unto you I say, and unto the rest in Thyatira, as many as have not this doctrine, and which have not known the depths of Satan, as they speak; I will put upon you none other burden.
Rev. 2:25
But that which ye have *already* hold fast till I come.
Rev. 2:26
And he that overcometh, and keepeth my works unto the end, to him will I give power over the nations:
Rev. 2:27
And he shall rule them with a rod of iron; as the vessels of a potter shall they be broken to shivers: even as I received of my Father.
Rev. 2:28
And I will give him the morning star.
Rev. 2:29
He that hath an ear, let him hear what the Spirit saith unto the churches.

In Verses 24-29, those faithful believers who were living during this church age were told to continue to be faithful and stand. He promises them that they will rule nations along with Jesus Christ. He stated that He will give them the "morning star." The "morning star" is Jesus Christ. The time of this rule will be when Jesus returns to earth to set up His Millennial Reign, just after the Seven-Year Tribulation Period.

Rev. 22:16
[16]I Jesus have sent mine angel to testify unto you these things in the churches. I am the root and the offspring of David, *and* the bright and morning star.

Letter to the Church of Sardis – Reformed Church
A.D. 1517-1730

Christians began to make a stand against the rule of the Papal Church during this church era. It was considered the Protestant Reformation era. Some of the great theologians of this period were Martin Luther, Zwingli, John Calvin, John Knox, Roger Williams, etc.

Rev. 3:1
And unto the angel of the church in Sardis write; These things saith he that hath the seven Spirits of God, and the seven stars; I know thy works, that thou hast a name that thou livest, and art dead.

The "seven Spirits of God" are also found in Rev. 4:5 and 5:6, where we are told they are the "seven eyes" of God. In Zec. 4:10 below, we see the "seven eyes" are the all-seeing eyes of God, seeing everything that goes on throughout the earth. This characteristic of God speaks of His omniscience, all knowing, and omnipresence, being everywhere at all times. Therefore, He is reminding this church that nothing can hide from Him and He sees everything.

Zec. 4:10
[10]For who hath despised the day of small things? for they shall rejoice, and shall see the plummet in the hand of Zerubbabel *with* those seven; they *are* the eyes of the LORD, which run to and fro through the whole earth.

Rev. 3:2
Be watchful, and strengthen the things which remain, that are ready to die: for I have not found thy works perfect before God.
Rev. 3:3
Remember therefore how thou hast received and heard, and hold fast, and repent. If therefore thou shalt not watch, I will come on thee as a thief, and thou shalt not know what hour I will come upon thee.
Rev. 3:4
Thou hast a few names even in Sardis which have not defiled their garments; and they shall walk with me in white: for they are worthy.
Rev. 3:5
He that overcometh, the same shall be clothed in white raiment; and I will not blot out his name out of the book of life, but I will confess his name before my Father, and before his angels.
Rev. 3:6
He that hath an ear, let him hear what the Spirit saith unto the churches.

In this church era, we see those who are making a stand against the paganism and control exerted by the Papal Church.

Obviously the Papal Church did not exist at the writing of this letter to Sardis. However, the church at Sardis must have allowed some forms of paganism to creep into their liturgy as did the Papacy. To make a stand against the Papacy teachings was to place a mark of death on your life. This could be the meaning of the phrase "thou has a name that thou livest, and are dead."

Some of these reformers did not go all the way against the paganism found in the Papacy. This could be the meaning of the rebuke that their works were not perfect. We must stand against "watered-down" theology, regardless of the cost. "Not defiled their garments," means they have not compromised fundamental Biblical scripture and have stood true to Bible doctrine and Biblical practices. A Christian's garments, in the spiritual sense, relates to his/her righteousness before God. After salvation, our righteous desires should be to serve God and accomplish His purpose for us on earth. Before salvation, "all our righteousness are as filthy rags" before God. In other words, we cannot work our way into heaven.

Is. 64:6a
⁶ᵃBut we are all as an unclean *thing*, and all our righteousnesses *are* as filthy rags;...

Letter to the Church of Philadelphia – Missionary Church
A.D. 1730-1900

Preachers and missionaries around the world became bold in the Lord and preached the Word of God in truth during this church era. Untold numbers of people throughout the world were led to the Lord as a result of the power and boldness of the Holy Spirit that resided on men and women of this time period. This era was also known as the "Great Awakening." Some of the great theologians of this period were Jonathan Edwards, John Wesley, George Whitfield, William Carey, David Livingston and D. L. Moody.

Rev. 3:7
And to the angel of the church in Philadelphia write; These things

saith he that is holy, he that is true, he that hath the key of David, he that openeth, and no man shutteth; and shutteth, and no man openeth;

Rev. 3:8

I know thy works: behold, I have set before thee an open door, and no man can shut it: for thou hast a little strength, and hast kept my word, and hast not denied my name.

Rev. 3:9

Behold, I will make them of the synagogue of Satan, which say they are Jews, and are not, but do lie; behold, I will make them to come and worship before thy feet, and to know that I have loved thee.

Rev. 3:10

Because thou hast kept the word of my patience, I also will keep thee from the hour of temptation, which shall come upon all the world, to try them that dwell upon the earth.

Rev. 3:11

Behold, I come quickly: hold that fast which thou hast, that no man take thy crown.

Rev. 3:12

Him that overcometh will I make a pillar in the temple of my God, and he shall go no more out: and I will write upon him the name of my God, and the name of the city of my God, *which is* new Jerusalem, which cometh down out of heaven from my God: and *I will write upon him* my new name.

We are told that those who trust Christ as Lord and Savior, "overcometh," will be sealed with God's name and have a part in the city of God, which is called the "New Jerusalem." I will discuss New Jerusalem toward the end of this book.

Rev. 3:13

He that hath an ear, let him hear what the Spirit saith unto the churches.

This church and church era are credited as being on "fire" for God. God has opened doors to send the gospel of truth throughout the world. When God opens, no man can shut and when God shuts, no man can open. Even though Satan, through many different ways, tried to stop this great mission movement, he could not. God moved on the hearts of true

Christian men and women to send them to areas of the world who had never heard the truth of the gospel. They, by God's drawing, left home, family and almost everything to heed the call of God on them to go to a lost and dying world.

In Verse 10, God promises true Christians who are alive at the Rapture that they will not have to suffer the Tribulation Period that will come upon the earth. This specifically refers to the Rapture, which we will discuss later.

Letter to the Church of Laodiceans – Apostate Church
A.D. 1900-?

This era of time, which continues into the current age in which we live, has seen the church become watered down and lukewarm. Liberalism has crept into the church. Christianity and the Bible are under constant attack and very few theologians are willing to make a stand. Most churches have mingled worldly activity to the point that the churches have become one big social club. Liberalism, compromise of the church with Darwinism, the World Council of Churches and Ecumenicalism have brought heresies into the churches and there have become very few churches that make a bold stand for Christ and His Word. Some of the champions of this period were and some still are C. I. Scofield, Billy Sunday, John R. Rice, Billy Graham and the list goes on.

Rev. 3:14
And unto the angel of the church of the Laodiceans write; These things saith the Amen, the faithful and true witness, the beginning of the creation of God;
Rev. 3:15
I know thy works, that thou art neither cold nor hot: I would thou wert cold or hot.
Rev. 3:16
So then because thou art lukewarm, and neither cold nor hot, I will spue thee out of my mouth.
Rev. 3:17
Because thou sayest, I am rich, ind increased with goods, and have

need of nothing; and knowest not that thou art wretched, and miserable, and poor, and blind, and naked:
Rev. 3:18
I counsel thee to buy of me gold tried in the fire, that thou mayest be rich; and white raiment, that thou mayest be clothed, and *that* the shame of thy nakedness do not appear; and anoint thine eyes with eyesalve, that thou mayest see.
Rev. 3:19
As many as I love, I rebuke and chasten: be zealous therefore, and repent.
Rev. 3:20
Behold, I stand at the door, and knock: if any man hear my voice, and open the door, I will come in to him, and will sup with him, and he with me.
Rev. 3:21
To him that overcometh will I grant to sit with me in my throne, even as I also overcame, and am set down with my Father in his throne.
Rev. 3:22
He that hath an ear, let him hear what the Spirit saith unto the churches.

Notice that He begins with "the faithful and true witness," speaking of Jesus Himself. Once again, His introduction describes the era. This era is filled with progressing apostasy. Finding a church today that has not "watered-down" scripture is hard to find. Christ reminds them of "the beginning of creation" which probably relates to the error of this era of mingling evolution with creation. Evolution is anti-God and should never be mingled. However, this era of time in which we live today, finds churches justifying evolution as being used of God to create everything. Evolution and creation are diametrically opposed.

We see the social gospel prominent during this last church era. Most people feel their riches and easy living means they have no need for God. It is full of church-going "fence-straddling" people, and this makes God sick. This era of time in church history will be the last era of the church before the Tribulation will begin. Many churches that stood strong on the principles of God during the Philadelphia Era are no longer standing strong with the gospel as they did before.

As I mentioned in the beginning of this chapter, these letters were sent to specific churches in Asia Minor, which we call Turkey today. However, as you have seen, these letters had a multi-purpose function:

1. They were specifically to inform the church of that day.

2. They were to be prophetic messages relating to the church age and condition that would exist throughout the history of the church.

3. They were to show that there would be people throughout each era that could be characterized by each church letter.

After Verse 22, the Church is not mentioned again until Revelation 19. The Rapture now occurs.

2

The Rapture Occurs

Rev. 4:1
After this I looked, and, behold, a door *was* opened in heaven: and the first voice which I heard *was* as it were of a trumpet talking with me; which said, Come up hither, and I will show thee things which must be hereafter.

John is now taken up into heaven to view what will happen in the future. Everyone would love to time travel and go back in time or forward into the future. Most people would probably want to travel into the future to see what it holds for them. John is one of a very few individuals who have been awarded the opportunity to travel forward into the future. He is given a seat on the 50-yard line or as the circus crowd would say, "a ring side seat." He will view what is going to happen in the future and try to describe it in terms understandable to him in his day and time. What an awesome opportunity, but at the same time an awesome responsibility. He, through the guidance of the Holy Spirit, will pen some of the most shocking scriptures of the Bible. It will be his duty to describe in his own words, the events that are about to unfold. Yes, they are in his own vocabulary, but they are guided by the Holy Spirit and it is the Word of God. John is not being translated to heaven and thrust into the future for his own personal gain, like the film "Back to the Future." He is to record the events in Godly real time, so he can warn mankind of the prophecy that will occur.

At this point the saved in Christ will be raptured to escape the wrath to come during the seven years of tribulation. The

Rapture is the resurrection of the body of all Church Age believers, both dead and alive. Scholars differ as to who is involved in this Rapture/resurrection. Some believe that it includes all the Old Testament saints, since they are also dead in Christ. Actually all believers from the beginning of Adam to the last believer saved are considered "dead in Christ." Others believe that the Rapture refers only to the Church Age believers since they are considered the Bride of Christ. Those who believe that it involves only the Church Age believers, also believe the Old Testament saints will be resurrected at the beginning of the Millennial Reign of Christ. Neither camp can be dogmatic on their premise, but the fact remains that there will be a Rapture and the Old Testament saints will also be resurrected either at the Rapture or just before the Millennium. For this study, I have included only the Church Age believers in this Rapture/resurrection and the resurrection of the Old Testament saints at the beginning of the Millennium.

John, being taken up to the third heaven, is a picture of the "Rapture" and here pictures the future Rapture of the saved. Rapture is a Latin word meaning "to be caught up or taken up." Someone might say at this point, "The word Rapture is not found in the Bible." That is correct and neither is the word "Bible" found anywhere in scripture. However, to use other words to describe an event or subject is not uncommon or unscriptural. In verse 1, I would like to point out the words "voice," "trumpet," "come up." These words flow with some of the scripture relating to the Rapture. The following scriptures help lend more credence to the Rapture of those who are saved before the Seven-Year Tribulation Period begins.

I Thess 4:13-18

[13]But I would not have you to be ignorant, brethren, concerning them which are asleep, that ye sorrow not, even as others which have no hope.

[14]For if we believe that Jesus died and rose again, even so them also which sleep in Jesus will God bring with him.

[15]For this we say unto you by the word of the Lord, that we which are alive and remain unto the coming of the Lord shall not prevent them which are asleep.

[16]For the Lord himself shall descend from heaven with a shout, with the voice of the archangel, and with the trump of God: and the dead in Christ shall rise first:

[17]Then we which are alive and remain shall be caught up together with them in the clouds, to meet the Lord in the air: and so shall we ever be with the Lord.

[18]Wherefore comfort one another with these words.

The saved dead and alive will be "caught up," raptured, to meet the Lord in the air. This is not the 2nd coming to earth, because we will meet the Lord in the air. At the 2nd coming to earth, after the Seven-Year Tribulation Period, Jesus will come with His saints in the clouds. In other words, to come with Him we would have to have been taken to be with Him prior to this. Verse 15 the word "prevent" in the KJV is used. This word means to "precede" or "come before." Notice verse 16 and Revelation 4:1 use the words "trump" and "trumpet." I believe this trumpet is the voice of Jesus Himself. The same words are used below in I Corinthians.

I Cor. 15:51-57

[51]Behold, I shew you a mystery; We shall not all sleep, but we shall all be changed,

[52]In a moment, in the twinkling of an eye, at the last trump: for the trumpet shall sound, and the dead shall be raised incorruptible, and we shall be changed.

[53]For this corruptible must put on incorruption, and this mortal must put on immortality.

[54]So when this corruptible shall have put on incorruption, and this mortal shall have put on immortality, then shall be brought to pass the saying that is written, Death is swallowed up in victory.

[55]O death, where is thy sting? O grave, where is thy victory?

[56]The sting of death is sin; and the strength of sin is the law.

[57]But thanks be to God, which giveth us the victory through our Lord Jesus Christ.

Both the dead and living in Christ, at the time of the Rapture, will be changed instantly and raised to an immortal life victorious over death.

John 14:1-3

¹Let not your heart be troubled: ye believe in God, believe also in me.

²In my Father's house are many mansions: if it were not so, I would have told you. I go to prepare a place for you.

³And if I go and prepare a place for you, I will come again, and receive you unto myself; that where I am, there ye may be also.

Jesus stated that He will come again and receive the saved unto Himself.

I Thess. 1:10

¹⁰And to wait for his Son from heaven, whom he raised from the dead, even Jesus, which delivered us from the wrath to come.

The saved will be delivered from the wrath to come. The wrath to come is the Seven-Year Tribulation.

I Thess. 5:4-11

⁴But ye, brethren, are not in darkness, that that day should overtake you as a thief.

⁵Ye are all the children of light, and the children of the day: we are not of the night, nor of darkness.

⁶Therefore let us not sleep, as do others; but let us watch and be sober.

⁷For they that sleep sleep in the night; and they that be drunken are drunken in the night.

⁸But let us, who are of the day, be sober, putting on the breastplate of faith and love; and for an helmet, the hope of salvation.

⁹For God hath not appointed us to wrath, but to obtain salvation by our Lord Jesus Christ,

¹⁰Who died for us, that, whether we wake or sleep, we should live together with him.

¹¹Wherefore comfort yourselves together, and edify one another, even as also ye do.

We are told that we are "not in darkness" that His coming "should overtake us as a thief." In other words, we will expect His coming. A similar statement will be made in Revelation 16 just before the Second Coming to earth. However, the Tribulation Saints are told to watch and be ready because Jesus comes as a "thief."

God has not appointed His saved to suffer wrath. Therefore, we will not go through the Tribulation.

II Thess. 2:1-3

¹Now we beseech you, brethren, by the coming of our Lord Jesus Christ, and by our gathering together unto him,
²That ye be not soon shaken in mind, or be troubled, neither by spirit, nor by word, nor by letter as from us, as that the day of Christ is at hand.
³Let no man deceive you by any means: for that day shall not come, except there come a falling away first, and that man of sin be revealed, the son of perdition;

Mic. 7:1-4

¹Woe is me! for I am as when they have gathered the summer fruits, as the grapegleanings of the vintage: there is no cluster to eat: my soul desired the firstripe fruit.
²The good man is perished out of the earth: and there is none upright among men: they all lie in wait for blood; they hunt every man his brother with a net.
³That they may do evil with both hands earnestly, the prince asketh, and the judge asketh for a reward; and the great man, he uttereth his mischievous desire: so they wrap it up.
⁴The best of them is as a brier: the most upright is sharper than a thorn hedge: the day of thy watchmen and thy visitation cometh; now shall be their perplexity.

Micah speaks of gathering "firstripe fruits," which I believe pertains to those who accepted Christ as their personal Savior and become a part of the resurrection of the first fruits. There will be several gatherings/resurrections of other dead believers that will be mentioned later in our study, who will be part of what is called the First Resurrection.

Also notice that there will be a time on earth when there will be no righteous person. The best of people left on earth are described in verses 3-4 as being a "brier" or "thorn hedge." This could only happen if the Lord raptures all the saved and then what is left is total unrighteousness and confusion. Notice the word "perplexity" in verse 4, which means confusion. There is no other possible time that such a situation could exist except there be a rapture of the saved and then total unrighteousness immediately follows. There has never been a time like this in the past nor present. Therefore, it has to be in the future. There has to be a Rapture and these verses prove it. The last part of verse 2 describes the beginning of the Tribulation Period.

Is. 57:1-2

[1]The righteous perisheth, and no man layeth it to heart: and merciful men are taken away, none considering that the righteous is taken away from the evil to come.
[2]He shall enter into peace: they shall rest in their beds, each one walking in his uprightness.

Isaiah also stated that "the righteous is taken away from the evil to come." This scripture also leads us to assume, as stated in Micah above, that if the righteous are taken away, then the unrighteous will rule.

Gen. 5:24

[24]And Enoch walked with God: and he *was* not; for God took him.

Heb. 11:5

[5]By faith Enoch was translated that he should not see death; and was not found, because God had translated him: for before his translation he had this testimony, that he pleased God.

Enoch was the great-grandfather of Noah and the Bible teaches us that Enoch was translated directly to heaven, just as was Elijah. Enoch is also a picture of the Rapture. He was taken out of the world before the Flood began.

I hope these scripture references have supplied enough Biblical proof to show that the Rapture of the Church will occur before the Seven-Year Tribulation Period begins.

3

The Judgment Seat of Christ

Sometime during the seven years of tribulation on earth, the Judgment Seat of Christ takes place in heaven. I believe it takes place immediately after the Rapture (see Rev. 4:4). Revelation 4:4 provides us a scene in heaven with the twenty-four elders sitting on their thrones and all have their crowns and white robes. Therefore, I believe the Judgment Seat of Christ takes place just before Revelation 4:4.

This rewards judgment will be for Christians only and will take place in heaven. The Judgment Seat is a judgment of the works done by believers while they were on earth. The judgment is for believers to receive rewards or lose rewards based on their love for Christ and others. It is not a judgment of their salvation. Being raptured signified their acceptance as Jesus Christ as their personal Savior and their salvation and entrance into the abode of God. This judgment of believers will determine if their works would stand the test of God's fire, whether good or bad, whether wood, hay or stubble or precious stone, gold, silver. We will be judged in how well have we behaved on earth as it relates to being good stewards of what God has bestowed upon us. A good steward encompasses many things such as witnessing to others, handling finances that God entrusted to us, giving to God's work monetarily or with our time, our attitude, self-control, love for others, our willingness to die for Christ, promoting the Gospel, patience, excitement about Jesus' Second Coming, faithfulness to feed the flock and much more. Crowns will be given and white robes put on everyone present. Jesus was referring to this in Matthew:

Mt. 6:20-21

²⁰But lay up for yourselves treasures in heaven, where neither moth nor rust doth corrupt, and where thieves do not break through nor steal:

²¹For where your treasure is, there will your heart be also.

Jesus was telling us to lay up treasures in heaven in the form of good works. He is not teaching that good works save a person, but that after someone is saved he/she will want to make their works count in heaven and stand the test of fire at the Judgment Seat of Christ.

Rom. 14:10

¹⁰But why dost thou judge thy brother? or why dost thou set at nought thy brother? for we shall all stand before the judgment seat of Christ.

II Cor. 5:10

¹⁰For we must all appear before the judgment seat of Christ; that every one may receive the things done in his body, according to that he hath done, whether it be good or bad.

I Cor. 3:9-15

⁹For we are labourers together with God: ye are God's husbandry, ye are God's building.

¹⁰According to the grace of God which is given unto me, as a wise masterbuilder, I have laid the foundation, and another buildeth thereon. But let every man take heed how he buildeth thereupon.

¹¹For other foundation can no man lay than that is laid, which is Jesus Christ.

¹²Now if any man build upon this foundation gold, silver, precious stones, wood, hay, stubble;

¹³Every man's work shall be made manifest: for the day shall declare it, because it shall be revealed by fire; and the fire shall try every man's work of what sort it is.

¹⁴If any man's work abide which he hath built thereupon, he shall receive a reward.

¹⁵If any man's work shall be burned, he shall suffer loss: but he himself shall be saved; yet so as by fire.

Notice that some people's works will be burned, but the person himself is not burned. Again, this is a test of Christian works, not salvation. Sometimes our works are of a selfish nature so that man will recognize it and pat us on the back or reward us. This type of work will burn because it is not geared toward uplifting Christ. Instead it is directed toward uplifting self. Some give their tithes out of a "have to" instead of a merry heart. These type of works will burn also. Notice that every work which is motivated by self and self-recognition will be burned. God's plan for us is to lose "self" and love Him and others first. If you want to lay up treasures, or righteousness, in heaven, then lose your selfish desires and let your desires be directed towards the best for others. I truly believe that the greatest sin of both the saved and the unsaved is "selfishness." From this stems all manner of sin. When a person comes to the point of self-judgment and gives himself or herself truly to God, then that is when they begin laying up treasures in heaven. The interest rate is out of this world. Literally!

Five Crowns Awarded

What kind of crowns will be awarded at the Judgment Seat and for what reasons? The following are the crowns that a believer can obtain in heaven according to his works on earth:

1. <u>Incorruptible Crown</u>. This crown is given to those Christians who deny themselves and their old nature and become controlled by God. These people could be considered those who are self-controlled and brought their desires under control of the Holy Spirit. They do not become angered very easily, they control their tongue, they flee temptation, they do for others before they do for themselves, etc. This is the unselfish crown. By the way, there will never be a selfish crown. All selfish works will be burned.

   1 Cor. 9:25

   [25]And every man that striveth for the mastery is temperate in all things. Now they *do it* to obtain a corruptible crown; but we an incorruptible.

2. <u>Crown of Rejoicing</u>. This crown is given to those who love to win people to Christ. Their desire is to see

people saved and they go about their job of soul-winning. To me, this would be the greatest crown to receive. How exciting to know that you had a part in saving a soul from Hell and will see them at this same Judgment Seat. I am sure there will be smiles everywhere from those who see the individuals who receive this crown. Oh, the joy of knowing that some of those standing in these lines were there because you cared. This should be the desire of every Christian.

1 Thess.2:19-20

[19]For what *is* our hope, or joy, or crown of rejoicing? *Are* not even ye in the presence of our Lord Jesus Christ at his coming?
[20]For ye are our glory and joy.

Prov. 11:30

[30]The fruit of the righteous *is* a tree of life; and he that winneth souls *is* wise.

Dan. 12:3

[3]And they that be wise shall shine as the brightness of the firmament; and they that turn many to righteousness as the stars for ever and ever.

3. Crown of Righteousness. This crown will be given to those who look forward to the Second Coming of Jesus Christ. I believe this also could be talking about those who love and look forward to the Rapture of the Church. One of the reasons I decided to write this book is the excitement it brings to the heart of a Christian from knowing that the Rapture could happen at any time. There is no other doctrine or Bible event, other than salvation, that excites the Christian more than the Second Coming and the Rapture. I am not writing this book to get this crown, for if that were the case, I would certainly not receive this crown. That would be considered selfishness on my behalf. No, I am writing this book so that others can become as excited as I am about Jesus' Second Coming. If you are not excited about His coming then one of the following must permeate your life: you are either not saved or you are saved and out of fellowship with God, or you are a

new Christian and do not understand the Second
Coming, or you have been saved for a long time and
your teachers and preachers have not taught you about
the Second Coming. I sincerely hope that by reading
and studying this book, you will become the excited
Christian that Christ wants you to become.

2 Tim. 4:8

[8]Henceforth there is laid up for me a crown of righteousness,
which the Lord, the righteous judge, shall give me at that day: and
not to me only, but unto all them also that love his appearing.

4. <u>Crown of Glory</u>. This crown will be given to those
   who are called to teach and/or preach the gospel. Will
   all saved teachers and preachers receive this crown?
   Absolutely not! Again, this will be for those who are
   faithful to teach and preach without self-gratification.
   They do it because they love to feed the flock of God
   and want to help others understand God's Word. There
   are some teachers and preachers that decide they
   would go into full-time ministry because it seemed like
   a good vocation. They thought they could do good.
   God is the only one, through the Holy Spirit, that calls
   teachers and preachers to the ministry. Unfortunately,
   there are many teachers and preachers that are teaching
   falsehood and misleading God's people. As Paul told
   Timothy in II Timothy 4:2-3, "Preach the word; be instant
   in season, out of season; reprove, rebuke, exhort with all
   longsuffering and doctrine. For the time will come when they will
   not endure sound doctrine; but after their own lusts shall they
   heap to themselves teachers, having itching ears." Therefore,
   teachers and preachers, be faithful to expound the truth
   of God's Word. Woe to that teacher or preacher who
   would rob a Christian of his/her joy in the Lord.

1 Pet. 5:2-4

[2]Feed the flock of God which is among you, taking the oversight
thereof, not by constraint, but willingly; not for filthy lucre, but of
a ready mind;
[3]Neither as being lords over *God's* heritage, but being ensamples
to the flock.
[4]And when the chief Shepherd shall appear, ye shall receive a

crown of glory that fadeth not away.

Verse 3 certainly rebukes any organization, church, priest, preacher, teacher or anyone who tries to influence a Christian through a "lordship" style of control. Leaders and organizations are supposed to be examples and not "lords." If you are being controlled in this way, run and find a church that practices by example and "walks the talk." A true Christian leader will joy in guiding someone who truly wants the truth. A true Christian leader will encourage Bible reading and study and not discourage it. They will encourage questions and discussions about the Word of God from anyone who has a desire to know the truth. And these same leaders will allow the Bible to interpret itself, as opposed to inserting their man-made doctrines. If you cannot not back up your statement with scripture, it is best to leave it alone. Do not accept that just because a church leader states something to be true, it is true. Search the scriptures so you can discern for yourself.

5. Crown of Life. This crown will be given to those Christians who have given their life for the Gospel's sake and to those who have been persecuted for the Gospel's sake and endured. It is sometimes referred to as the Martyr's Crown. I am sure that there are not too many people who would want to win this crown, purposefully. However, as with any of these crowns, no one actually strives to win a crown. These are given as a result of their Christian life on earth and dedication out of their love for Christ. I feel sure Stephen, in the book of Acts, will be in this line to receive this crown. The book "Foxe's Book of Martyrs" tells the stories of many who died for their faith. Many of them will receive this crown. Peter and Paul and many others died for their faith in Christ and will probably receive this crown. John endured until the end the persecution and exile to the Isle of Patmos.

He will probably receive this crown.

Rev. 2:10

[10]Fear none of those things which thou shalt suffer: behold, the devil shall cast *some* of you into prison, that ye may be tried; and ye shall have tribulation ten days: be thou faithful unto death, and I will give thee a crown of life.

4

Christ On His Heavenly Throne

John has been caught up into heaven to be shown what is about to happen in the future as we saw in Revelation 4:1. The scene is majestic to say the least. The glory of heaven is beyond human thought and understanding and hard to describe in human terms. John tries to relate to us the beauty of the one sitting upon His throne, Jesus and the glory that emanates from Him.

Rev. 4:2
And immediately I was in the spirit: and, behold, a throne was set in heaven, and *one* sat on the throne.
Rev. 4:3
And he that sat was to look upon like a jasper and a sardine stone: and *there was* a rainbow round about the throne, in sight like unto an emerald.

Look at the majestic aura about God's throne. If we could see this with our human eye, we would be awestruck, as was John. Can you imagine how John must have felt to have the opportunity to see this scene in heaven and have to describe it in his own words? The rainbow was a sign from God, after He judged the world with the flood, that He will never destroy the world with a flood again. Every time I see a rainbow, I am amazed! Everyone I know who has ever seen a rainbow in the sky, cannot help but continue to watch and view the majesty of its colors and brilliance. There is an ever-present rainbow surrounding God's throne, which makes it even more pleasing to the human eye.

Rev. 4:4
And round about the throne *were* four and twenty seats: and upon the seats I saw four and twenty elders sitting, clothed in white raiment; and they had on their heads crowns of gold.

Verse 4 seems to indicate that the Judgment Seat has already taken place, because these twenty-four elders have already been awarded their white robes and crowns. Some scholars believe that these elders could be a combination of twelve Old Testament and twelve New Testament saints.

Dan. 7:9

[9]I beheld till the thrones were cast down, and the Ancient of days did sit, whose garment *was* white as snow, and the hair of his head like the pure wool: his throne *was* *like* the fiery flame, *and* his wheels *as* burning fire.

In addition, Daniel saw these thrones "cast down" which actually means being set in place, but not occupied at the time of his vision. Now the thrones are occupied by the twenty-four elders.

Rev. 4:5
And out of the throne proceeded lightnings and thunderings and voices: and *there were* seven lamps of fire burning before the throne, which are the seven Spirits of God.

From the throne proceeds "lightnings and thunderings and voices," which shows us that the view of the throne is a view of judgment. In the past, we have seen a throne of grace as other New Testament writers describe to us. I believe this description shows that the judgment of the world is about to begin, even though grace is always present in God's judgment.

Rev. 4:6
And before the throne *there was* a sea of glass like unto crystal: and in the midst of the throne, and round about the throne, *were* four beasts full of eyes before and behind.

These four beasts, or "living creatures," are created beings. We will see them mentioned many times in the Book of Revelation.

Rev. 4:7
And the first beast *was* like a lion, and the second beast like a calf, and the third beast had a face as a man, and the fourth beast *was* like a flying eagle.

The language "like a" carries some symbolism to its meaning. In other words these creatures were "like a lion" but not necessarily "a lion," etc. The likeness could represent the offices of Christ as lion/king, calf or ox/servant, man/humanity and eagle/deity.

Rev. 4:8
And the four beasts had each of them six wings about *him*; and *they were* full of eyes within: and they rest not day and night, saying, Holy, holy, holy, Lord God Almighty, which was, and is, and is to come.

This verse seems to describe these four living creatures as some type of holy angel similar to the Cherubim and the Seraphim as described in Ezekiel Chapter 1 and 10. I will not speculate any further, because the exact identification is not presented in scripture. The fact is that these creatures are always seen around the throne of God and continue to praise Him, attribute to the facts of the characteristics of the Godhead and pronounce the righteousness of God's judgments. They are certainly eyewitnesses of virtually everything that proceeds from God's throne and they testify to His glory and majesty.

Rev. 4:9
And when those beasts give glory and honour and thanks to him that sat on the throne, who liveth for ever and ever,
Rev. 4:10
The four and twenty elders fall down before him that sat on the throne, and worship him that liveth for ever and ever, and cast their

crowns before the throne, saying,
Rev. 4:11
Thou art worthy, O Lord, to receive glory and honour and power:
for thou hast created all things, and for thy pleasure they are and
were created.

Only God is to receive glory, honor and power for He is the
creator of everything. God created everything! Nothing
evolved and God did not use evolution in His creation.
Evolution is the lie of Satan and should never be used in
conjunction with God's creation, because they are
diametrically opposed, as I stated earlier.

Search to Determine Who is Worthy to Open the Seven Sealed Book

The book of the seven seals is introduced and the Seven-
Year Tribulation is about to begin. The search now begins to
find out who is worthy to open the book.

Rev. 5:1
And I saw in the right hand of him that sat on the throne a book
written within and on the backside, sealed with seven seals.
Rev. 5:2
And I saw a strong angel proclaiming with a loud voice, Who is
worthy to open the book, and to loose the seals thereof?
Rev. 5:3
And no man in heaven, nor in earth, neither under the earth, was
able to open the book, neither to look thereon.
Rev. 5:4
And I wept much, because no man was found worthy to open and to
read the book, neither to look thereon.
Rev. 5:5
And one of the elders saith unto me, Weep not: behold, the Lion of
the tribe of Juda, the Root of David, hath prevailed to open the
book, and to loose the seven seals thereof.

Jesus is the Lamb, the Lion of the tribe of Judah, the Root
of David, who is the only one who has the right to open the

book and begin the Seven-Year Tribulation.

Is. 11:1

¹And there shall come forth a rod out of the stem of Jesse, and a Branch shall grow out of his roots:

Lk. 1:32

³²He shall be great, and shall be called the Son of the Highest: and the Lord God shall give unto him the throne of his father David:

Mt. 1:1

¹The book of the generation of Jesus Christ, the son of David, the son of Abraham.

Rev. 5:6

And I beheld, and, lo, in the midst of the throne and of the four beasts, and in the midst of the elders, stood a Lamb as it had been slain, having seven horns and seven eyes, which are the seven Spirits of God sent forth into all the earth.

Rev. 5:7

And he came and took the book out of the right hand of him that sat upon the throne.

Rev. 5:8

And when he had taken the book, the four beasts and four *and* twenty elders fell down before the Lamb, having every one of them harps, and golden vials full of odours, which are the prayers of saints.

Rev. 5:9

And they sung a new song, saying, Thou art worthy to take the book, and to open the seals thereof: for thou wast slain, and hast redeemed us to God by thy blood out of every kindred, and tongue, and people, and nation;

Jesus, the Lamb who was slain, is shown here as all-powerful (seven horns, which represent all-powerful or His omnipotence) and all-knowing (seven eyes, which represent all-knowing or omniscience). His other characteristic is being everywhere at all times through the work of the Holy Spirit or omnipresence.

Rev. 5:10

And hast made us unto our God kings and priests: and we shall reign on the earth.

Verse 10 is a statement of the future Millennium on earth to begin shortly after the Seven-Year Tribulation Period. Notice that we will reign on earth during this period.

Rev. 5:11
And I beheld, and I heard the voice of many angels round about the throne and the beasts and the elders: and the number of them was ten thousand times ten thousand, and thousands of thousands;

In other words, there is an innumerable number of angels.

Rev. 5:12
Saying with a loud voice, Worthy is the Lamb that was slain to receive power, and riches, and wisdom, and strength, and honour, and glory, and blessing.
Rev. 5:13
And every creature which is in heaven, and on the earth, and under the earth, and such as are in the sea, and all that are in them, heard I saying, Blessing, and honour, and glory, and power, *be* unto him that sitteth upon the throne, and unto the Lamb for ever and ever.

It has been said that just before many natural disasters occur, such as earthquakes, tsunamis, volcanic eruptions, etc., the animals seem to know or sense them approaching. Obviously, all of creation is in God's control and He very well may warn them.

Rev. 5:14
And the four beasts said, Amen. And the four *and* twenty elders fell down and worshipped him that liveth for ever and ever.

5

The Antichrist Arrives

At some point, just after the Rapture of the saints, a very strong personality appears on the scene. He is the Antichrist. He will be someone well known during this time and very crafty, with a strong charismatic personality. He will be one who can and will deceive the nations, especially Israel. I have placed Rev. 13:1-2 here to show that he is introduced somewhere in the beginning of the Tribulation Period, just after the Rapture.

Rev. 13:1
And I stood upon the sand of the sea, and saw a beast rise up out of the sea, having seven heads and ten horns, and upon his horns ten crowns, and upon his heads the name of blasphemy.
Rev. 13:2
And the beast which I saw was like unto a leopard, and his feet were as *the feet* of a bear, and his mouth as the mouth of a lion: and the dragon gave him his power, and his seat, and great authority.

The Antichrist will also head up a ten-nation confederacy, which many scholars believe to be the European Union or the Revived Roman Empire. His power and authority is given to him by Satan himself (the dragon). The "sea" is considered to be people or nations. He will probably become the head of the European Union and base his headquarters out of Rome for the first 3½ years of the Tribulation Period.

The seven heads refer to seven hills and the ten horns refer to ten powers or nations. It is very obvious that none of these kings believe in God for each are considered blasphemous.

The leopard could refer to his cunningness, the bear to his sternness, and the lion to his authority.

Dan. 11:21-22

[21]And in his estate shall stand up a vile person, to whom they shall not give the honour of the kingdom: but he shall come in peaceably, and obtain the kingdom by flatteries.

Verse 21 means that the Antichrist has not been awarded the title of "kingship" but that he will win it through his flatteries and deceit. The Antichrist will be very cunning, deceitful, flattering and full of lies. However, the people, and especially Israel, will believe him and welcome him with open arms.

[22]And with the arms of a flood shall they be overflown from before him, and shall be broken; yea, also the prince of the covenant.

Verse 22 talks about the battle mentioned in Ez. 38-39:16 which is discussed in Chapter 7. This verse refers to the upcoming battle in which the overflowing forces coming against the Antichrist and Israel will be defeated and broken. We will see who these forces are in Chapter 7.

Dan. 9:27a

[27a]And he shall confirm the covenant with many for one week:...

Dan. 11:23a

[23a]And after the league made with him he shall work deceitfully:...

As seen in Dan. 9:27a and 11:23a, the Antichrist signs or confirms the seven-year treaty with Israel and the Tribulation actually begins. The word "week" in Daniel is referring to the last week or 7 years of Daniel's prophecy of the 70 weeks of years.

The Tribulation Period will begin at the signing or confirmation of the seven-year treaty with Israel by the

Antichrist. The Hebrew word used in Daniel 9:27 for "confirm" is "gabar," which means to put to more strength, make stronger or to confirm. The Hebrew word for "covenant" is "beriyth" which means to make a compact or league or treaty.

> Mt. 24:5-8
> [5]For many shall come in my name, saying, I am Christ; and shall deceive many.
> [6]And ye shall hear of wars and rumours of wars: see that ye be not troubled: for all these things must come to pass, but the end is not yet.
> [7]For nation shall rise against nation, and kingdom against kingdom: and there shall be famines, and pestilences, and earthquakes, in divers places.
> [8]All these are the beginning of sorrows.

As seen in Matthew, there will be many antichrists, but at this time The Antichrist has appeared on the scene. There will be "wars and rumours of wars," but this is not "the end." Verse 8 states that this is the "beginning of sorrows." The Tribulation Period has begun.

6

The Two Witnesses Arrive

I believe that the "two witnesses," as described in the scriptures to follow, will appear on the scene at the same time the Antichrist signs or confirms a treaty with Israel, at which time the Seven-Year Tribulation clock begins. I have placed them here so the next few chapters of this book flow in an unbroken manner.

Rev. 11:3
And I will give *power* unto my two witnesses, and they shall prophesy a thousand two hundred *and* threescore days, clothed in sackcloth.

Mal. 4:5-6
[5]Behold, I will send you Elijah the prophet before the coming of the great and dreadful day of the LORD:
[6]And he shall turn the heart of the fathers to the children, and the heart of the children to their fathers, lest I come and smite the earth with a curse.

Just before the seven seals are opened and judgment is to begin on the earth, God raises up two godly witnesses to appear on the scene in Jerusalem, who will perform their miracles during the first half of the Seven-Year Tribulation Period or 3½ years or 1260 days. Bible months were considered 30 days per month. Therefore, 1260 days divided by 30 days equals 3½ years.

Rev. 11:4
These are the two olive trees, and the two candlesticks standing before the God of the earth.

Zech. 4:11, 13-14

[11]Then answered I, and said unto him, What are these two olive trees upon the right side of the candlestick and upon the left side thereof?

[13]And he answered me and said, Knowest thou not what these be? And I said, No, my lord.

[14]Then said he, These are the two anointed ones, that stand by the LORD of the whole earth.

Most Bible scholars believe that one of these witnesses is Elijah and the other could be Moses or Enoch. I will not speculate about who the other witness is, but show scripture supporting that one of them will very probably be Elijah. Obviously, the plagues and miracles performed during this period are very similar to some of the plagues that Moses performed in Egypt, but that does not necessarily mean that Moses has to perform them here. The only two individuals who have never seen death were Enoch and Elijah. Moses died and his body was buried by God. As seen in the scripture below, no one will be able to hurt or kill either of these two men until their ministry is complete (see also Rev. 11:7-12).

Rev. 11:5

And if any man will hurt them, fire proceedeth out of their mouth, and devoureth their enemies: and if any man will hurt them, he must in this manner be killed.

Zech. 4:12

[12]And I answered again, and said unto him, What be these two olive branches which through the two golden pipes empty the golden oil out of themselves?

Notice the statement "empty golden oil out of themselves." When the oil is lit, it turns into fire, which is golden in color as Revelation 11:5 states. Does this mean they will be "fire breathing" humans? I think this suggests that the two witnesses will have the power to call down fire or lightning from heaven to strike those who try to hurt them.

Rev. 11:6
These have power to shut heaven, that it rain not in the days of their prophecy: and have power over waters to turn them to blood, and to smite the earth with all plagues, as often as they will.

These two witnesses have great power that God has allowed. They have the power to not allow it to rain for 1260 days or 3½ years. We have to assume, according to this wording, that it did not rain for 3½ years. They will be able to perform some of the same miracles that Moses performed on the Egyptians, by turning water into blood and causing all types of plagues on earth.

7

Russia and Her Allies Attack Israel

Scholars agree to disagree as to when the Battle of Gog and Magog described in Ezekiel 38-39:16 occurs. Some believe it will happen just after the Rapture, or at the beginning of the Tribulation Period, which is called the post-Rapture view. Others believe that it will happen at the middle of the Tribulation Period or the mid-tribulation view. And still others believe this is the same as the Battle of Armageddon, which occurs at the end of the Tribulation Period. I am not about to split hairs with those individuals and by no means do I intend to sound dogmatic in my premise. However, I believe scripture seems to support the idea that Russia (Gog, the land of Magog) and her allies will attack Israel just after the Rapture occurs and just after the Antichrist signs a seven-year treaty with Israel. The fact that this battle will happen sometime during the Tribulation seems certain because the same language used in Ezekiel of the "latter years," "latter days," and "in that day" is used to refer to the Tribulation Period through the Millenium. We are also told that the Jews will have returned to their land from all corners of the world.

Let me show a few reasons why I believe this Battle of Gog and Magog is <u>not</u> the same as the Battle of Armageddon. I will summarize from Dr. Tim LaHaye and Dr. Thomas Ice's book: *(Charting the End Times, Harvest House Publishers, page 92)*

1. Ezekiel mentions <u>definite allies</u> who will attack Israel and a few nations that will oppose the attack, whereas, at the Battle of Armageddon, <u>all the nations</u> are allied together against the Lord of Hosts of Heaven.

2. Ezekiel's invasion of <u>specific nations</u> come mainly from the north and at the Battle of Armageddon, <u>all nations</u> come from everywhere.

3. Ezekiel's invaders are coming to gain riches and a spoil and the invaders at Armageddon are come to destroy the Jews and the hosts of heaven.

4. In Ezekiel, the Jews dwell securely, but at Armageddon the Jews are far from secure and are even experiencing deep persecution, murder and destruction.

5. In Ezekiel, the Jews seem to be present in their land, whereas, during the Battle of Armageddon, the remnant Jews have fled to the mountains of Petra and are in hiding.

6. In Ezekiel, there are protests from other nations against the invasion and at Armageddon there are no protests from other nations.

7. In Ezekiel, the invaders are destroyed by supernatural earthquakes in the mountains of Israel and at the end of the Battle of Armageddon, the invaders are destroyed by Jesus Christ at His Second Coming and totally consumed by fire.

8. In Ezekiel, only five-sixths of the invading armies are destroyed in the mountains of Israel, whereas, at the Battle of Armageddon all the invaders are destroyed in many different areas of Israel and especially the valleys of Israel.

9. In Ezekiel, it will take seven months to bury the dead, whereas at the end of the Battle of Armageddon there will be no burying of the dead because they would have been completely destroyed or consumed by fire or eaten by birds and beasts or left to decay on earth. Jeremiah 25 speaks about the Battle of Armageddon and the destruction of unsaved mankind throughout the world, not just in Israel. It also states their bodies will not be buried, but left to decay.

Jer. 25:33

[33]And the slain of the LORD shall be at that day from

> *one* end of the earth even unto the *other* end of the earth:
> they shall not be lamented, neither gathered, nor buried;
> they shall be dung upon the ground.

10. In Ezekiel, it will take seven years to burn the weapons of the invaders, while at the end of Armageddon, once again, the weapons will be destroyed by fire almost immediately.

Now let us show a few reasons why I do <u>not</u> believe that this battle, in Ezekiel, takes place in the middle of the Tribulation Period. There is certainly less evidence to compare against this theory than there is against the Battle of Armageddon theory, and therefore the mid-tribulation view and the post-Rapture view are both within reason. However, I will present a few reasons why I believe this battle is post-Rapture and not mid-Tribulation.

1. In Ezekiel, it is stated that the Jews dwell securely and the Jews will be secure just before the middle of the Tribulation. However, in the middle of the Tribulation, the Jews will experience more deep persecution, murder and destruction than ever before, at the hand of the Antichrist. We are told that the Jews will bury the dead from this battle for seven months and burn the weapons of war for seven years. In addition, we are told that the Jews will hire people to bury the dead even beyond the seven month period as "continual employment." As you will see later in this book, the middle of the Tribulation will find the Jews being raped, killed, and tortured, and their temple being desecrated. I believe they will not expose themselves to bury the dead of the armies from Russia for fear of being caught. In addition, because of the new Antichrist's economic system of purchasing and selling that will be instituted in the middle of the Tribulation, people will not have the money to spend on burying the dead and especially of the dead from an army that hated them.

2. In Ezekiel, the Jews seem to be present in their land,

whereas, in the middle of the Tribulation, the remnant Jews will flee to the mountains of Petra and hide there until the return of the Lord. Most of the other Jews who are left will be killed by the Antichrist and his cohorts.

3. Ezekiel 39:10 states that the Jews will "spoil those that spoiled them and rob those that robbed them," but the problem is the same as mentioned in item 1 above. The Jews will be the ones who will be spoiled and robbed and raped in the middle of the Tribulation Period by the Antichrist and his armies. The Jews could very well spoil and rob those who came against them if this battle happens just after the Rapture.

As you can see, there is more evidence supporting the two theories of this battle happening shortly after the Rapture or at the middle of the Tribulation as opposed to the end of the Tribulation or the Battle of Armageddon. I believe that this battle will take place shortly after the Rapture of the Church and will be an opportunity for the Antichrist to come on the scene as a great conqueror and provider of peace to Israel. After the Rapture, the actual length of time when the Seven-Year Tribulation begins is not clear in scripture. However, most scholars believe it could be within a few months to no longer than a year after the Rapture. It could be immediately after the Rapture, but I believe it to be within a few months.

As previously stated, the Antichrist will come into power and sign or confirm a treaty with Israel and this will infuriate Russia and her allies. I believe Russia sees an opportunity to gain riches, while her allies just hate Israel and are bent on her destruction. You will see that the allies with Russia are currently almost all Muslim countries who are vowed to destroy Israel. The confirming of the peace treaty will begin the seven (7) years of The Tribulation. The first four seals will happen in rapid succession. I believe that this battle is also seen in the first four seal judgments and correlates very well with them as you will see later in our study.

Ez. 38:1-23
[1]And the word of the LORD came unto me, saying,
[2]Son of man, set thy face against Gog, the land of Magog, the chief prince of Meshech and Tubal, and prophesy against him,

The land of Magog is considered to be Russia and some of the provinces that were a part of the old Soviet Union, which is the area where the descendants of Magog, son of Japheth, grandson of Noah, settled. "Magog, the chief prince of Meshech and Tubal" can also be translated as "prince of Rosh, Meshech and Tubal," from which is derived the name Russia. Ezekiel 38:15, which states they come from "the north parts," can also be translated as coming from the "uttermost parts of the north." Meshech and Tubal were also sons of Japheth, grandsons of Noah.

[3]And say, Thus saith the Lord GOD; Behold, I *am* against thee, O Gog, the chief prince of Meshech and Tubal:
[4]And I will turn thee back, and put hooks into thy jaws, and I will bring thee forth, and all thine army, horses and horsemen, all of them clothed with all sorts *of armour, even* a great company *with* bucklers and shields, all of them handling swords:

God is the one who draws this band of armies toward Israel. Some have suggested that the reason Russia wants to control Israel is because of the abundance of potash found in the Dead Sea that could be used for fertilizer and in producing explosives. Israel is the second largest producer of bromine in the world and the fifth largest producer of potash in the world. It has been estimated that the value of potash, bromine and other chemical salts in the Dead Sea could be well over 2 trillion dollars. Since today the Russian economy is in terrible condition and with many of their people lacking food, this natural resource could boost their economy and food production.

Israel is also the center for technical intelligence

according to the CIA. Jews from around the world have been considered the most brilliant scientist for centuries. The military technology possessed by Israel could thrust Russia into the leading military power overnight. Of course, as history has proven, control of Israel means potential control of all the areas surrounding Israel, Africa and many other nations. Israel has always been the route in which armies of the past have used as a stepping-stone to Africa and the Middle East.

[5]Persia, Ethiopia, and Libya with them; all of them with shield and helmet:

Persia is modern day Iran. Ethiopia or the South African nations, and Libya or the North African nations, are still the same names today. These nations are considered Muslim nations. At the writing of this book, the UN and especially the USA and the UK are attempting to stop Iran from continuing their nuclear processes and the building of a nuclear weapon. It just so happens, that Russia has volunteered to partner with Iran to be the "watch-dog" for the UN to ensure that Iran does not produce a nuclear weapon. Anyone familiar with these passages of scripture will stand against this Russian/Iranian alliance.

[6]Gomer, and all his bands; the house of Togarmah of the north quarters, and all his bands: *and* many people with thee.

Some believe that Gomer is Germany and parts of the eastern block of Europe. Others believe that Gomer is part of what is known as the Western portion of modern day Turkey. Togarmah is also considered to be Turkey and probably the Eastern portion. Once again, these are mostly Muslim nations. It has been suggested that by 2020 AD, Germany could become a majority Muslim nation due to the large growth of Muslims within Germany today.

[7]Be thou prepared, and prepare for thyself, thou, and all thy company that are assembled unto thee, and be thou a guard unto them.
[8]After many days thou shalt be visited: in the latter years thou shalt come into the land *that is* brought back from the sword, *and is* gathered out of many people, against the mountains of Israel, which have been always waste: but it is brought forth out of the nations, and they shall dwell safely all of them.

The last phrase, "dwell safely," can also mean "dwell securely." Israel is secure and their land has been "brought back from the sword" because it will not be at war. The Antichrist's treaty will give Israel this "false" security. Even though there is currently turmoil within the state of Israel and the surrounding areas, the people are dwelling securely. The same could be said of the United States. We dwell safely and securely, however, we are always in constant threat of being attacked by terrorists. Therefore, we could conclude that Israel, in its current state, is secure in their land. It will definitely be secure after the Antichrist's treaty, for a short time.

The Jewish people were scattered throughout all the nations of the world beginning 70 A.D., after the destruction of their temple. They have not had a nation to call their own until just after World War II. Since the creation of the nation of Israel in 1948, Jews from all over the world have been moving back to Israel. In the last two decades, since the fall of the Soviet empire, Jews have been moving to Israel in record numbers and especially from the old Soviet Union. Of all the nations on this earth, Israel is the only nation who has been "gathered out of many people" in such a short time. The times in which we live have seen Israel become a nation and an unprecedented return of its people from every nation on earth. Israel, at the writing of this book, has a population of over 6.6 million people of which 80% are Jewish. It is said that, in the streets of Jerusalem alone, you can find over 125 nations represented.

⁹Thou shalt ascend and come like a storm, thou shalt be like a cloud to cover the land, thou, and all thy bands, and many people with thee.

Dan. 11:23-27

²³And after the league *is made* with him he shall act deceitfully, for he shall come up and become strong with a small *number of* people.

This verse tells us that the Antichrist will become strong with a small people. Israel was chosen by God because He loved them, not because they were large in number. In fact, they were the smallest in number among the nations.

Deu. 7:6-7

⁶For thou *art* an holy people unto the LORD thy God: the LORD thy God hath chosen thee to be a special people unto himself, above all people that *are* upon the face of the earth.

⁷The LORD did not set his love upon you, nor choose you, because ye were more in number than any people; for ye *were* the fewest of all people:

²⁴He shall enter peaceably, even into the richest places of the province; and he shall do *what* his fathers have not done, nor his forefathers: he shall disperse among them the plunder, spoil, and riches; and he shall devise his plans against the strongholds, but *only* for a time.

²⁵And he shall stir up his power and his courage against the king of the south with a great army; and the king of the south shall be stirred up to battle with a very great and mighty army; but he shall not stand: for they shall forecast devices against him.

"Forecast devices" could mean that the king of the south is destroyed almost immediately by missiles or aircraft or by some quick means.

²⁶Yea, they that feed of the portion of his meat shall destroy him, and his army shall overflow: and many shall fall down slain.
²⁷And both of these kings' hearts shall be to do mischief, and they shall speak lies at one table; but it shall not prosper: for yet the end shall be at the time appointed.

Israel has the technology and they seem to work with their new-found "friend" the Antichrist to help destroy these nations. Daniel also tells us that the Antichrist will see the king of the south begin to attack and he will go to battle against him.

We will now continue in Ezekiel.

¹⁰Thus saith the Lord GOD; It shall also come to pass, *that* at the same time shall things come into thy mind, and thou shalt think an evil thought:
¹¹And thou shalt say, I will go up to the land of unwalled villages; I will go to them that are at rest, that dwell safely, all of them dwelling without walls, and having neither bars nor gates,
¹²To take a spoil, and to take a prey; to turn thine hand upon the desolate places *that are now* inhabited, and upon the people *that are* gathered out of the nations, which have gotten cattle and goods, that dwell in the midst of the land.
¹³Sheba, and Dedan, and the merchants of Tarshish, with all the young lions thereof, shall say unto thee, Art thou come to take a spoil? hast thou gathered thy company to take a prey? to carry away silver and gold, to take away cattle and goods, to take a great spoil?

Israel has an abundance of cattle and goods and has developed fertilizer from the potash found in the Dead Sea. Farming and agriculture have become a large export for Israel, which was at one time a desolate place. Israel is considered a leading nation in "agriscience." It is currently in the process of transforming the Negev Desert, which is in the south of Israel, into a thriving agricultural community. They are developing scientific ways to transform desert land into land that produces an abundance of crops and fruits.

In addition, in 2005, the Temple Institute located in Old City Jerusalem, has completed the making of the utensils for the third temple that is to be built. I believe the rebuilding of this third temple could happen just before or during the Tribulation. Most of these utensils are made from pure gold and silver. They have also completed all the garments, crowns and articles, which they deem necessary for worship in the third Temple. If you are interested in further study of these exciting events, you may visit the following websites: www.templeinstitute.com and www.templemount.org. I am not endorsing these sites, but believe anyone interested in the Second Coming of Jesus Christ will be excited to know what is happening in Jerusalem and Israel at this day and time.

Sheba and Dedan are considered to be Arabia and Tarshish is considered to be Spain and the UK. Lion is the symbol of the UK. "Young lions" could possibly refer to North America, since the USA and Canada are young nations founded by England and Spain. However, this would certainly be a theory and is not necessarily supported in scripture. Notice that these nations do not seem to be involved in the war, but are concerned as to the intentions of this band of invaders. It could be that these nations, although not involved militarily, may be against what is happening and possibly are verbally and financially supporting the Antichrist's attempt to stop these invaders. This is my theory and there is no biblical basis to substantiate this premise, either.

[14]Therefore, son of man, prophesy and say unto Gog, Thus saith the Lord GOD; In that day when my people of Israel dwelleth safely, shalt thou not know *it*?
[15]And thou shalt come from thy place out of the north parts, thou,

and many people with thee, all of them riding upon horses, a great company, and a mighty army:

Verse 15 speaks of the invaders coming from the "north parts," which I previously mentioned, could be translated "from the uttermost parts of the north." As stated above, this lends credence to the fact that because Russia is in the uttermost part as relates to the land of Israel, therefore Russia is the one referred to as king of the north. If you notice on virtually any map, Moscow is true north of Jerusalem. Notice the correlation of the nations in both Ezekiel and Daniel.

Dan. 11:40-44

[40]And at the time of the end shall the king of the south push at him: and the king of the north shall come against him like a whirlwind, with chariots, and with horsemen, and with many ships; and he shall enter into the countries, and shall overflow and pass over.
[41]He shall enter also into the glorious land, and many countries shall be overthrown: but these shall escape out of his hand, even Edom, and Moab, and the chief of the children of Ammon.

It is possible that Edom escapes unharmed, for two reasons:

> 1. Edom, which is modern day southern portion of Jordan, has a treaty with Israel and shares open tourism with each other today.
> 2. Petra is the mountainous fortress city found in southern Jordan and is believed to be the city in which the remnant of Jews will flee during the middle of the Tribulation or the 3½-year period from the beginning of the Tribulation. The number one tourist site visited in Jordan today by Jews is Petra.

[42]He shall stretch forth his hand also upon the countries: and the land of Egypt shall not escape.

⁴³But he shall have power over the treasures of gold and of silver, and over all the precious things of Egypt: and the Libyans and the Ethiopians shall be at his steps.
⁴⁴But tidings out of the east and out of the north shall trouble him: therefore he shall go forth with great fury to destroy, and utterly to make away many.

As seen in Daniel 11:40-44, the Antichrist will fight against this host of invaders and will overthrow them.

Once again, we continue speaking of Russia and her allies from Ezekiel:

¹⁶And thou shalt come up against my people of Israel, as a cloud to cover the land; it shall be in the latter days, and I will bring thee against my land, that the heathen may know me, when I shall be sanctified in thee, O Gog, before their eyes.
¹⁷Thus saith the Lord GOD; *Art* thou he of whom I have spoken in old time by my servants the prophets of Israel, which prophesied in those days *many* years that I would bring thee against them?
¹⁸And it shall come to pass at the same time when Gog shall come against the land of Israel, saith the Lord GOD, *that* my fury shall come up in my face.
¹⁹For in my jealousy *and* in the fire of my wrath have I spoken, Surely in that day there shall be a great shaking in the land of Israel;
²⁰So that the fishes of the sea, and the fowls of the heaven, and the beasts of the field, and all creeping things that creep upon the earth, and all the men that *are* upon the face of the earth, shall shake at my presence, and the mountains shall be thrown down, and the steep places shall fall, and every wall shall fall to the ground.
²¹And I will call for a sword against him throughout all my mountains, saith the Lord GOD: every man's sword shall be against his brother.

Verse 21 speaks of "every man's sword shall be against his brother," correlates wonderfully with Revelation 6:4, 8.

Rev. 6:4,8

⁴And there went out another horse that was red: and power was given to him that sat thereon to take peace

from the earth, and that they should kill one another: and there was given unto him a great sword.
[8]And I looked, and behold a pale horse: and his name that sat on him was Death, and Hell followed with him. And power was given unto them over the fourth part of the earth, to kill with sword, and with hunger, and with death, and with the beasts of the earth.

[22]And I will plead against him with pestilence and with blood; and I will rain upon him, and upon his bands, and upon the many people that *are* with him, an overflowing rain, and great hailstones, fire, and brimstone.

Notice here and in Ezekiel 39:2, that God will destroy these armies.

[23]Thus will I magnify myself, and sanctify myself; and I will be known in the eyes of many nations, and they shall know that I *am* the LORD.

Ez. 39:1-16
[1]Therefore, thou son of man, prophesy against Gog, and say, Thus saith the Lord GOD; Behold, I *am* against thee, O Gog, the chief prince of Meshech and Tubal:
[2]And I will turn thee back, and leave but the sixth part of thee, and will cause thee to come up from the north parts, and will bring thee upon the mountains of Israel:
[3]And I will smite thy bow out of thy left hand, and will cause thine arrows to fall out of thy right hand.

Verse 2 correlates with Revelation 6:8. Over 83% of these Northern Alliance of armies will be destroyed in the mountains of Israel. God will miraculously destroy them. It is very obvious from these passages that the nations who align with Russia will be virtually annihilated. This means that Russia and its Muslim allies will no longer be of influence on earth at this time. Israel will certainly feel safe and secure now that almost all these Muslim nations, who currently hate Israel, will no longer exist as any religious or world power.

⁴Thou shalt fall upon the mountains of Israel, thou, and all thy bands, and the people that *is* with thee: I will give thee unto the ravenous birds of every sort, and *to* the beasts of the field to be devoured.

Verses 4 correlates with Revelation 6:8.

⁵Thou shalt fall upon the open field: for I have spoken *it*, saith the Lord GOD.
⁶And I will send a fire on Magog, and among them that dwell carelessly in the isles: and they shall know that I *am* the LORD.
⁷So will I make my holy name known in the midst of my people Israel; and I will not *let them* pollute my holy name any more: and the heathen shall know that I *am* the LORD, the Holy One in Israel.
⁸Behold, it is come, and it is done, saith the Lord GOD; this *is* the day whereof I have spoken.
⁹And they that dwell in the cities of Israel shall go forth, and shall set on fire and burn the weapons, both the shields and the bucklers, the bows and the arrows, and the handstaves, and the spears, and they shall burn them with fire seven years:

Verse 7 uses the word "pollute" which means "to profane." I believe He is stating that this Russian Alliance will not "profane' His "holy name any more." It could be because they are virtually annihilated. The "heathen" will know that He is God, but that does not mean they will trust Him as Lord and Savior. Verse 9 tells us that Israel will burn these weapons for seven years. As I stated earlier, I believe this is one of the reasons why this battle will occur toward the beginning of the Tribulation.

¹⁰So that they shall take no wood out of the field, neither cut down *any* out of the forests; for they shall burn the weapons with fire: and they shall spoil those that spoiled them, and rob those that robbed them, saith the Lord GOD.
¹¹And it shall come to pass in that day, *that* I will give unto Gog a place there of graves in Israel, the valley of the passengers on the east of the sea: and it shall stop the *noses* of the passengers: and there shall they bury Gog and all his multitude: and they shall call *it* The valley of Hamongog.
¹²And seven months shall the house of Israel be burying of them,

that they may cleanse the land.

[13]Yea, all the people of the land shall bury *them*; and it shall be to them a renown the day that I shall be glorified, saith the Lord GOD.

Israel will bury the dead of these Northern Allies for seven months.

[14]And they shall sever out men of continual employment, passing through the land to bury with the passengers those that remain upon the face of the earth, to cleanse it: after the end of seven months shall they search.
[15]And the passengers *that* pass through the land, when *any* seeth a man's bone, then shall he set up a sign by it, till the buriers have buried it in the valley of Hamongog.

After the seven months, they will hire people in continued employment to bury the rest of the dead that are found.

[16]And also the name of the city *shall* be Hamonah. Thus shall they cleanse the land.

Israel has been tormented by its Muslim neighbors, who have been militarily financed by Russia and China for many years. Most of her Muslim neighbors have threatened the annihilation of Israel since her existence. Now, neither them nor Russia will exist to continue this threat. There is no wonder that Israel will give all their allegiance to the Antichrist and credit him for most of this new peace. However, as we will see in 3½ years, they will see the true identity of this Antichrist and it will be in shocking horror. Until that time, Israel will continue to dwell in their land in unbelief in Jesus as their Messiah.

The Muslim religion today is the fastest growing religion in the world. With most of it destroyed, the False Harlot Church will have an open door to control the religions of the world that are left.

Some may question why stop at Ezekiel 39:16 and

not include verses 17-29. The answer is that verses 17-29 do not refer to the Battle of Gog and Magog, but do refer to the Battle of Armageddon. There is a definite change in the tone from verse 16 to verse 17 that creates what should be a new chapter at that point. I have already presented more than ten reasons why the Battle of Gog and Magog is not the same as the Battle of Armageddon and will not repeat these points.

Notice in verses 17-29, in your Bible, the language that is used refers to the Battle of Armageddon, which is at the time of Jesus' Second Coming to earth. Verse 22 coincides with the Second Coming because we are told "So the house of Israel shall know that I *am* the LORD their God from that day and forward." This will not happen during the Tribulation, but after the Battle of Armageddon ends. Verse 23 states that "all" the enemies of Israel die and not just five-sixths, as we have discussed about the Battle of Gog and Magog. Verses 25-26 state that Israel will be restored and not be afraid anymore. Certainly Israel will be horribly frightened during the last half of the Tribulation Period, therefore these verses relate to the Second Coming to earth. Verse 29 mentions that all those of Israel who are left after the Second Coming to earth will be saved. Before this time Israel as a nation will abide in mostly unbelief. I conclude that verses 17-29 are truly related to the Second Coming and the Battle of Armageddon and are not related to the Battle of Gog and Magog, that Ezekiel 38:1 through 39:16 refer.

8

The Harlot Religious System Revealed

Once the Antichrist signs or confirms the treaty with Israel and claims that he defeated Russia and her Muslim allies, he will consummate a worldwide religious system. This religious system is revealed in Revelation Chapter 17 and is called the "great whore." This religious system will be given the authority to control religious activity throughout the world as the "official government religion" recognized by the new world leader, the Antichrist. He will promote this religious system and have all of his followers promote it also. I believe the following verses describe the Church at Rome, with the Pope of that day as its leader. Most scholars believe the Antichrist will rule what is known as the Revived Roman Empire from Rome. We also know from history that during the latter years of the Old Roman Empire, the Catholic Church headed by the Pope in Rome was recognized as the "official government religion" of the world. Does this mean that I believe that the Pope will be the Antichrist? In fact, I do not believe the Pope will be the Antichrist. I believe the Antichrist will promote the Pope's religious system in a deceptive mode and then in the middle of the Tribulation have it completely destroyed. This shows the cunning ability of the Antichrist to draw most of the world to fall in love with him and follow him.

Before we begin our study of the Harlot Religious System, let us study some background supporting our Harlot Church theory. You will see me quote Dr. Harold Willmington throughout this book and for a good reason. Dr. Willmington is known as "Mr. Bible" because of his thorough knowledge of the Bible, history and his unique way of presenting arguments from both sides of many issues. He has published a large study book called *Willmington's Guide to the Bible*, which I recommend to everyone. Back in the early 1980's, I studied under his teachings through his series the "Liberty Home Bible Institute" and was impressed by his simple, easy to understand, yet detailed study of the complete Bible. Dr. Willmington is currently Dean of Liberty Bible Institute located in Lynchburg, Virginia. I will quote only his text relating to the description of this Harlot Church. Notice carefully the description of this "Harlot" religious system.

"IV.   The Destruction of the World's Religious System
(Rev. 17).
"And there came one of the seven angels which had the seven vials, and talked with me, saying unto me, come hither; I will shew unto thee the judgment of the great whore that sitteth upon many waters" (17:1).

This brutal, bloody, and blasphemous harlot is none other than the universal false church, the wicked wife of Satan. God had no sooner begun his blessed work in preparing for himself a people than the devil did likewise. In fact, the first baby to be born on this earth later became Satan's original convert. (See Gen. 4:8; 1 Jn. 3:12.) We shall now consider the historical, current, and future activities of this perverted prostitute.
A.   The harlot viewed historically.
1.   Satan's church began officially at the Tower of Babel in Genesis 11:1-9, nearly twenty-four centuries b.c. Here, in the fertile plain of Shinar, probably very close to the original Garden of Eden, the first spade of dirt was turned for the purpose of devil-worship.
2.   The first full-time minister of Satan was Nimrod, Noah's wicked and apostate grandson (Gen. 10:8-10).

3. Secular history and tradition tell us that Nimrod married a woman who was as evil and demonic as himself. Her name was Semerimus. Knowing God's promise of a future Savior (Gen. 3:15), Semerimus brazenly claimed that Tammuz, her first son, fulfilled this prophecy.

4. Semerimus thereupon instituted a religious system which made both her and her son the objects of divine worship. She herself became the first high priestess. Thus began the mother-child cult which later spread all over the world. The city of Babylon was the seat of Satan worship until it fell, in 539 B.C., to the Persians.

    a. From Babylon it spread to Phoenicia under the name of Ashteroth and Tammuz.

    b. From Phoenicia it traveled to Pergamos in Asia Minor. This is the reason for John's admonition to the church at Pergamos in the book of Revelation: "I know thy works, and where thou dwellest, even where Satan's seat is" (Rev. 2:13).

    c. In Egypt the mother-child cult was known as Isia and Horus.

    d. In Greece it became Aphrodite and Eros.

    e. In Rome this pair was worshiped as Venus and Cupid.

    f. In China it became known as Mother Shing Moo and her child.

        Dr. J. Dwight Pentecost writes:

        "Several years ago I visited an archeological museum in Mexico City. A recent find had just been put on display which Mexican archeologists had authenticated as belonging to the period about 200 years before Christ. The object was the center of religious worship among some of the early Indians in Mexico. To my amazement, it was an image of a mother with a child in her arms. This Babylonian religion spread abroad to become the religion of the world." (*Prophecy for Today,* p. 133)

5. What was the teaching of Semerimus' satanic church?

    a. That Semerimus herself was the way to God. She actually adopted the title "Queen of Heaven."

    b. That she alone could administer salvation to the sinner through various sacraments, such as the sprinkling of holy water.

    c. That her son Tammuz was tragically slain by a wild boar during a hunting trip.

    d. That he was, however, resurrected from the dead forty days later. Thus, each year afterward, the temple virgins of this cult would enter a forty-day fast as a memorial to Tammuz' death and resurrection.

    e. After the forty-day fast, a joyful feast called Ishtar took place. At this feast colored eggs were exchanged and eaten as a symbol of the resurrection. An evergreen tree was displayed and a yule log was burned. Finally, hot cakes marked with the letter T (to remind everybody of Tammuz) were baked and eaten.

6. About 2000 B.C., God called Abraham away from all this (see Josh. 24: 2, 3) and led him into the Promised Land. But by the ninth century B.C., Israel had returned to this devil worship under the influence of wicked Jezebel

(1 Ki. 16:30-33). At this time the cult was worshiped under the name of Baal.

7.   Both Ezekiel and Jeremiah warned against this hellish thing.

"Then he brought me to the door of the gate of the Lord's house which was toward the north; and behold, there sat women weeping for Tammuz" (Ezek. 8:14).

"The children gather wood, and the fathers kindle the fire, and the women knead their dough, to make cakes to the queen of heaven...to burn incense to the queen of heaven, and to pour out drink offerings unto her" (Jer. 7:18; 44:25).

8.   By the time of Christ, this cult had so influenced Roman life that the Caesars were not only crowned as emperors of Rome, but also bore the title *Pontifex Maximus,* meaning, "high priest." They were high priests of the Babylonian satanic church.

9.   During A.D. 306, a Roman emperor named Constantine was threatened by a very powerful enemy army. Realizing that his uneasy troops needed confidence, Constantine claimed to have seen a vision on the eve of battle. He saw a large blue flag with a red cross on it and heard a mighty voice which said, *In hoc signo vinces*—"In this sign conquer." He thereupon marched his troops into a shallow river, claimed them to be officially baptized, and ordered the sign of the cross painted on all his weapons. Thus inspired, he led his troops to victory and subsequently made Christianity the state religion of Rome.

The Roman priests of Tammuz soon discovered that they could easily make the transition into Christianity (with certain changes) and thereupon carried their traditions forward without interruption by promoting the Madonna-Child worship concept, the holy water sacrament, etc.

Thus for nearly 300 years the devil had desperately attempted to destroy the church from outside by his terrible persecutions. But with the advent of Constantine he changed his tactics, walking the aisle to work from within. The corrupted church was already flourishing in Christ's day, and the Savior delivered a scathing attack against some of its very deacons and elders (Mt. 23).

B. The harlot viewed currently. Is mystery Babylon at work today? She is indeed—stronger and more sinful than ever. At least three New Testament writers describe her latter-day activities and characteristics:

1. Paul.

"This know also, that in the last days perilous times shall come. For men shall be lovers of their own selves, covetous, boasters, proud, blasphemers, disobedient to parents, unthankful, unholy, without natural affection, trucebreakers, false accusers, incontinent, fierce, despisers of those who are good, traitors, heady, high-minded, lovers of pleasures more than lovers of God, having a form of godliness but denying the power thereof" (2 Tim. 3:1-5).

"For the time will come when they will not endure sound doctrine but after their own lusts shall they heap to themselves teachers, having itching ears; and they shall turn away their ears from the truth, and shall be turned unto fables" (2 Tim. 4:3, 4).

2. Peter.

"But there were false prophets also among the people, even as there shall be false teachers among you, who privily shall bring in damnable heresies, even denying the Lord that bought them" (2 Pet. 2:1).

3. John.

"I know thy works, that thou art neither cold nor hot; I would thou wert cold or hot. So then because thou art lukewarm, and neither cold nor hot, I will spue thee out of my mouth. Because thou sayest, I am rich and increased with goods, and have need of nothing, and

knowest not that thou art wretched, and miserable, and
poor, and blind, and naked" (Rev. 3:15-17).

> This harlot church will probably be
> composed of apostate masses from
> Protestantism, Catholicism, Judaism, and every
> other major world religion. It is entirely
> possible that the World Council of Churches
> will spearhead this latter-day ungodly union."
> *(Willmington's Guide to the Bible, Tyndale
> House Publishers Inc., pages 570-572)*

As Dr. Willmington stated, this Harlot Church will be
probably composed of many different religions and
denominations. I believe he is correct, because after the
Rapture, most of the "religious people" left on earth will turn
to the Pope for "religious" answers. As I have already stated,
the Muslim religion will be virtually erased or at least of no
effect after the Russian Alliance invasion of Israel. The
Antichrist will certainly tell everyone to follow the Pope's
advice. This is why I believe the Harlot Church of the
Tribulation Period will reside in Rome and it will be headed
by the Pope of that era. The Pope will seem to have power
over almost the whole world. This has always been the desire
of the Papacy since it came into power over 1500 years ago.
Even the Antichrist will "seemingly" respect the Pope as the
supreme spiritual authority. The Antichrist will be a master
deceiver.

Rev. 17:1
And there came one of the seven angels which had the seven vials,
and talked with me, saying unto me, Come hither; I will shew unto
thee the judgment of the great whore that sitteth upon many waters:

Even though none of the seven angels with the seven vials
have been introduced at this point, the description given and
the rule appointed to this religious system happened in the first
3½ years of the Tribulation. Revelation Chapter 17:1-15 is
considered a parenthetical vision or interlude. Interludes were

used throughout the Revelation to describe particular events. In a sense, it is like someone giving a summary of an event before the interlude and then the interlude steps back to describe the event in more detail. As you will see toward the middle of the Tribulation, this system will be completely destroyed by the one who promoted it the most, the Antichrist.

We are told that the woman "sitteth upon many waters." This is interpreted in Revelation 17:15 as people, nations and tongues. Therefore, this Harlot Church is accepted throughout the world and can be found throughout the world. Today there are over one billion professing Catholics worldwide and Catholicism is widely accepted throughout the world, even in Communist countries, dictatorships and other countries that will not allow Protestants or even cults to abide.

Rev. 17:2
With whom the kings of the earth have committed fornication, and the inhabitants of the earth have been made drunk with the wine of her fornication.

What other religious system has been accepted throughout the world and throughout its history by kings, princes and governments everywhere? Catholicism! Before Catholicism, there were pagan practices of the "gods," which as we have already seen, was nothing but Satan worship. This does not mean that it is accepted by God. Obviously, my statements will not be considered "politically correct," but neither were John the Baptist statements. I certainly do not mean to compare myself to John the Baptist, for I am but a fly as to a 747 Jetliner compared to him.

While on a mission trip to Haiti in the late 1970's, we were told by our missionary that the Haitians would attend a Catholic mass and turn right around and attend a voodoo service. It was obvious that the mass did not convict them of sin and many saw nothing wrong with mixing their paganism with Catholicism. Even though some Catholic apologists state their Church does not preach salvation by works, virtually all Catholics around the world have been taught that works are the way for salvation. How is it possible that most of these people around the world believe works are the way to heaven? The Bible teaches that salvation is "not of works." It is by the grace and mercy of God that we are saved. His grace and mercy are applied to us when we come to Him with a humble heart and confess our sin of unbelief and believe in our heart and soul that Jesus died, was buried and rose again the third day. Whosoever does this will be saved. Jesus is our priest and we need no other.

Eph. 2:8-9

[8]For by grace are ye saved through faith; and that not of yourselves: *it is* the gift of God:
[9]Not of works, lest any man should boast.

Tit. 3:4-5

[4]But after that the kindness and love of God our Saviour toward man appeared,
[5]Not by works of righteousness which we have done, but according to his mercy he saved us, by the washing of regeneration, and renewing of the Holy Ghost;

Rom. 10:13

[13]For whosoever shall call upon the name of the Lord shall be saved.

Rev. 17:3

So he carried me away in the spirit into the wilderness: and I saw a woman sit upon a scarlet coloured beast, full of names of blasphemy, having seven heads and ten horns.

Notice that John is not carried away into a heavenly type of setting, but into a gruesome setting called the "wilderness." This means a desolate place. This place is considered, in the eyes of God, as not being a spiritually desirable place. That does not seem to be the word that one would use to describe a religious system, does it? But this religious system is not considered a Godly system, to say the least.

The "woman" is the Harlot Church system. Is it just coincidence that Mary the mother of Jesus, has been exalted to the status of Co-Redeemer and Mediatrix in the Roman Catholic Church? According to Pope Pius XII: "The Blessed Virgin Mary is to be called Queen not only on account of her divine motherhood but also because by the will of God she had a great part in the work of our salvation. . . . In this work of redemption the blessed Virgin Mary was closely associated with her Christ. . . . Just as Christ, because he redeemed us, is by a special title our King and Lord, so too is Blessed Mary, our Queen and our Mistress, because of the unique way in which she co-operated in our redemption. She provided her very substance for his body, she offered him willingly for us, and she took a unique part in our salvation by desiring it, praying for it, and so obtaining it. . . . - - *Ad Coeli Reginam.*" Remember our discussion of identity of the "Queen of Heaven?" Semerimus has now been incorporated into the Roman Catholic Church in the form of "Mary." Semerimus was also known as the Mediatrix.

The beast could very well be the Antichrist. The phrase "sit upon a scarlet coloured beast" probably means that this religious system has the blessings of the Antichrist. The Antichrist will promote this religion, for a while. It will look as though the "woman" is controlling the Antichrist since she is sitting on the "beast." The beast is slyly allowing the woman to feel and look like she is in control, but as stated before, that will change toward the middle of the Tribulation. He will certainly be a magnificent and crafty statesman! The "ten horns" probably represent the ten-nation confederacy (European Union) or the Revived Roman Empire in which the Antichrist will be the head. The "seven heads" represent seven mountains upon which this religious system sits. (see Rev. 17:9).

Rev. 17:4
And the woman was arrayed in purple and scarlet colour, and decked with gold and precious stones and pearls, having a golden cup in her hand full of abominations and filthiness of her fornication:

Notice the colors and the gold and precious stones that are mentioned. These are the same colors representing the Pope and his Cardinals and Bishops. She is also arrayed with "gold and precious stones" and having a "golden cup." The Papacy, in all its splendor, is arrayed with these items. The Pope wears a scarlet tabarro or cloak, the Cardinals wear scarlet attire and the Bishops wear purple attire. Gold and precious stones are found on liturgical vestments, the Tiara (crown) and many other vessels found in the Vatican. The mass held by the Pope includes a golden chalice which contains the wine. I do realize that governments and royals have the same similar vestments and articles woven within their framework also. There is an economic/governmental system called Babylon and a religious system called Babylon, in the Revelation. However, I believe that this system is referring to a "religious" system at this point and not the governmental system.

Do all of these items alone qualify the Church of Rome to be the Harlot Church? Certainly not! However, when the description in the rest of these verses are seen, one must conclude there is no other religious system that fits this description other than Roman Catholicism. Its predecessor, the Babylonian Mysticism, has been incorporated within Roman Catholicism for over fourteen hundred years and fits this description. Before Roman Catholicism, it was the Roman gods, Greek gods, Egyptian gods, Babylonian gods and finally back to the tower of Babel itself which was headed up by Nimrod. No wonder it is called "Mystery Babylon!"

Rev. 17:5
And upon her forehead *was* a name written, MYSTERY, BABYLON THE GREAT, THE MOTHER OF HARLOTS AND ABOMINATIONS OF THE EARTH.
Rev. 17:6
And I saw the woman drunken with the blood of the saints, and with the blood of the martyrs of Jesus: and when I saw her, I wondered with great admiration.

John wonders who this woman could be. Roman Catholicism was unknown during John's day. Throughout history, we have seen that Rome and Roman Catholicism have been the leaders of the murder of untold numbers of Christian saints in the name of "religion." Many were considered heretic if they dared question the Pope or try to study scripture for themselves. The Bible teaches us to:

II Tim. 2:15

[15]Study to show thyself approved unto God, a workman that needeth not to be ashamed, rightly dividing the word of truth.

Why would any "church" or church leader not want their members to study the Word of God? Could it be because their lies, abominations and fornications will be unveiled to the public? Could it mean that the "church" would no longer control the public in a tyrannized fashion? Could it mean that they would lose control of the world? I think so!

Rev. 17:7

And the angel said unto me, Wherefore didst thou marvel? I will tell thee the mystery of the woman, and of the beast that carrieth her, which hath the seven heads and ten horns.

Rev. 17:8

The beast that thou sawest was, and is not; and shall ascend out of the bottomless pit, and go into perdition: and they that dwell on the earth shall wonder, whose names were not written in the book of life from the foundation of the world, when they behold the beast that was, and is not, and yet is.

We see some strange statements about this beast: he "was," "is not," "shall ascend out of the bottomless pit," "go into perdition" and "yet is." I have already established that the beast is the Antichrist. However, we will see that the Antichrist will be possessed by Satan in the middle of the Tribulation. We will also see that the Antichrist will receive a mortal head wound. These strange statements could mean the following:

1. "Was" meaning that the Antichrist comes to power, which happens at the beginning of the Tribulation, and his power is given to him by Satan.

2. "Is not" meaning he is killed, or there is a mock killing, which happens at the middle of the Tribulation.

3. "Yet is" meaning he will be possessed by Satan at

the middle of the Tribulation and will probably be revived by this Satanic possession.

4. "Shall ascend out of the bottomless pit" meaning the Antichrist's body will be cast into the Lake of Fire, but Satan will be cast into the "bottomless pit" at the Second Coming after the Tribulation Period and before the Millennium. Satan will be loosed from the bottomless pit at the end of the Millennium.

5. "Go into perdition" meaning that Satan will be cast into the Lake of Fire at the end of the Millennial Reign of Christ.

Notice that the unsaved, "whose names were not found written in the book of life," will wonder and be amazed at these happenings. These will be the people who believe that the Antichrist is God.

Verse 8 contains a whole prophecy of the end times relating to the Antichrist and Satan.

Rev. 17:9
And here *is* the mind which hath wisdom. The seven heads are seven mountains, on which the woman sitteth.

We have already discussed the seven mountains and determined that this is probably Rome.

Rev. 17:10
And there are seven kings: five are fallen, and one is, *and* the other is not yet come; and when he cometh, he must continue a short space.

The seven kings are probably the ruling world empires of the past and future. Part of this verse could relate to Daniel's dream interpretation found in Daniel Chapter 2 of the statue relating to the upcoming ruling world empires, which he described to Nebuchadnezzar. Daniel describes five of these empires. Before Daniel, the first world empire was Egypt and the second was Assyria.

Dan. 2:36-43

[36]"This *is* the dream; and we will tell the interpretation thereof before the king.

[37]Thou, O king, *art* a king of kings: for the God of heaven hath given thee a kingdom, power, and strength, and glory.

[38]And wheresoever the children of men dwell, the beasts of the field and the fowls of the heaven hath he given into thine hand, and hath made thee ruler over them all. Thou *art* this head of gold.

Babylon was the first world empire in Daniel's interpretation.

[39]And after thee shall arise another kingdom inferior to thee, and another third kingdom of brass, which shall bear rule over all the earth.

The second kingdom was the Medo-Persian and the third was the Greek Empire.

[40]And the fourth kingdom shall be strong as iron: forasmuch as iron breaketh in pieces and subdueth all *things*: and as iron that breaketh all these, shall it break in pieces and bruise.

The fourth kingdom was the Roman Empire.

[41]And whereas thou sawest the feet and toes, part of potters' clay, and part of iron, the kingdom shall be divided; but there shall be in it of the strength of the iron, forasmuch as thou sawest the iron mixed with miry clay.

[42]And *as* the toes of the feet *were* part of iron, and part of clay, *so* the kingdom shall be partly strong, and partly broken.

[43]And whereas thou sawest iron mixed with miry clay, they shall mingle themselves with the seed of men: but they shall not cleave one to another, even as iron is not mixed with clay.

The fifth kingdom will be the Revived Roman Empire, which I believe will be the European Union.

In Verse 10, the five that have fallen since John's time were Eqypt, Assyria, Babylon, Medo-Persia and Greece. The one that "is" is the Roman Empire, which existed during the period of John's writings. The other that "is not yet come" is the Revived Roman Empire. The Revived Roman Empire, or possibly what is the European Union, will come into power during the Tribulation Period. This will be the shortest period any empire has ever ruled.

Rev. 17:11
And the beast that was, and is not, even he is the eighth, and is of the seven, and goeth into perdition.

The Antichrist is probably sharing the rule of the Revived Roman Empire with the Harlot Church, but will become the sole ruler at the middle of the Tribulation Period after he destroys the Harlot Church. He will take complete rule of the Empire and will be the "eighth and is of the seven." We have already spoken of the fact that he will go into "perdition" or the Lake of Fire.

Rev. 17:12
And the ten horns which thou sawest are ten kings, which have received no kingdom as yet; but receive power as kings one hour with the beast.

These ten kings, which we have already discussed, "will receive power as kings for one hour with the beast." This may be a prophecy of when these ten kings team up with the Antichrist to destroy the Harlot Church at the middle of the Tribulation Period. We will see this in Revelation 17:16-18. Verses 17-18 are events which happen at the middle of the Tribulation. It could very well mean that the Harlot Church and city of Rome will be destroyed in one hour, similar to the destruction of the rebuilt city of Babylon, which is discussed toward the end of the Tribulation.

Rev. 17:13
These have one mind, and shall give their power and strength unto the beast.
Rev. 17:14
These shall make war with the Lamb, and the Lamb shall overcome them: for he is Lord of lords, and King of kings: and they that are

with him *are* called, and chosen, and faithful.

Verses 13 and 14 will be listed again because their occurrence will be later in time. I left them here to show continuity to verse 15. Verse 13 is a prophecy of the middle of the Tribulation when these ten kings will pledge allegiance to the Antichrist. Verse 14 is a prophecy of the Battle of Armageddon and the Second Coming of Christ at the end of the Tribulation.

Rev. 17:15
And he saith unto me, The waters which thou sawest, where the whore sitteth, are peoples, and multitudes, and nations, and tongues.

I have already mentioned in the beginning of this chapter, that this verse supplies the meaning to the word "waters" found in Revelation 17:1. The Harlot Church will have power and control over the multitudes throughout the world. This has always been the goal of the Roman Papacy since its inception. It will not be popular during this time to make a stand for Christ, because you will suffer immeasurable persecution and probably death. However, as a true Christian you have to make your stand, win others to Christ and expose this Harlot Church for who she really is: "Mystery Babylon," the worship of Satan himself. Thank God there will be a lot of "Stephens" during this time who stand strong for Christ regardless of the cost. Thank God that He will give that dying grace to those who are martyred for the cause of Christ. Remember Stephen's death? It was like going to sleep and waking up to see Jesus standing before him in Paradise, which is heaven.

Now that the Harlot Church has become the "religion" of the first half of the Tribulation, God's wrath will now begin to fall on mankind, in unfathomable judgments, during the seven years of the Tribulation.

9

The Seal Judgments Opened

In the Introduction I posed several questions, one of which was "Will there be a judgment day?" The judgment day nightmares about which many people today have concern are about to begin and will be seen throughout the Tribulation Period. The seven seal judgments are about to be released upon mankind in rapid succession.

Zech. 6:1, 4-5

¹And I turned, and lifted up mine eyes, and looked, and, behold, there came four chariots out from between two mountains; and the mountains were mountains of brass.

⁴Then I answered and said unto the angel that talked with me, What are these, my lord?

⁵And the angel answered and said unto me, These are the four spirits of the heavens, which go forth from standing before the LORD of all the earth.

Zechariah sees these horses and chariots moving just behind each other in seemingly rapid succession.

These first four seal judgments are probably released just before or during the battle mentioned in Ezekiel in which we have seen in Chapter 7 of this book.

The First Seal is Opened - Antichrist Conquering

Rev. 6:1

And I saw when the Lamb opened one of the seals, and I heard, as it were the noise of thunder, one of the four beasts saying, Come and see.

Rev. 6:2

And I saw, and behold a white horse: and he that sat on him had a bow; and a crown was given unto him: and he went forth conquering, and to conquer.

> Matt. 24:6
> [6]And ye shall hear of wars and rumours of wars: see that ye be not troubled: for all these things must come to pass, but the end is not yet.

The first seal is opened and we see the white horse of a conqueror going about conquering. This is none other than the Antichrist.

> Zech. 6:3,6
> [3]And in the third chariot white horses; and in the fourth chariot grisled and bay horses.
> [6]The black horses which are therein go forth into the north country; and the white go forth after them; and the grisled go forth toward the south country.

Notice, in Zechariah, the special directions in which these chariots ride, as they relate to the battle mentioned in Chapter 7 of this book, with the king of the north and king of the south. Zechariah's vision and John's vision seem to be one in the same. "Grisled and bay horses" mentioned in Zechariah's vision are also considered pale in color, which corresponds with the pale horses in John's vision.

> Ez. 38:15
> [15]And thou shalt come from thy place out of the north parts, thou, and many people with thee, all of them riding upon horses, a great company, and a mighty army:

As we have just discussed the battle mentioned in Ezekiel, we can see that the rider in Revelation 6:2 is the Antichrist who is head of the ten-nation confederacy, the European Union. This is not Jesus' Second Coming, which happens seven years in the future. As we saw in Chapter 7 of this book, this ruler will conquer these nations who are attacking Israel.

The Second Seal is Opened – Peace Taken From the Earth

Rev. 6:3
And when he had opened the second seal, I heard the second beast say, Come and see.
Rev. 6:4
And there went out another horse *that was* red: and *power* was given to him that sat thereon to take peace from the earth, and that they should kill one another: and there was given unto him a great sword.

   The second seal is opened and the red horse is revealed. Peace is taken from the earth temporarily and people go about killing each other. The Antichrist will kill with a sword.

Zech. 6:2
[2]In the first chariot were red horses; and in the second chariot black horses;

Matt. 24:7-8
[7]For nation shall rise against nation, and kingdom against kingdom: and there shall be famines, and pestilences, and earthquakes, in divers places.
[8]All these *are* the beginning of sorrows.

   Matthew states this is "the beginning of sorrows," meaning the beginning of the Tribulation Period.

Ez. 38:21
[21]And I will call for a sword against him throughout all my mountains, saith the Lord GOD: every man's sword shall be against his brother.

Mic. 7:3-6
[3]That they may do evil with both hands earnestly, the prince asketh, and the judge asketh for a reward; and the great man, he uttereth his mischievous desire: so they wrap it up.
[4]The best of them is as a brier: the most upright is sharper than a thorn hedge: the day of thy watchmen and thy visitation cometh; now shall be their perplexity.
[5]Trust ye not in a friend, put ye not confidence in a guide: keep the doors of thy mouth from her that lieth in thy bosom.
[6]For the son dishonoureth the father, the daughter riseth up against her mother, the daughter in law against her mother in law; a man's enemies are the men of his own house.

Notice that Micah is describing a time when there are no righteous people on earth. This happened just after the Rapture as we discussed in Chapter 2. It also states that "the day of thy watchmen and thy visitation cometh" which speaks of the Tribulation Period. Notice it also states that "now begins their perplexity." The word "perplexity" means confusion. There will be total confusion after the Rapture. Verses 5-6 states that you can no longer trust family or friend during this time because they will rise up against you.

Lk. 21:16
[16]And ye shall be betrayed both by parents, and brethren, and kinsfolks, and friends; and some of you shall they cause to be put to death.

The Third Seal is Opened – Famine Across the Earth

Rev. 6:5
And when he had opened the third seal, I heard the third beast say, Come and see. And I beheld, and lo a black horse; and he that sat on him had a pair of balances in his hand.
Rev. 6:6
And I heard a voice in the midst of the four beasts say, A measure of wheat for a penny, and three measures of barley for a penny; and see thou hurt not the oil and the wine.

The third seal is opened and the black horse is revealed. Verses 5-6 speak of a probable famine and a very high cost of living and cost of goods during this period. There may also be food rationing. "Balances" in verse 5 refers to famine or rationing of food.

Zech. 6:6,8
[6]The black horses which are therein go forth into the north country; and the white go forth after them; and the grisled go forth toward the south country.
[8]Then cried he upon me, and spake unto me, saying, Behold, these that go toward the north country have quieted my spirit in the north country.

This verse probably refers to the destruction of over 83% of the Russian Alliance mentioned in the Chapter 7 of this book.

Matt. 24:7
[7]For nation shall rise against nation, and kingdom against kingdom: and there shall be famines, and pestilences, and earthquakes, in divers places.

Ez. 14:21
[21]For thus saith the Lord GOD; How much more when I send my four sore judgments upon Jerusalem, the sword, and the famine, and the noisome beast, and the pestilence, to cut off from it man and beast?

The Fourth Seal is Opened – One Fourth of the Population is Killed

---

Rev. 6:7
And when he had opened the fourth seal, I heard the voice of the fourth beast say, Come and see.

Rev. 6:8
And I looked, and behold a pale horse: and his name that sat on him was Death, and Hell followed with him. And power was given unto them over the fourth part of the earth, to kill with sword, and with hunger, and with death, and with the beasts of the earth.

The fourth seal is opened and the pale horse is revealed with Death and Hell following in this vision. This means that probably only the unsaved are killed. One fourth of the earth's population is killed. Today's population is around 6.5 billion people. If we consider 10% of today's population to be truly Christian, then this 10% or 650 million people will rapture just before the Tribulation begins. No one knows how many will be saved after the Rapture, but we do know that during the Seven-Year Tribulation Period, there will be an unprecedented number of people who trust in Christ Jesus as their Lord and Savior. Let us hypothetically assume that at least 4.5 billion people who are left on earth are not saved. A "fourth part" of them being killed, as stated in Verse 8, would equate to over one billion people being killed during this judgment. Much of this one billion are probably those killed during the war with Russia and its allies. I have already stated that over 83% of this Russian Alliance will be killed. However, these Seal Judgments are not limited to affecting just these warring armies, but their effects are worldwide.

Matt. 24:7

[7]For nation shall rise against nation, and kingdom against kingdom: and there shall be famines, and pestilences, and earthquakes, in divers places.

Zech. 6:3, 6-7

[3]And in the third chariot white horses; and in the fourth chariot grisled and bay horses.

[6]The black horses which are therein go forth into the north country; and the white go forth after them; and the grisled go forth toward the south country.

[7]And the bay went forth, and sought to go that they might walk to and fro through the earth: and he said, Get you hence, walk to and fro through the earth. So they walked to and fro through the earth.

Ezekiel speaks of the death of these invaders and especially Russia. They will die by the sword, hunger and by the beasts of the earth.

Ez. 39:2, 4-6, 11

[2]And I will turn thee back, and leave but the sixth part of thee, and will cause thee to come up from the north parts, and will bring thee upon the mountains of Israel:

[4]Thou shalt fall upon the mountains of Israel, thou, and all thy bands, and the people that is with thee: I will give thee unto the ravenous birds of every sort, and to the beasts of the field to be devoured.

[5]Thou shalt fall upon the open field: for I have spoken it, saith the Lord GOD.

[6]And I will send a fire on Magog, and among them that dwell carelessly in the isles: and they shall know that I am the LORD.

[11]And it shall come to pass in that day, that I will give unto Gog a place there of graves in Israel, the valley of the passengers on the east of the sea: and it shall stop the noses of the passengers: and there shall they bury Gog and all his multitude: and they shall call it The valley of Hamongog.

The Fifth Seal is Opened – Scene in Heaven

Revelation 6:9-11 depicts a scene in heaven of many souls of those true believers who are murdered during the Tribulation.

Rev. 6:9
And when he had opened the fifth seal, I saw under the altar the souls of them that were slain for the word of God, and for the testimony which they held:
Rev. 6:10
And they cried with a loud voice, saying, How long, O Lord, holy and true, dost thou not judge and avenge our blood on them that dwell on the earth?
Rev. 6:11
And white robes were given unto every one of them; and it was said unto them, that they should rest yet for a little season, until their fellowservants also and their brethren, that should be killed as they *were*, should be fulfilled.

The fifth seal is opened and these saints are asking God when will their blood be avenged. They are told that many other true believers must die and then vengeance will come. We will see this prayer answered in Revelation Chapters 8 and 19. People today become offended when a Christian attempts to witness to them about Jesus. Today we receive sneers, jeers and ridicule. During the Tribulation, these Christians will be murdered for their faith. This will be far worse than the ridicule we receive today.

Mt. 24:9
[9]Then shall they deliver you up to be afflicted, and shall kill you: and ye shall be hated of all nations for my name's sake.

The Sixth Seal is Opened – Earthquake, Sun Blackened, Moon Red, Atmosphere Changes, Mountain and Hills Moved Out of Their Places

When the sixth seal is opened we see a great earthquake,

the sun is darkened, the moon becomes as blood, stars fall from the sky, the atmosphere is rolled back like a scroll and the mountains and hills are moved out of their places. All of these possibly describe the results of the explosion of a nuclear bomb or bombs. The description is literally what happens when a nuclear bomb is exploded.

Rev. 6:12
And I beheld when he had opened the sixth seal, and, lo, there was a great earthquake; and the sun became black as sackcloth of hair, and the moon became as blood;

We have seen the destructive force as a result of an earthquake and the eruption of Mt. Saint Helen and many other volcanoes throughout the world in the 20th and 21st centuries. This seal will bring with it, the largest earthquake known to the history of man.

Ez. 38:19-20
[19]For in my jealousy *and* in the fire of my wrath have I spoken, Surely in that day there shall be a great shaking in the land of Israel;
[20]So that the fishes of the sea, and the fowls of the heaven, and the beasts of the field, and all creeping things that creep upon the earth, and all the men that *are* upon the face of the earth, shall shake at my presence, and the mountains shall be thrown down, and the steep places shall fall, and every wall shall fall to the ground.

Joel 2:30-32
[30]And I will show wonders in the heavens and in the earth, blood, and fire, and pillars of smoke.
[31]The sun shall be turned into darkness, and the moon into blood, before the great and the terrible day of the LORD come.
[32]And it shall come to pass, *that* whosoever shall call on the name of the LORD shall be delivered: for in mount Zion and in Jerusalem shall be deliverance, as the LORD hath said, and in the remnant whom the LORD shall call.

Rev. 6:13
And the stars of heaven fell unto the earth, even as a fig tree casteth her untimely figs, when she is shaken of a mighty wind.

Ez. 38:22-23
[22]And I will plead against him with pestilence and with blood; and

I will rain upon him, and upon his bands, and upon the many people that *are* with him, an overflowing rain, and great hailstones, fire, and brimstone.
[23]Thus will I magnify myself, and sanctify myself; and I will be known in the eyes of many nations, and they shall know that I *am* the LORD.

Rev. 6:14
And the heaven departed as a scroll when it is rolled together; and every mountain and island were moved out of their places.
Rev. 6:15
And the kings of the earth, and the great men, and the rich men, and the chief captains, and the mighty men, and every bondman, and every free man, hid themselves in the dens and in the rocks of the mountains;
Rev. 6:16
And said to the mountains and rocks, Fall on us, and hide us from the face of him that sitteth on the throne, and from the wrath of the Lamb:
Rev. 6:17
For the great day of his wrath is come; and who shall be able to stand?

Do these people, upon whom these disasters fall, turn to God for forgiveness? Not at all! They flee to the caves and rocks to try to hide from Him. Notice the parallel in Isaiah 2 below.

Is. 2:9-22
[9]And the mean man boweth down, and the great man humbleth himself: therefore forgive them not.
[10]Enter into the rock, and hide thee in the dust, for fear of the LORD, and for the glory of his majesty.
[11]The lofty looks of man shall be humbled, and the haughtiness of men shall be bowed down, and the LORD alone shall be exalted in that day.
[12]For the day of the LORD of hosts *shall be* upon every *one that is* proud and lofty, and upon every *one that is* lifted up; and he shall be brought low:
[13]And upon all the cedars of Lebanon, *that are* high and lifted up, and upon all the oaks of Bashan,
[14]And upon all the high mountains, and upon all the hills *that are* lifted up,

¹⁵And upon every high tower, and upon every fenced wall,
¹⁶And upon all the ships of Tarshish, and upon all pleasant pictures.
¹⁷And the loftiness of man shall be bowed down, and the haughtiness of men shall be made low: and the LORD alone shall be exalted in that day.
¹⁸And the idols he shall utterly abolish.
¹⁹And they shall go into the holes of the rocks, and into the caves of the earth, for fear of the LORD, and for the glory of his majesty, when he ariseth to shake terribly the earth.
²⁰In that day a man shall cast his idols of silver, and his idols of gold, which they made *each one* for himself to worship, to the moles and to the bats;
²¹To go into the clefts of the rocks, and into the tops of the ragged rocks, for fear of the LORD, and for the glory of his majesty, when he ariseth to shake terribly the earth.
²²Cease ye from man, whose breath *is* in his nostrils: for wherein is he to be accounted of?

The 144,000 Are Sealed

Just before the trumpet judgments are sounded, God seals 144,000 Jewish witnesses on earth, 12,000 from each of the tribes of Israel except Dan and Ephraim. I do not know why Dan and Ephraim were excluded. God alone knows. These witnesses will be the greatest evangelists to have walked the earth. Millions will be saved as a result of their testimony and preaching during the Tribulation Period. Notice Matthew 24:14, that possibly as a result of these 144,000 preachers, the gospel will be preached unto all nations during the Tribulation Period.

Mt. 24:14
¹⁴And this gospel of the kingdom shall be preached in all the world for a witness unto all nations; and then shall the end come.

Rev. 7:1
And after these things I saw four angels standing on the four corners of the earth, holding the four winds of the earth, that the wind should not blow on the earth, nor on the sea, nor on any tree.

Notice that God has and always will control the wind.

Regardless of who may state that God lost control of this universe at the fall of Adam, God has never and will never lose control of this universe and all His creation.

Rev. 7:2
And I saw another angel ascending from the east, having the seal of the living God: and he cried with a loud voice to the four angels, to whom it was given to hurt the earth and the sea,
Rev. 7:3
Saying, Hurt not the earth, neither the sea, nor the trees, till we have sealed the servants of our God in their foreheads.
Rev. 7:4
And I heard the number of them which were sealed: *and there were* sealed an hundred *and* forty *and* four thousand of all the tribes of the children of Israel.
Rev. 7:5
Of the tribe of Judah *were* sealed twelve thousand. Of the tribe of Reuben *were* sealed twelve thousand. Of the tribe of Gad *were* sealed twelve thousand.
Rev. 7:6
Of the tribe of Aser *were* sealed twelve thousand. Of the tribe of Nepthalim *were* sealed twelve thousand. Of the tribe of Manasses *were* sealed twelve thousand.
Rev. 7:7
Of the tribe of Simeon *were* sealed twelve thousand. Of the tribe of Levi *were* sealed twelve thousand. Of the tribe of Issachar *were* sealed twelve thousand.
Rev. 7:8
Of the tribe of Zabulon *were* sealed twelve thousand. Of the tribe of Joseph *were* sealed twelve thousand. Of the tribe of Benjamin *were* sealed twelve thousand.

In Revelation 7:1-2 the angels with the first four trumpet judgments are told not to allow the wind to blow on the earth, sea, nor any tree and not to hurt the earth, sea or trees until the 144,000 are sealed by God. The command "not to hurt" relates to the upcoming four trumpet judgments that are to sound. All of these first four trumpet judgments affect the earth, sea and trees.

The Seventh Seal is Opened – Silence in Heaven for One-Half Hour

Rev. 8:1
And when he had opened the seventh seal, there was silence in heaven about the space of half an hour.

Today we have moments of silence for those loved ones who have died, those who are having problems, silent prayer and silence for many other occasions. There is silence during war to hear the coming of the enemy. Sometimes total silence can be frightful.

I do not know why there is ½ hour of silence, but it could be because of the upcoming trumpet judgments that are to sound. It could also be that God is about to answer the prayers of saints for all ages, asking when God would show vengeance upon the evil that has been thrust on the saints for ages. Only God knows why there is ½ hour of complete silence in heaven at this particular time.

10

The Trumpet Judgments Sound

The time frame for this chapter is around the 21st through the 42nd month of the first 3½ years of the Tribulation Period. This chapter will be one of the most action packed chapters in this book. We will see, as the seven trumpets sound, the significance once again of the fraction one-third. An additional one-third of the trees and all the green grass are burned up, one-third of the seas become as blood, along with one-third of sea life and shipping are destroyed. One-third of all fresh water becomes undrinkable. One-third of the sun, moon and stars are darkened. In addition, we will see locust-like demons with scorpion-like stingers who will plague unsaved mankind. There will also be a 200 million demon army go about the earth killing an additional one-third of mankind. We will see the gospel will have been preached to all the nations during these trumpet judgments.

Other events that unfold in this chapter are: the temple will be defiled by the Antichrist, the two witnesses will be murdered, war in heaven will occur and Satan and his demonic angels will be kicked out of heaven onto earth, the Harlot Church will be destroyed along with the city in which it resides, the Antichrist supposedly is killed and brought back to life, the False Prophet and the number 666 appear, many of the Jews will be persecuted and killed and the Jewish remnant will flee to the mountains of Petra.

As you can see by the introduction to this chapter, many events will unfold in rapid succession, therefore let us begin.

Rev. 8:2

And I saw the seven angels which stood before God; and to them were given seven trumpets.

Rev. 8:3

And another angel came and stood at the altar, having a golden censer; and there was given unto him much incense, that he should offer *it* with the prayers of all saints upon the golden altar which was before the throne.

Rev. 8:4

And the smoke of the incense, *which came* with the prayers of the saints, ascended up before God out of the angel's hand.

Incense in the bible is a symbol of prayers of the saints. Here their prayers, and especially the prayers of those mentioned in Revelation 6:9-11, are answered.

Rev. 8:5

And the angel took the censer, and filled it with fire of the altar, and cast *it* into the earth: and there were voices, and thunderings, and lightnings, and an earthquake.

Rev. 8:6

And the seven angels which had the seven trumpets prepared themselves to sound.

As seen in Verse 5, the incense censer, filled with fire, is cast into the earth. These are prayers for God's vengeance upon the evil that is present on earth. The number of prayers causes their voices to be loud like thunder and specific like lightning which results in an earthquake. God then releases the seven trumpet judgments in answer to these prayers.

The First Trumpet Sounds – 1/3 Trees Burned Up and All Green Grass Burned Up

---

Notice in the trumpet judgments to follow, God judges the idols of mankind. As you study scripture, God seems to bring judgment on the idols of that time period being studied. The judgments on Babel were to bring confusion to man because they were worshipping the deeds of humanism and being able to communicate without hindrance. Therefore God confounded their languages and they could no longer communicate. Confusion was the result. The judgments on Egypt during Moses' era were directly related to the Egyptian idols, so were the judgments on Babylon during Belshazzar's reign and so forth. God will judge the idols of the era of the Tribulation Period, which are the sun, earth, moon, stars, trees, sea, economics, etc. We have groups today who worship each of these idols and the main area of worship is evolution, which states that life evolved from the sea.

In addition, notice the word "one-third" is used frequently. Three is the number of grace. God's grace still prevails even during His harshest judgments. Had He destroyed all of the trees, seas, etc. there would have been no oxygen left on earth for mankind and animals to breathe. He wants man to turn to Him for salvation even during His wrath. He truly is a loving God, but we must understand that God has to judge sin and sinful man. Anyone at anytime can turn from his sin and trust Him and He will save that person immediately.

The trumpet judgments are probably sounded toward the last half of the first 3½ years of the Tribulation Period or during months 21 through 42.

Rev. 8:7
The first angel sounded, and there followed hail and fire mingled with blood, and they were cast upon the earth: and the third part of trees was burnt up, and all green grass was burnt up.

The first trumpet judgment sounds and one third of trees and all green grass are burned up. Consider the fact that the majority of our oxygen production comes from algae in the ocean, trees, grass and plants of all kinds. These judgments will impact all industries such as housing, building, food, livestock and a host of others. Farmers will be put out of business, unemployment will skyrocket because of the lack of wood to build buildings, people will starve for lack of food because livestock will die, etc.

Joel 1:15-20

[15]Alas for the day! for the day of the LORD *is* at hand, and as a destruction from the Almighty shall it come.

[16]Is not the meat cut off before our eyes, *yea*, joy and gladness from the house of our God?

[17]The seed is rotten under their clods, the garners are laid desolate, the barns are broken down; for the corn is withered.

[18]How do the beasts groan! the herds of cattle are perplexed, because they have no pasture; yea, the flocks of sheep are made desolate.

[19]O LORD, to thee will I cry: for the fire hath devoured the pastures of the wilderness, and the flame hath burned all the trees of the field.

[20]The beasts of the field cry also unto thee: for the rivers of waters are dried up, and the fire hath devoured the pastures of the wilderness.

Isn't it wonderful how scripture interprets scripture! For those who mistakenly believe that the Old Testament is no longer to be used, be advised that all scripture is to be used to interpret scripture. As you have seen and will see, there are more scripture relating to the end of times found in the Old Testament than found in the New Testament.

The Second Trumpet Sounds – 1/3 Sea Became Blood, 1/3 Creatures In Sea Die, 1/3 Shipping Destroyed

The second trumpet sounds and we see judgment on the sea.

Rev. 8:8
And the second angel sounded, and as it were a great mountain burning with fire was cast into the sea: and the third part of the sea became blood;
Rev. 8:9
And the third part of the creatures which were in the sea, and had life, died; and the third part of the ships were destroyed.

One third of the seas become as blood, one third of sea life is destroyed and one third of shipping is destroyed. Just these first two trumpet judgments have now brought the world's economy to its knees. We will see towards the middle of the Seven-Year Tribulation, the two Godly witnesses mentioned earlier will be credited by mankind for causing these judgments during the first half of the tribulation along with most of the seal and trumpet judgments (Rev. 11:10).

The Third Trumpet Sounds – 1/3 of Fresh Water Becomes Bitter and Undrinkable

---

Rev. 8:10
And the third angel sounded, and there fell a great star from heaven, burning as it were a lamp, and it fell upon the third part of the rivers, and upon the fountains of waters;
Rev. 8:11
And the name of the star is called Wormwood: and the third part of the waters became wormwood; and many men died of the waters, because they were made bitter.

The third trumpet sounds and a star call Wormwood falls from the sky and one-third of all fresh waters are made bitter and undrinkable. Wormwood means bitter. Bitter relates to the wickedness of man and could be the reason for such a judgment, for during the Tribulation Period, man is extremely wicked. At this point, one-third of all the waters both salt and fresh are destroyed. People will probably kill each other for a bottle of fresh water. I feel sure many will die from dehydration and thirst during this time. If you are living during this period and reading this book and this judgment has not already occurred, I would begin to store as much bottled water as possible. However, trusting in Jesus who is the "living water" will allow you to depend on Him to provide. He will direct your paths.

Joel 1:20
[20]The beasts of the field cry also unto thee: for the rivers of waters are dried up, and the fire hath devoured the pastures of the wilderness.

Jer. 23:10-15
[10]For the land is full of adulterers; for because of swearing the land mourneth; the pleasant places of the wilderness are dried up,

and their course is evil, and their force *is* not right.
[11]For both prophet and priest are profane; yea, in my house have I found their wickedness, saith the LORD.

These judgments come because of the perversion that is dominant over the world.

[12]Wherefore their way shall be unto them as slippery *ways* in the darkness: they shall be driven on, and fall therein: for I will bring evil upon them, *even* the year of their visitation, saith the LORD.
[13]And I have seen folly in the prophets of Samaria; they prophesied in Baal, and caused my people Israel to err.
[14]I have seen also in the prophets of Jerusalem an horrible thing: they commit adultery, and walk in lies: they strengthen also the hands of evildoers, that none doth return from his wickedness: they are all of them unto me as Sodom, and the inhabitants thereof as Gomorrah.

Even the prophets, priests and preachers are involved with and promote this wicked perversion. These priests have told people that it is alright to indulge in sinful acts to satisfy the desires of their flesh. What an abomination!

[15]Therefore thus saith the LORD of hosts concerning the prophets; Behold, I will feed them with wormwood, and make them drink the water of gall: for from the prophets of Jerusalem is profaneness gone forth into all the land.

The Fourth Trumpet Sounds – 1/3 Sun, Moon and Stars Darkened

Rev. 8:12
And the fourth angel sounded, and the third part of the sun was smitten, and the third part of the moon, and the third part of the stars; so as the third part of them was darkened, and the day shone not for a third part of it, and the night likewise.

The fourth trumpet sounds and one-third of the sun, moon and stars are darkened. Instead of 24 hours in a full day, there are now only 16 hours to a day because 8 hours (one-third) are removed from the 24-hour day, 4 hours from the night and 4 hours from the day. We can assume that there are 8 hours of darkness and 8 hours of daylight. God has now shortened time. There are still the same number of days in the calendar, but they pass by much faster.

Mt. 24:22

22 And except those days should be shortened, there should no flesh be saved: but for the elect's sake those days shall be shortened.

Notice that God's grace is shown again in verse 12 and predicted by Jesus in Matthew 24. God shortens the day to keep everyone from being destroyed. However, he does this for the sake of those who are saved during the Tribulation, not for the unsaved.

Lk. 21:25a

25a And there shall be signs in the sun, and in the moon, and in the stars;...

Luke 21 tells us there will be signs in the heavens. I believe that Revelation 8:12 could be considered a major sign to all of mankind during this time, that there truly is a God and His name is Jesus. Who else could cause a shortening of a day? Sure, volcanic eruptions could block the sun and moon from shining, but that would not cause the 24-hour day to be shortened permanently. It would only be a temporary circumstance. I am sure the Antichrist will blame it on the "ozone depletion." However, even trying to explain it away could never replace the fact that only a Supreme Being could have performed such a miracle.

Let me summarize these first four trumpet judgments and the disasters that they have reaped upon the universe. At this time one-third of all these are destroyed: trees, seas, creatures in the sea, shipping in the sea, fresh water, sun, moon and stars. All the green grass is destroyed. No one can comprehend the toll this takes upon mankind. We are also told that many die as a result of the bitter waters. We have already seen in the seal judgments that over one-fourth of mankind died. People are dying on the earth by the millions and billions during this Tribulation Period.

Rev. 8:13
And I beheld, and heard an angel flying through the midst of heaven, saying with a loud voice, Woe, woe, woe, to the inhabiters of the earth by reason of the other voices of the trumpet of the three angels, which are yet to sound!

In Verse 13 we see an angel pronouncing three woes on those who are on earth. These three woes are the next three trumpet judgments and they are obviously more horrible than anything we have seen thus far. Could it get any worse? Yes! And it will!

The Fifth Trumpet Sounds - Locust/Scorpion-Like Demons Torment Unsaved Mankind Five Months

---

Rev. 9:1
And the fifth angel sounded, and I saw a star fall from heaven unto the earth: and to him was given the key of the bottomless pit.
Rev. 9:2
And he opened the bottomless pit; and there arose a smoke out of the pit, as the smoke of a great furnace; and the sun and the air were darkened by reason of the smoke of the pit.
Rev. 9:3
And there came out of the smoke locusts upon the earth: and unto them was given power, as the scorpions of the earth have power.
Rev. 9:4
And it was commanded them that they should not hurt the grass of the earth, neither any green thing, neither any tree; but only those men which have not the seal of God in their foreheads.
Rev. 9:5
And to them it was given that they should not kill them, but that they should be tormented five months: and their torment *was* as the torment of a scorpion, when he striketh a man.
Rev. 9:6
And in those days shall men seek death, and shall not find it; and

shall desire to die, and death shall flee from them.
Rev. 9:7
And the shapes of the locusts *were* like unto horses prepared unto battle; and on their heads *were* as it were crowns like gold, and their faces *were* as the faces of men.
Rev. 9:8
And they had hair as the hair of women, and their teeth were as *the teeth* of lions.
Rev. 9:9
And they had breastplates, as it were breastplates of iron; and the sound of their wings *was* as the sound of chariots of many horses running to battle.
Rev. 9:10
And they had tails like unto scorpions, and there were stings in their tails: and their power was to hurt men five months.
Rev. 9:11
And they had a king over them, *which is* the angel of the bottomless pit, whose name in the Hebrew tongue *is* Abaddon, but in the Greek tongue hath *his* name Apollyon.

The fifth trumpet sounds and the bottomless pit is opened and a horde of locust-like demons are released upon earth to torment the unsaved for five months. These locust demons are commanded not to touch nor torment the saved. It is obvious that the spiritual world of demons and angelic beings can see or recognize the mark of God on the saved, because they are told to only torment the unsaved. They have stingers in their tails much like a scorpion. Their sting torments mankind for 5 months and yet no one will die from their stings. However, men will wish to die due to the unbearable pain they receive as a result of their stings. These are not grass or green leaf-eating locusts, as locusts are today. They are prepared for a specific purpose and time and have evidently been contained and controlled in the bottomless pit until this time. Their description is beyond human reason and understanding as John tries his best to describe them.

Some scholars have speculated that these locust-like creatures could be an Apache helicopter. However, I do not believe that it is a warship or something that we can describe in our own finite minds. An Apache helicopter or any other warship, though it fits the pictorial description given by John, is used for killing and not wounding. If you have seen the destruction in the Iraq war that is transpiring at the writing of this book, you will see plainly that these helicopters are not used for wounding, but to destroy life. The demon locust will not destroy life, but cause excruciating pain for five months even to the point that mankind will want to die and cannot.

Even though the saved are not affected by this plague and many other plagues, they still experience the events that are taking place during this Tribulation Period. We hurt when others hurt, whether they are saved or unsaved. As a saved individual, our whole heart is to reach the unsaved so they will not go through this torment. I feel sure that many saved individuals who have been witnessing to their unsaved friends during this time will see their friends go through this torment. It is very possible that many of these unsaved individuals who go through this torment by the locust, later profess Jesus Christ as their personal Savior after the five months of excruciating pain. Let's pray this will be the case!

Verses 1-11 were the inspiration for the cover for this book. Verse 1 seems to refer to "Satan" or "a star fall from heaven." He is temporarily given the key to the bottomless pit. This key is controlled by Jesus and Jesus will allow Satan to loose these demon locust for this plague.

Rev. 1:18

[18]I *am* he that liveth, and was dead; and, behold, I am alive for evermore, Amen; and have the keys of hell and of death.

Satan does not keep the key, as we see in Revelation 20:1.

Rev. 20:1

[1]And I saw an angel come down from heaven, having the key of the bottomless pit and a great chain in his hand.

Verses 2-10 describe these locust demons, but how did they get into the bottomless pit?

Jude 1:6-7

[6]And the angels which kept not their first estate, but left their own habitation, he hath reserved in everlasting chains under darkness unto the judgment of the great day.

[7]Even as Sodom and Gomorrha, and the cities about them in like manner, giving themselves over to fornication, and going after strange flesh, are set forth for an example, suffering the vengeance of eternal fire.

II Pet. 2:4

[4]For if God spared not the angels that sinned, but cast *them* down to hell, and delivered *them* into chains of darkness, to be reserved unto judgment;

We see in Jude and II Peter that some angels have been chained until judgment. It stands to reason that other demons were chained and reserved in the bottomless pit to be used at this point in the Tribulation for whatever purpose God desires.

Verse 11 speaks about the king of these locust demons. His name is "Abaddon" or "Apollyon" which means "destroyer." This is not Satan, but must be Satan's right-hand demonic angel. As Michael may be considered God's right-hand holy angel, so Apollyon is Satan's right-hand evil angel.

The Sixth Trumpet Sounds – Four Demons Released From Euphrates River

Now that the demon locusts have had their time of torment and are considered the first woe, the second woe which is the sixth trumpet is about to sound. As I stated earlier, times are progressively getting worse. Yet, we will see in Revelation 9:21, that many still do not turn to Christ for salvation, but continue in their defiance towards Him. A simple, yet sincere, "Lord Jesus forgive me and save me" is all it takes to become a child of God, yet pride and stubbornness control people during the Tribulation, as it does today. Are you willing to risk your soul because of your pride? I certainly hope not!

Rev. 9:12
One woe is past; *and*, behold, there come two woes more hereafter.

Rev. 9:13
And the sixth angel sounded, and I heard a voice from the four horns of the golden altar which is before God,
Rev. 9:14
Saying to the sixth angel which had the trumpet, Loose the four angels which are bound in the great river Euphrates.

The sixth trumpet is considered the second woe. It has now sounded. As we see in Verse 14, another demonic force is released and this time from the Euphrates River in Iraq. These four demonic angels are loosed and evidently become the leaders of the upcoming 200 million demon army found in Verse 16.

> 2 Pet. 2:4
> [4]For if God spared not the angels that sinned, but cast *them* down to hell, and delivered *them* into chains of darkness, to be reserved unto judgment;
> Jude 6
> [6]And the angels which kept not their first estate, but left their own habitation, he hath reserved in everlasting chains under darkness unto the judgment of the great day.
> Lk. 8:31
> [31]And they besought him that he would not command them to go out into the deep.

As we see in these verses and many verses in Revelation, many fallen angels have been bound and chained in different places. Some are loose and were active throughout history and are still active today and will be in the future. These four fallen angels, along with the 200 million found in Verse 16, will kill another one-third of mankind. These four demonic angels could be Satan's match to the four heavenly beasts that stand before God's throne continuously. Satan usually has an evil match to God's holy beings or Godhead. Some of these are: Holy Trinity versus Evil Trinity (Satan, Antichrist, False Prophet), Holy Angels versus Demonic Fallen Angels, Jesus Christ versus Antichrist, Four Holy Beasts versus Four Demonic Angels, etc.

Rev. 9:15
And the four angels were loosed, which were prepared for an hour, and a day, and a month, and a year, for to slay the third part of men.

Notice in Verse 15, that these four demonic angels have been chained until an absolute specific time, even down to the very hour. God knows exactly when these are to be loosed and this proves that God is in absolute control of the universe. As I stated before, there are some "so-called Bible teachers" today stating that God lost control of the universe for a while. They have stated that God has no authority over this universe. God has never lost one iota of control over His universe or mankind at anytime during His existence, nor will He ever lose one iota of control. As to His existence, He is the beginning and the end and is, has been and will always be in complete control of every molecule throughout this universe and all other universes that may exist. I believe these individuals have been reading the wrong book or taking heed to bad influences. The Bible teaches emphatically that God has all power and will never lose power and authority over His creation. If He ever did lose authority or one ounce of power, He would not be God. I am passionately against all forms of deceit and hypocrisy.

As to these four demonic angels, God knows how man will react and He knows just when to loose these angels.

Rev. 9:16
And the number of the army of the horsemen *were* two hundred thousand thousand: and I heard the number of them.

Verse 16 has been a verse encompassed with much controversy. Some say it is the army from China, others believe it is strictly symbolic and yet others, including myself, believe it is an army of 200 million demons, led by the four demonic angels from the Euphrates. Verse 19 helps me to eliminate the army from China. Chinese, along with the rest of mankind, do not have tails like a serpent. I realize that this could be symbolic language to describe some apparatus or weapon that this 200 million army uses. Regardless, it is a huge army that will reap havoc upon the earth. We know from the Bible's description of demons, they are horrible, powerful and full of evil.

Rev. 9:17
And thus I saw the horses in the vision, and them that sat on them, having breastplates of fire, and of jacinth, and brimstone: and the heads of the horses *were* as the heads of lions; and out of their mouths issued fire and smoke and brimstone.

Verse 17 describes this army with breastplates of fire, jacinth and brimstone. The heads of their horses are like lions. They seem to spew fire, smoke and brimstone from their mouths. If you try to visualize these creatures, you would almost visualize fire-breathing dragons. I did not say they were fire-breathing dragons, so please do not stop your study of this book and say "he is loony!" Thank God, those saved before the Tribulation will not have to witness these creatures.

However, we do see another demonic force riding on demonic beasts that are indescribable. Could this be major volcanic eruptions caused by this army? Fire, smoke and brimstone (sulfur) are certainly characteristics of erupting volcanoes. We know from history that volcanic eruptions can wipe out a civilization almost instantly.

Rev. 9:18
By these three was the third part of men killed, by the fire, and by the smoke, and by the brimstone, which issued out of their mouths.
Rev. 9:19
For their power is in their mouth, and in their tails: for their tails *were* like unto serpents, and had heads, and with them they do hurt.

Verses 18 and 19 tell us that this army will kill 1/3 of all mankind with fire, smoke and brimstone. They will do this with the power from within their mouths and tails. This will equate to about 1.7 billion additional people killed during this plague alone. Up to this point over 3.5 billion people would have been killed during the 1st half of the Tribulation alone (less than 3½ years). This will now leave less than 3 billion people on earth. Remember, using today's population of over 6.5 billion, the death rate is overwhelming to say the least. The stench alone would be unbearable not considering the disease caused by the decaying bodies.

Rev. 9:20
And the rest of the men which were not killed by these plagues yet repented not of the works of their hands, that they should not worship devils, and idols of gold, and silver, and brass, and stone, and of wood: which neither can see, nor hear, nor walk:
Rev. 9:21
Neither repented they of their murders, nor of their sorceries, nor of their fornication, nor of their thefts.

In Verses 20-21, even with all of what has happened during this first 3½ years, people will stubbornly choose not to believe in Jesus as Savior. God is merciful, because He still does not annihilate all of mankind. If we were God we would say "I have tried and tried, but you still will not respond to me. Forget you and make ready to die." Thank God we are not God!

Notice the word "sorceries." We derive our word "pharmacy" from this word. In other words they continue with their drugs. This plague and the death it causes seems to only affect the unsaved. Verse 20 states "the rest of the men which were not killed... repented not...." Therefore, it seems to indicate that those who were killed were unsaved.

A Mighty Angel and the Little Sweet/Bitter Book

Rev. 10:1
And I saw another mighty angel come down from heaven, clothed with a cloud: and a rainbow *was* upon his head, and his face *was* as it were the sun, and his feet as pillars of fire:

As we see beginning in Revelation 10:1, a "mighty angel" is described. Scholars differ as to who this angel may be. Some believe it is an archangel with no specific name, others believe it is Michael the Archangel or Gabriel the Archangel and others believe it is a post-resurrection appearance of Christ. I believe this is a description of Jesus Christ. No one can be dogmatic with any theory, including myself. However, the Bible is filled with many pre-incarnate appearances of Christ in the Old Testament, which are called a "Christophany." These Christophanies were usually seen where you find "the angel of the Lord" in the Old Testament.

This appearance in Revelation seems to be a post-resurrection appearance of Jesus Christ, whom John sees as a "mighty angel" and Daniel sees a one of "two men" clothed in linen. Some do not believe that this could be an appearance of Jesus since it has not been prophesied or predicted. However, most of the Old Testament Christophanies were not necessarily prophesied in advance either. This appearance does not take away from the 2nd Coming to earth to rule and reign. It seems to be an appearance to show that Jesus is the owner and creator of all the earth and sea and has all authority over them and is about to judge it through the Wrath of God. In addition, this angel states in Verse 6 that "time is no longer." This phrase could also be interpreted as "delay no longer." Who, other than Jesus Himself, has the authority to make such an announcement?

I will try not to debate this issue too much because the identity of this messenger is not the true meaning of the context of this scripture. However, I will supply references to support my theory and give you opportunity to determine the meaning for yourself. The message in Revelation 10 is the precursor to the beginning of the last half of the Seven-Year Tribulation Period or the last 3½ years.

Now let's see the description of this "mighty angel" and provide the proof to our theory that this is a description of Jesus Christ.

John used Michael the archangel's name in Rev. 12:7, so I

believe that he would have no problem using it here, if this were Michael. See the references below describing Jesus Christ:

"Clothed with a cloud"

Ex. 13:21

[21] And the LORD went before them by day in a pillar of a cloud, to lead them the way; and by night in a pillar of fire, to give them light; to go by day and night:

Ex. 19:9,16

[9] And the LORD said unto Moses, Lo, I come unto thee in a thick cloud, that the people may hear when I speak with thee, and believe thee for ever. And Moses told the words of the people unto the LORD.

[16] And it came to pass on the third day in the morning, that there were thunders and lightnings, and a thick cloud upon the mount, and the voice of the trumpet exceeding loud; so that all the people that *was* in the camp trembled.

Ex. 40:38

[38] For the cloud of the LORD *was* upon the tabernacle by day, and fire was on it by night, in the sight of all the house of Israel, throughout all their journeys.

Acts 1:9

[9] And when he had spoken these things, while they beheld, he was taken up; and a cloud received him out of their sight.

"Rainbow was upon his head"

Ez.1:28

[28] As the appearance of the bow that is in the cloud in the day of rain, so *was* the appearance of the brightness round about. This *was* the appearance of the likeness of the glory of the LORD. And when I saw *it*, I fell upon my face, and I heard a voice of one that spake.

Rev.4:3

[3] And he that sat was to look upon like a jasper and a sardine stone: and *there was* a rainbow round about the throne, in sight like unto an emerald.

"Face was as it were the sun"

Mal. 4:2

[2] But unto you that fear my name shall the Sun of righteousness arise with healing in his wings; and ye shall go forth, and grow up as calves of the stall.

Mt. 17:2

²And was transfigured before them: and his face did shine as the sun, and his raiment was white as the light.

Acts 26:13

¹³At midday, O king, I saw in the way a light from heaven, above the brightness of the sun, shining round about me and them which journeyed with me.

Rev. 1:16

¹⁶And he had in his right hand seven stars: and out of his mouth went a sharp twoedged sword: and his countenance *was* as the sun shineth in his strength.

"His feet as pillars of fire"

Ex. 13:21

²¹And the LORD went before them by day in a pillar of a cloud, to lead them the way; and by night in a pillar of fire, to give them light; to go by day and night:

Rev. 1:15

¹⁵And his feet like unto fine brass, as if they burned in a furnace; and his voice as the sound of many waters.

Rev. 10:2

And he had in his hand a little book open: and he set his right foot upon the sea, and *his* left *foot* on the earth,

Dan. 12:5-6

⁵Then I Daniel looked, and, behold, there stood other two, the one on this side of the bank of the river, and the other on that side of the bank of the river.

⁶And *one* said to the man clothed in linen, which *was* upon the waters of the river, How long *shall it be to* the end of these wonders?

In Daniel 12:5-6, we find in Daniel's vision the question is being asked as to when will be the "end of these wonders?" We find in these verses that Daniel seems to have the same vision as John. Notice that Daniel sees two men on either side of the bank of the river. Could these two that Daniel sees possibly be Jesus and John? Is this a prophecy vision of John as we see him in Revelation 10:2, that Daniel sees hundreds of years before? I think so! Notice that Daniel sees the "one clothed in linen" stand upon the "waters of the river" and John sees the angel stand upon the "sea" and the "earth." These are not contradictions. The location could very well be found at the mouth of a river flowing into the sea. This act of standing on the sea and the earth could relate to the complete authority Jesus the creator has over his dominion. It also foretells the upcoming vial judgments that are to plague both the earth and the sea and all creation. Jesus has full authority to judge in His righteousness.

Ps. 8:6

⁶Thou madest him to have dominion over the works of thy hands; thou hast put all *things* under his feet:

Heb. 2:8

⁸Thou hast put all things in subjection under his feet. For in that he put all in subjection under him, he left nothing *that is* not put under him. But now we see not yet all things put under him.

Rev. 10:3

And cried with a loud voice, as *when* a lion roareth: and when he had cried, seven thunders uttered their voices.

"lion roareth"
Jesus is referred to as the "Lion of the Tribe of Juda"

Rev. 5:5

⁵And one of the elders saith unto me, Weep not: behold, the Lion of the tribe of Juda, the Root of David, hath prevailed to open the book, and to loose the seven seals thereof.

Hos. 11:10

¹⁰They shall walk after the LORD: he shall roar like a lion: when he shall roar, then the children shall tremble from the west.

"seven thunders"

Ps. 29:3

³The voice of the LORD *is* upon the waters: the God of glory thundereth: the LORD *is* upon many waters.

In Psalms Chapter 29, the "voice of the Lord" is mentioned seven times. This chapter also describes the voice of the Lord and the effects.

Ps. 18:13

¹³The LORD also thundered in the heavens, and the Highest gave

his voice; hail *stones* and coals of fire.

Rev. 10:4
And when the seven thunders had uttered their voices, I was about to write: and I heard a voice from heaven saying unto me, Seal up those things which the seven thunders uttered, and write them not.

Both John and Daniel were told to "seal" and not to write, the things which were uttered.

Dan. 12:9
⁹And he said, Go thy way, Daniel: for the words *are* closed up and sealed till the time of the end.

Rev. 10:5
And the angel which I saw stand upon the sea and upon the earth lifted up his hand to heaven,

Rev. 10:6
And sware by him that liveth for ever and ever, who created heaven, and the things that therein are, and the earth, and the things that therein are, and the sea, and the things which are therein, that there should be time no longer:

Dan. 12:7
⁷And I heard the man clothed in linen, which *was* upon the waters of the river, when he held up his right hand and his left hand unto heaven, and sware by him that liveth for ever that *it shall be* for a time, times, and an half; and when he shall have accomplished to scatter the power of the holy people, all these *things* shall be finished.

Heb. 6:13
¹³For when God made promise to Abraham, because he could swear by no greater, he sware by himself,

As we see in Revelation 10:5-6, this person lifts his hands to heaven and "sware by him that liveth for ever and ever" and is seen by both Daniel and John. To swear by someone, that "someone" had to be greater in authority than yourself. Jesus is swearing to God the Father in heaven and stating that the time for the judgments to cease will be 3½ years ("time, times and an half"). Once again, times are determined by Jesus Christ and no one else. Notice that the person in Daniel's vision states that the "the power of the holy people" will be scattered and then the judgments will be finished. This is a prophesy of the upcoming persecution of the Jewish remnant that we will see in Revelation 12. Jesus is God, so He swore by Himself.

Rev. 10:7
But in the days of the voice of the seventh angel, when he shall begin to sound, the mystery of God should be finished, as he hath declared to his servants the prophets.

As I stated in the introduction to Revelation 10 above, the phrase "time no longer" in Verse 6 can also be interpreted as "delay no longer." Some scholars believe when you take Verse 6 and 7 together in context, "time no longer" possibly relates to time no longer to preach the gospel, "mystery of God," found in Verse 7. If this is true, then it would mean that at this time of the Tribulation, just after the 7th trumpet is sounded, the gospel would have been preached throughout the world to all human beings, fulfilling the Great Commission in Matthew 28. It would also fulfill:

Mt 24:14
^{14}And this gospel of the kingdom shall be preached in all the world for a witness unto all nations; and then shall the end come.

This does not limit people from being saved during the last half of the Tribulation. It means that all would have heard the gospel and many will turn to Christ during the terrible judgments to come. Today, many turn to Christ after having heard the gospel through song, witness, preaching or reading the Word. There may have been many days, months or years pass since the time they heard the gospel, but finally they turn from their sin and are saved as a result of what they heard in the past. God's Word will not return unto Him void.

Is. 55:10
^{10}So shall my word be that goeth forth out of my mouth: it shall not return unto me void, but it shall accomplish that which I please, and it shall prosper in the thing whereto I sent it.

Some scholars suggest that it could not mean that the

gospel will no longer be preached at this time, because Revelation 14:6 states that an angel will preach the gospel. This does not impact the fact that the gospel has been preached as I have just stated. This angel's message occurs just before the 7 vial judgments are poured out on the earth and just after the 7th trumpet judgment is sounded. Therefore, these two events mentioned in Revelation 10 and Revelation 14 coincide just after the 7th trumpet begins to sound. They tend to lend more credence to the "end of preaching of the gospel" theory.

Others believe that it speaks of the Wrath of God, or "mystery of God," will no longer be delayed. Once again, neither camp can be dogmatic on their theory. I believe it means the fulfillment of the preaching of the gospel throughout the world at the 7th trumpet sounding, because the "mystery of God" refers to the gospel itself. By the way, who else could make the decision that the gospel would no longer be preached, other than Jesus Christ Himself? Once again, this is another reason I believe that this "mighty angel" is Jesus Christ.

Rev. 10:8
And the voice which I heard from heaven spake unto me again, and said, Go *and* take the little book which is open in the hand of the angel which standeth upon the sea and upon the earth.

Dan. 12:9
[9]And he said, Go thy way, Daniel: for the words *are* closed up and sealed till the time of the end.

Is this the book that Daniel is told to seal? This point in time is certainly "the time of the end."

Rev. 10:9
And I went unto the angel, and said unto him, Give me the little book. And he said unto me, Take *it*, and eat it up; and it shall make thy belly bitter, but it shall be in thy mouth sweet as honey.

Ps. 119:103
[103]How sweet are thy words unto my taste! *yea, sweeter* than honey to my mouth!

This little book will be sweet to the taste, yet bitter to the stomach. Have you ever had a wonderful meal that satisfied your tastes, but later find out you have food poisoning? This is similar to the meaning of this verse. It is probably speaking of the Word of God and specifically the Book of Revelation. The sweet taste relates to the first half of the Tribulation Period, where the unsaved are judged with plagues and disasters. This is part of the answer to prayers of those who prayed for God to avenge their blood.

The Jewish people enjoy a false peace during the first half of the Tribulation. The last half of the Tribulation, known as the Time of Jacob's Trouble, will be a time of persecution of the Jewish State, the Jewish saved remnant and all the others who have trusted Jesus Christ as their personal Savior. It will be the bitter portion of the taste. You could relate it to a rival football game where the home team has "taken it" to the visitors in the first half. The visitors are overwhelmed in the first half. We have scored time and time again and everyone are on their feet with excitement and joy. However, the second half begins and the visitors come back with score after score and the home team has nothing to be excited about. Many of our players have been put out of the game. This seems to become a bitter defeat until our Supreme Quarterback comes into the game for the last play. He will score the winning touchdown for the home team and the celebration will begin. The losers will go down in agony and defeat.

Rev. 10:10
And I took the little book out of the angel's hand, and ate it up; and it was in my mouth sweet as honey: and as soon as I had eaten it, my belly was bitter.
Rev. 10:11
And he said unto me, Thou must prophesy again before many peoples, and nations, and tongues, and kings.
Dan. 12:10
[10]Many shall be purified, and made white, and tried; but the wicked shall do wickedly: and none of the wicked shall understand; but the wise shall understand.

Verse 11 states that John will preach and prophesy again to many people, nations, languages and kings. Some might say, how could that be since he was banished to the Isle of Patmos? The words he has penned have been preaching and prophesying to billions over these past 2000 years. People of all nationalities have read the Book of Revelation. People today are studying the end times more than anytime in history because of the wide distribution of the Word and the ability to read it from many different medias, in addition to fulfillment of prophecy in these last days.

The Third Temple is Measured and the Length of the Last Half of the Tribulation Period is Foretold

Rev. 11:1
And there was given me a reed like unto a rod: and the angel stood, saying, Rise, and measure the temple of God, and the altar, and them that worship therein.
Rev. 11:2
But the court which is without the temple leave out, and measure it not; for it is given unto the Gentiles: and the holy city shall they tread under foot forty *and* two months.

In Verses 1-2, we see the temple is measured, but the outer court is not measured. The fact that the temple is measured tells us that the 3rd temple had to be built prior to this time. This means that the Dome of the Rock, which still stands in Jerusalem on the Temple Site at the publishing date of this book, must have been destroyed at least several years earlier or the temple was built on another spot. Could the Dome of the Rock have been destroyed at the beginning of the Tribulation, just before the Tribulation began or even before the Rapture? Could it be that the battle with Russia and her Muslim allies, mentioned earlier, caused the destruction of the Dome of the Rock? There would certainly not be a major Muslim outcry about this third temple being built, since most of the Muslim population, at the beginning of the Tribulation, would have been killed. We are not told in scripture, but I do believe something had to happen to the Dome of the Rock for the Jewish third Temple to have been built on the same spot, if it is built on the same spot. *(See the following picture of the Dome of the Rock as it exists today).*

(Photograph Courtesy of John and Jana Nowell)

This is the first time the earthly temple is mentioned in the book of Revelation. I assume it has existed for some period of time up to this point. We will see later in our study that this Temple is desecrated by the Antichrist. We are told that the Gentiles will occupy Jerusalem and the outer court of the temple for 42 months or 1260 days or 3½ years.

Lk. 21:20

[20]And when ye shall see Jerusalem compassed with armies, then know that the desolation thereof is nigh.

Notice that the Anitchrist's armies will encompass Jerusalem first and then the Antichrist will take over.

This probably happens just before the Antichrist kills the two witnesses.

The Significance of the 3½ Years or 42 Months or 1260 Days

From this point in the Tribulation Period, which is the middle point, we will see events unfold in very rapid succession. The middle of the Tribulation will be a very busy time. As seen in Verse 2 above, the time period of 42 months or 3½ years or 1260 days is mentioned. We will see this period of time mentioned many times during the next several events.

So much will happen in such a short time. We will see events unfold in a matter of hours within the next few chapters of Revelation. Because of the quick unfolding of events, and many occurring within possibly one day, it is difficult to determine the exact order in which they occur. However, I will try to arrange them so that they will flow as best as possible. Virtually all of the following events begin the last half of the Tribulation or last 3½ years or last 42 months or last 1260 days. Some of the events that will occur in possibly the very same day, or within just a few days, will be:

1. The Temple is measured, as seen above.
2. The Temple is defiled by the Antichrist. The abomination of desolation occurs.
3. The murder of the two Godly witnesses.
4. The seventh trumpet is sounded.
5. War in heaven and Satan and his fallen angels are kicked out of heaven.
6. Harlot Church and Rome are destroyed.
7. The Antichrist supposedly receives a mortal head wound and comes back to life and is possessed by Satan himself.
8. The False Prophet appears and the number 666 is instituted and the Antichrist is worshipped as God.
9. Persecution of the Jews.

10. The Jewish remnant flee to Petra.

Since we are now at the middle of the Tribulation Period, the Antichrist has left Rome and is now in Jerusalem for a short time. Eventually, he will leave Jerusalem and set up his main headquarters in Babylon, Iraq.

We know that when the Antichrist defiles the Temple (the abomination that makes desolate) there will be 1260 days or 3½ years left in the Tribulation. We also know that at the end of the 1260 days ministry of the Two Witnesses, they will be murdered. The remnant Jews will flee to Petra and will stay there for 3½ years. Therefore, the arrangement of these events do signify specific time periods and therefore happen in very quick succession and very possibly the same day.

The Abomination of Desolation Occurs

At this point the Antichrist breaks the seven-year treaty with Israel and his true colors are shown. He commits the abomination of desolation by placing his statue in the Holy of Holies and demanding that everyone worship him. He defiles the Temple and sets himself up to be God. The only one allowed to enter the Holy of Holies is the High Priest. This could possibly be the time when many orthodox Jews, who have not believed that Jesus is the Messiah, come to trust Him as Lord and Savior. They will now know for sure that the Antichrist is not the true Messiah.

Mt. 24:15

[15]When ye therefore shall see the abomination of desolation, spoken of by Daniel the prophet, stand in the holy place, (whoso readeth, let him understand:)

Dan. 9:27

[27]And he shall confirm the covenant with many for one week: and in the midst of the week he shall cause the sacrifice and the oblation to cease, and for the overspreading of abominations he shall make *it* desolate, even until the consummation, and that determined shall be poured upon the desolate.

Daniel speaks of "one week: and in the midst of the week." This is part of Daniel's prophecy of the Seventy Weeks of Years and is speaking specifically of the last week and even more specifically of the middle of the last week. The week that is referred to is actually 7 years. We will not discuss the whole of the prophecy of the Seventy Weeks of Years or 490 years that is foretold in Daniel 9 beginning in verse 24. However, the first 483 years were completed at the death of Jesus Christ ("shall Messiah be cut off"). There is a gap between the 483rd year and the beginning of the 484th year. The last seven years, the Tribulation Period, would not begin until the Antichrist signed or confirmed the treaty with Israel. The midst of the year is the middle or 3½ years into the Tribulation Period. We saw this signing or confirming of the treaty with Israel at the very beginning of the Tribulation, which started the seven-year clock. We are now at the middle of that period.

Dan. 11:28-36

^{28}Then shall he return into his land with great riches; and his heart *shall be* against the holy covenant; and he shall do *exploits*, and return to his own land.

^{29}At the time appointed he shall return, and come toward the south; but it shall not be as the former, or as the latter.

^{30}For the ships of Chittim shall come against him: therefore he shall be grieved, and return, and have indignation against the holy covenant: so shall he do; he shall even return, and have intelligence with them that forsake the holy covenant.

At the time of the writing of the Book of Revelation, "Chittim" usually designated generally the islands and coasts of the Mediterranean and the nations that inhabit them. Although I usually do not use translations from Catholic bibles, the Douay-Rheims Bible translates Daniel 11:30 as "the galleys and the Romans" instead of "ships of Chittim." This was interpreted from the Latin Vulgate into English around 1582 AD to 1610 AD.

We have already discussed the probability that Catholicism, with a mixture of Protestants, could be the recognized world religion during this first 3½-year period headed up by the Pope of this era. Could it be that the Pope and his allied armies at this time are attempting to take over Jerusalem and the Temple, and the Antichrist is furious at his intent? Could it be that some of the nations that are not members of the ten-nation confederacy join with Rome against the Antichrist? Could some of these nations be the USA or Canada? Obviously, I would be reading into scripture if I were to be dogmatic here. However, we will see later that the Antichrist along with his ten-nation confederacy will have the religion of Rome destroyed around this same time period. This is when he will set himself up to be God and demand that the world worship him.

³¹And arms shall stand on his part, and they shall pollute the sanctuary of strength, and shall take away the daily *sacrifice*, and they shall place the abomination that maketh desolate.
³²And such as do wickedly against the covenant shall he corrupt by flatteries: but the people that do know their God shall be strong, and do *exploits*.
³³And they that understand among the people shall instruct many: yet they shall fall by the sword, and by flame, by captivity, and by spoil, *many* days.
³⁴Now when they shall fall, they shall be holpen with a little help: but many shall cleave to them with flatteries.
³⁵And *some* of them of understanding shall fall, to try them, and to purge, and to make *them* white, *even* to the time of the end: because *it is* yet for a time appointed.
³⁶And the king shall do according to his will; and he shall exalt himself, and magnify himself above every god, and shall speak marvellous things against the God of gods, and shall prosper till the indignation be accomplished: for that that is determined shall be done.

Dan. 12:11-13

¹¹And from the time *that* the daily *sacrifice* shall be taken away, and the abomination that maketh desolate set up, *there shall be* a thousand two hundred and ninety days.

[12]Blessed *is* he that waiteth, and cometh to the thousand three hundred and five and thirty days.

[13]But go thou thy way till the end *be*: for thou shalt rest, and stand in thy lot at the end of the days.

I must clarify two periods of time that seem to be different from the typical 1260 days mentioned throughout our study. The difference between the 1260 days and the two other periods mentioned here, 1290 days and 1335 days, are 30 days plus 45 days respectively or a total of 75 days. Why is there a difference? Some theories could be postulated. We know from previous discussions that the Seven-Year Tribulation Period will cease when Jesus returns in His Second Coming to earth. We will see that after His Second Coming there will be a judgment of the "sheep and goat" nations, which we will discuss later. We will also see later that the Temple will be reused during the Millennium or one thousand-year reign of Jesus Christ on earth after going through the abomination of desolation by the Antichrist at the middle of the Tribulation. It could be that it takes 30 days to cleanse the temple. It could be that it takes 30 days for all the people on earth who are still alive at his coming, to transport to Jerusalem for the judgment of nations. As to the additional 45 days, it could be that this is the length of time it takes for the judgment of the sheep and goat nations. Whatever the meaning of these two differences of time, God only knows. This does not, in any way, contradict nor take away from the 1260 days of the last half of the Tribulation.

Ps. 79:1

[1]O God, the heathen are come into thine inheritance; thy holy temple have they defiled; they have laid Jerusalem on heaps.

The Two Witnesses Are Murdered

You will recall in the very beginning of the Tribulation, two godly witnesses appeared on the scene. These, as I stated, could be Elijah and Enoch. We discussed this in Chapter 6. The Bible stated that they would minister on earth for 1260 days or 3½ years. That time is now over and we are about to see these two godly men murdered in the streets of Jerusalem. No one could harm them until they had "finished their testimony." Now their testimony has finished and God will allow the "beast," the Antichrist, to take their lives.

Rev. 11:7
And when they shall have finished their testimony, the beast that ascendeth out of the bottomless pit shall make war against them, and shall overcome them, and kill them.

Ps. 79:1-2
[1]O God, the heathen are come into thine inheritance; thy holy temple have they defiled; they have laid Jerusalem on heaps.
[2]The dead bodies of thy servants have they given *to be* meat unto the fowls of the heaven, the flesh of thy saints unto the beasts of the earth.

Notice that Psalms 79 states the heathen are in Jerusalem, the Holy Temple is defiled and Jerusalem is virtually destroyed. The second verse speaks of the Two Witnesses being killed and lying outside for the fowls to feed upon. This verse leads us into Revelation 11:8.

Rev. 11:8
And their dead bodies *shall lie* in the street of the great city, which spiritually is called Sodom and Egypt, where also our Lord was crucified.

Here it states that their dead bodies are left in the streets of Jerusalem. Notice the term "which spiritually is called Sodom and Egypt." Sodom relates to the fact that Jerusalem has committed abominations before the Lord in the past and present. Egypt relates to the fact that Jerusalem has mingled more with the world than with their true Savior. "Spiritually Egypt" usually refers to someone who has compromised with worldly ways instead of Godly ways. The clarity of where this city is located comes into view within the next phrase: "where also our Lord was crucified." Therefore, we know for sure that this city is Jerusalem.

Rev. 11:9
And they of the people and kindreds and tongues and nations shall see their dead bodies three days and an half, and shall not suffer their dead bodies to be put in graves.

> Ps. 79:3
> [3]Their blood have they shed like water round about Jerusalem; and *there was* none to bury *them*.

Their dead bodies will lie in the streets of Jerusalem for 3½ days and will not be allowed to be buried. This is significant in that these 3½ days could also be a prediction of how long the rest of the Tribulation could last in years. Regardless, this length of time for dead bodies to lie in the sun and the heat would create abrupt decaying of these bodies. When Jesus was about to raise Lazarus from the dead, Martha told him:

> Jn. 11:39b
> [39b]... by this time he stinketh: for he hath been *dead* four days.

> Lazarus' body had been prepared for burial with spices and burial clothes before being laid in the tomb or cave. The people in those days knew that the body would have already decayed even after this preserving process and the odor would not be pleasant.

We are told in verse 9 that virtually everyone will see their dead bodies lying in the streets. Can you think of a time in history where this would have been possible? The present age in which we live, is the only time in history in which this could take place. People throughout the world watched their television and computers via the Internet, as the American coalition freed Afghanistan and Iraq. We even saw pictures on the battlefield, where villages watched battles unfold in their neighborhoods via their own television sets. Some of these huts seem to be built in the style of block and adobe (mud), yet they owned a television. This shows us that even though some people seem to not have a lot of money for food, they will find a way to buy a television. All the news channels throughout the world were broadcasting live as the battles unfolded.

The technology which exists in the 21st Century is difficult to fathom. With the invention of television, satellite and the Internet, people all over the world can view instances in real-time video. The conclusion is, that this event could never have taken place in the past, because technology did not exist to allow this prophecy to be fulfilled. This is one more reason why these events are future in nature and can be taken literally.

Rev. 11:10
And they that dwell upon the earth shall rejoice over them, and make merry, and shall send gifts one to another; because these two prophets tormented them that dwelt on the earth.

These two witnesses are now given credit by mankind for causing all of the plagues and disasters that happened during the first 3½ years of the Tribulation. The world is so happy these are dead, that they create their own Satanic Christmas (Anti-Christmas) by exchanging gifts to celebrate their death. They probably now think since these two men are dead, that there will be no more plagues and disasters. How surprised they will be to find the next 3½ years to be worse than the first 3½ years. As a matter of fact, we are told that the last 3½ years will be the worst period of time which mankind will ever witness.

Rev. 11:11
And after three days and an half the spirit of life from God entered into them, and they stood upon their feet; and great fear fell upon them which saw them.

Can you imagine the looks on everyone's faces as they are watching real-time television, all the cameras focused on these dead bodies, people throughout the world rejoicing, partying, getting drunk and all of a sudden these two dead bodies stand up on their own two feet? I believe this will become the world's most "sobering" moment. All the coffee in the world, all the cold showers, all the slapping in the face to sober someone, could not compare to the antidote this event will have. I have witnessed to drunks and seen the mighty hand of God sober them and save them immediately. This event will bring shock to the world and fear will come upon them. Have you ever talked about someone behind their back, to find out they heard everything you said? These people probably said, "Oh No! They are going to plague us big time now!"

Rev. 11:12
And they heard a great voice from heaven saying unto them, Come up hither. And they ascended up to heaven in a cloud; and their enemies beheld them.

Ps. 79:10-11
[10]Wherefore should the heathen say, Where *is* their God? let him be known among the heathen in our sight *by* the revenging of the blood of thy servants *which is* shed.
[11]Let the sighing of the prisoner come before thee; according to the greatness of thy power preserve thou those that are appointed to die;

Everyone hears a "great voice from heaven" calling the Two Witnesses to come up to heaven. Hopefully, many who see this event will turn to God for salvation. We know from previous passages that most of them will most likely continue to curse God.

Rev. 11:13
And the same hour was there a great earthquake, and the tenth part of the city fell, and in the earthquake were slain of men seven thousand: and the remnant were affrighted, and gave glory to the God of heaven.

We are told in Verse 13, in the exact same hour in which the witnesses are taken into heaven, that there is a great earthquake and one-tenth of the city is destroyed and 7000 men are killed. As I stated earlier, these events happen in a short period of time. "Men" in this verse refers to mankind or human beings. This earthquake seems to have only happened in Jerusalem.

Ps. 79:4-9, 12-13

[4]We are become a reproach to our neighbours, a scorn and derision to them that are round about us.
[5]How long, LORD? wilt thou be angry for ever? shall thy jealousy burn
like fire?
[6]Pour out thy wrath upon the heathen that have not known thee, and upon the kingdoms that have not called upon thy name.
[7]For they have devoured Jacob, and laid waste his dwelling place.
[8]O remember not against us former iniquities: let thy tender mercies speedily prevent us: for we are brought very low.
[9]Help us, O God of our salvation, for the glory of thy name: and deliver us, and purge away our sins, for thy name's sake.
[12]And render unto our neighbours sevenfold into their bosom their reproach, wherewith they have reproached thee, O Lord.
[13]So we thy people and sheep of thy pasture will give thee thanks for ever: we will show forth thy praise to all generations.

Notice in verse 12, the prayer of the remnant is to render to those who are persecuting them sevenfold. This could very well be the prayer that God hears to pour out the upcoming seven vials of judgment on the earth.

Rev. 11:14
The second woe is past; *and*, behold, the third woe cometh quickly.

The Seventh Trumpet Sounds – Christ's Reign Over Creation is Predicted

Rev. 11:15
And the seventh angel sounded; and there were great voices in heaven, saying, The kingdoms of this world are become *the kingdoms* of our Lord, and of his Christ; and he shall reign for ever

and ever.

The seventh trumpet sounds and we see that Christ's reign over all creation is predicted. Notice, "he shall," which means "in the not too distant future." We are also told in Verse 14 that the second woe is past and the third woe will come quickly. We will see in Revelation 12:12 that the third woe is when Satan and his fallen angels are kicked out of the heaven and cast into the earth.

The Work of Satan in the Past

Revelation 12:1-5 are parenthetical verses or an interlude as I described earlier. However, these verses paint a picture in history, which leads us to Verse 6, which is not parenthetical. We are about to embark on a history lesson all the way back to the birth of Jesus. This lesson, given to us by John, is to teach us to see how Satan has been active throughout history to destroy the nation of Israel before it could give birth to Jesus the Messiah. Since Satan failed to destroy Israel in the past, he will attempt to destroy her during the Tribulation. Satan is alive and will not be chained until after the Second Coming.

Rev. 12:1
And there appeared a great wonder in heaven; a woman clothed with the sun, and the moon under her feet, and upon her head a crown of twelve stars:

The "woman" is the nation Israel and the "twelve stars" are the twelve tribes of Israel. In Genesis 37, Joseph dreamed that his brothers would bow to him. The sun represented Jacob, the moon was Rachel and the eleven stars were the other eleven sons of Jacob. Joseph was the twelfth son. In verse 10, Jacob understood the dream and tells us the meaning. Now this dream was literally fulfilled later in Genesis when Joseph was vice president of Egypt. However, the definition of the "woman" is the object of our study and this woman is Israel.

Gen. 37:9-10

[9]And he dreamed yet another dream, and told it his brethren, and said, Behold, I have dreamed a dream more; and, behold, the sun and the moon and the eleven stars made obeisance to me.
[10]And he told *it* to his father, and to his brethren: and his father rebuked him, and said unto him, What *is* this dream that thou hast dreamed? Shall I and thy mother and thy brethren indeed come to bow down ourselves to thee to the earth?

Rev. 12:2
And she being with child cried, travailing in birth, and pained to be delivered.

The "child" is Jesus and He is about to be born into the Jewish family of Joseph and Mary, via the virgin birth.

Rev. 12:3
And there appeared another wonder in heaven; and behold a great red dragon, having seven heads and ten horns, and seven crowns upon his heads.
Rev. 12:4
And his tail drew the third part of the stars of heaven, and did cast them to the earth: and the dragon stood before the woman which was ready to be delivered, for to devour her child as soon as it was born.

The "red dragon" is none other than Satan himself. The "third part of the stars" are the fallen angels (demons) who sided with Satan at the beginning of time when they rebelled against God. As seen in Verse 4, they are ready to devour the "child" Jesus as He is born. Since Satan's fall and removal as one of God's "anointed cherub" angels, Satan has attempted to destroy any possibility of the lineage of Jesus, so he could destroy God's plan of salvation for mankind. Cain was the first example of this when Satan convinced Cain to murder Abel. Poor Eve! She thought when Cain was born, that he would be the Messiah. Boy was she wrong!

Gen. 4:1

[1]And Adam knew Eve his wife; and she conceived, and bare Cain, and said, I have gotten a man from the LORD.

As you study the Old Testament and the New Testament, you will see that Satan has actively tried to destroy this lineage throughout history. Satan has tried to influence mankind to worship him as God instead of Jehovah God. Even after God destroyed unrighteous mankind with the flood, Satan found someone to worship him. Nimrod set up Satan worship in Babylon, from which all pagan gods and pagan religions derive their rituals. In Matthew Chapter 2, Satan, through Herod, tried to kill Jesus when He was born. Herod told the wise men to report back to him when they found this "King of the Jews" that was born. However, the wise men did not report back to Herod and therefore Herod ordered every child in Bethlehem under the age of two to be killed. The wise men's visit was when Jesus was about two years of age. Therefore, this was the reason for Herod's order to kill all children who were two years old and younger.

Rev. 12:5
And she brought forth a man child, who was to rule all nations with a rod of iron: and her child was caught up unto God, and *to* his throne.

Ps. 2:9

[9]Thou shalt break them with a rod of iron; thou shalt dash them in pieces like a potter's vessel.

Rev. 19:15

[15]And out of his mouth goeth a sharp sword, that with it he should smite the nations: and he shall rule them with a rod of iron: and he treadeth the winepress of the fierceness and wrath of Almighty God.

Jesus is the rod of iron and will rule at the Second Coming. Once again, Satan thought he had won the victory when he convinced the hypocritical Jews to have Jesus crucified. Satan wanted to make sure Jesus did not come out of the grave, so he convinced the guards to seal the tomb with a huge stone and place guards to secure the tomb. However, three days later Jesus rose from the grave and the stone did not keep him captive. Forty days later, Jesus took His seat on His throne in heaven. Satan lost again! But does Satan give up? No!

Satan and His Demon Angels Are Cast Out of Heaven

Rev. 12:7
And there was war in heaven: Michael and his angels fought against the dragon; and the dragon fought and his angels,
Rev. 12:8
And prevailed not; neither was their place found any more in heaven.
Rev. 12:9
And the great dragon was cast out, that old serpent, called the Devil, and Satan, which deceiveth the whole world: he was cast out into the earth, and his angels were cast out with him.

Verse 9 tells us who the dragon is and his name is the Devil, Satan. We see that Satan and his angels are kicked out of heaven and cast into the earth. This event happens during the middle of the Tribulation Period. They no longer have access to heaven. Yes, Satan has entrance to God's abode today and in the past to accuse the saints before the throne of God (Revelation 12:10). Remember that Job's problems were a result of a "dare" by Satan to God, before the throne of God? Do not misunderstand the word "dare" that I use. God cannot be tempted. But God in His sovereignty knew Job would not succumb to Satan. Satan has been and is actively accusing the saints before God. However, we have our lawyer, Jesus, who is called our Advocate. He pleads our case before God. Essentially, all Jesus has to say on behalf of the saved that are being accused by Satan, is "they have accepted my sacrifice for them and I plead my blood in their behalf." The quotes are mine, but the idea is the same. God sees us through the blood of Christ and Satan has no case.

Unlike some, who believe that Satan has been bound and chained in the bottomless pit, I believe without question, that Satan has not been chained. I believe, that if you allow scripture to interpret scripture, you will come to the same conclusion. He and his fallen angels have been very active throughout history and the present, as I mentioned earlier.

1 Pet. 5:8-9

[8]Be sober, be vigilant; because your adversary the devil, as a roaring lion, walketh about, seeking whom he may devour:
[9]Whom resist stedfast in the faith, knowing that the same afflictions are accomplished in your brethren that are in the world.

Notice the Devil is not chained at this time, which was written long after the ascension of Christ to heaven.

Eph. 2:2

[2]Wherein in time past ye walked according to the course of this world, according to the prince of the power of the air, the spirit that now worketh in the children of disobedience:

Once again, the Devil is still active, not chained. He will not be chained until after the Tribulation Period is complete. If Satan and all his demons were bound, as some believe, when were they loosed for the Apostles to cast them out of human beings after the Ascension? Even though some fallen angels were bound as we studied earlier, most of them and Satan have been walking to and fro throughout this earth causing havoc and destruction to mankind. Remember, Satan was the first to rebel and then he deceived Eve, and Adam chose to sin, and the rest is history.

Rev. 12:10

And I heard a loud voice saying in heaven, Now is come salvation, and strength, and the kingdom of our God, and the power of his Christ: for the accuser of our brethren is cast down, which accused them before our God day and night.

Up until the middle of the Tribulation Period, before Satan was cast out of heaven, he accused the "brethren" before God "day and night." Now, he no longer has access to heaven and he will begin to reap havoc on mankind like he has never done before.

Rev. 12:11
And they overcame him by the blood of the Lamb, and by the word of their testimony; and they loved not their lives unto the death.

As I stated earlier, the saints overcame Satan's accusations by pleading the blood of the Lamb.

Rev. 12:12
Therefore rejoice, *ye* heavens, and ye that dwell in them. Woe to the inhabiters of the earth and of the sea! for the devil is come down unto you, having great wrath, because he knoweth that he hath but a short time.

The third woe is past. This "woe" is about Satan and his demons being cast out of heaven to earth. The first half of the Tribulation has been a Sunday School picnic in comparison to the second half. We saw in the first half, most of the plagues were directed mainly toward the unsaved. The last half is where we will see the Antichrist, possessed by Satan, persecute the remnant Jews and the saved who are left on earth. Many will die for their faith during this last half of the Tribulation.

The Harlot Church and Rome are Destroyed

We see another event, which probably takes place in the same period of time. The Antichrist gives an order to the ten-nation confederacy who gives their allegiance to him, to destroy the Church of Rome and the city of Rome. As I mentioned at the very beginning of the Tribulation, the Antichrist promoted this religious system to the world, but now betrays it and has it destroyed.

Rev. 17:13
These have one mind, and shall give their power and strength unto the beast.

The ten-nation confederacy gives their armies over to the

Antichrist for him to command and control.

Rev. 17:16
And the ten horns which thou sawest upon the beast, these shall hate the whore, and shall make her desolate and naked, and shall eat her flesh, and burn her with fire.

At this time, the ten-nation confederacy attacks Rome and destroys the city and the world religious system of that day. Why would the Antichrist want to destroy them who seem to be loyal to him?

Dan. 11:30
[30]For the ships of Chittim shall come against him: therefore he shall be grieved, and return, and have indignation against the holy covenant: so shall he do; he shall even return, and have intelligence with them that forsake the holy covenant.

I believe, as I stated earlier, that the Pope of Rome of this era, who very possibly has some of the Mediterranean coastal areas loyal to him (ships of Chittim), may try to take over control of Jerusalem for himself. As seen in Daniel, the Antichrist will be furious at this attempt and will consult with "them that forsake the holy covenant," the ten-nation confederacy to determine what to do. Their meeting brings about the agreement and the action to have Rome and the Harlot religious system destroyed. The Antichrist does not leave Jerusalem to perform this destruction, because the ten-nation confederacy armies are sent to perform this act of destruction. As we will see shortly, the Antichrist has several other plans of his own to carry out in Israel and Petra.

Rev. 17:17
For God hath put in their hearts to fulfil his will, and to agree, and give their kingdom unto the beast, until the words of God shall be fulfilled.

Verse 17 states that it is God's will for the destruction to take place and for these nations to give everything to the charge of the Antichrist.

Rev. 17:18
And the woman which thou sawest is that great city, which reigneth over the kings of the earth.

The "woman" refers to Rome "that great city." Remember earlier, I asked the question, "Why would the Antichrist want to destroy them who seem to be loyal to him?" The reason is, and has always been, so that the Antichrist himself could become the object of worship. This has always been Satan's goal, to be worshipped by mankind instead of God, and he will get his wish for a short span of time.

Antichrist's "So-Called" Death Experience, "So-Called" Resurrection and His Possession by Satan Himself

Rev. 13:3
And I saw one of his heads as it were wounded to death; and his deadly wound was healed: and all the world wondered after the beast.

We are told that the Antichrist will receive "as it were" a mortal head wound. It could be that some of the Orthodox Jews of that era, after seeing the abomination of desolation take place in the Temple's Holy of Holies, take it upon themselves to try to kill the Antichrist for desecrating their Temple. However, it does seem certain that the Antichrist is wounded in the head by a sword of some nature. The language seems to suggest that it may not have been an actual death experience. Remember, Satan is the master of deception and knowing his past, he will pull a masterful lie about this "so-called" death experience of the Antichrist. Some believe he will actually die and God will allow him to be resurrected. However, I believe that because the Antichrist is a human being, once an unsaved person is dead, they immediately are cast into Hades where there is no possibility of return or another chance to live again. Therefore, I personally believe

the master of liars, Satan, will pull another "fast one."
Revelation 13:14 tells us that the "wound" was inflicted by a
"sword" of some nature.

II Thess. 2:8-12

[8]And then shall that Wicked be revealed, whom the Lord shall
consume with the spirit of his mouth, and shall destroy with the
brightness of his coming:
[9]*Even him*, whose coming is after the working of Satan with all
power and signs and lying wonders,
[10]And with all deceivableness of unrighteousness in them that
perish; because they received not the love of the truth, that they
might be saved.
[11]And for this cause God shall send them strong delusion, that
they should believe a lie:
[12]That they all might be damned who believed not the truth, but
had pleasure in unrighteousness.

We see in II Thessalonians that the Antichrist will
deceive people with a master deception. This scripture
relates to a period of time just after the Rapture.
However, the context of this scripture shows how
deceptive Satan truly is. The Devil, the father of lies
who possesses the Antichrist, is so cunning, he pulls
off this lie of the ages and brings the Antichrist back to
life. At least he will convince everyone that he was
resurrected.

John 8:44

[44]Ye are of *your* father the devil, and the lusts of your father ye
will do. He was a murderer from the beginning, and abode not in
the truth, because there is no truth in him. When he speaketh a lie,
he speaketh of his own: for he is a liar, and the father of it.

Rev. 13:4
And they worshipped the dragon which gave power unto the beast:
and they worshipped the beast, saying, Who *is* like unto the beast?
who is able to make war with him?

At this point in time, I believe Satan himself possesses the
Antichrist and performs his masterful trick of the so-called
resurrection of the Antichrist from his mortal head wound.
This act is Satan's attempt to duplicate Jesus Christ's death

and resurrection. As we discussed earlier in this book, Satan has a counterfeit to match everything of God. These counterfeits are "unholy" to say the least.

Rev. 13:5
And there was given unto him a mouth speaking great things and blasphemies; and power was given unto him to continue forty and two months.

Satan, through the Antichrist, will speak his blasphemous language before mankind and convince most of the living at that time that he is God. He has always blasphemed God in the past and now God has given him more rope to hang himself even further. Satan knows he only has a short time, so he is going to make the best of the situation. We see once again the time period of 42 months or 1260 days or 3½ years. We have discussed previously this time period and its meaning. In Daniel we see the same time period mentioned again when the Antichrist will rule the world and persecute the saints of God for 3½ years. This is the last half of the Tribulation Period known as the "Great Tribulation" or "Jacob's Trouble."

Dan. 7:25
[25]And he shall speak *great* words against the most High, and shall wear out the saints of the most High, and think to change times and laws: and they shall be given into his hand until a time and times and the dividing of time.

Dan. 12:11
[11]And from the time *that* the daily *sacrifice* shall be taken away, and the abomination that maketh desolate set up, *there shall be* a thousand two hundred and ninety days.

Rev. 13:6
And he opened his mouth in blasphemy against God, to blaspheme his name, and his tabernacle, and them that dwell in heaven.

II Thess. 2:4,9
[4]Who opposeth and exalteth himself above all that is called God, or that is worshipped; so that he as God sitteth in the temple of God, showing himself that he is God.
[9]*Even him*, whose coming is after the working of Satan with all power and signs and lying wonders,

Rev. 13:7
And it was given unto him to make war with the saints, and to overcome them: and power was given him over all kindreds, and tongues, and nations.

The Antichrist, possessed by Satan, has now been given power over all the nations. He will kill many of those who are saved and many Jews and persecute the remnant Jews.

> Dan. 7:21
> [21] I beheld, and the same horn made war with the saints, and prevailed against them;
>
> Dan. 8:23-24
> [23] And in the latter time of their kingdom, when the transgressors are come to the full, a king of fierce countenance, and understanding dark sentences, shall stand up.
> [24] And his power shall be mighty, but not by his own power: and he shall destroy wonderfully, and shall prosper, and practice, and shall destroy the mighty and the holy people.

Rev. 13:8
And all that dwell upon the earth shall worship him, whose names are not written in the book of life of the Lamb slain from the foundation of the world.

Satan is receiving what he has always wanted, to be worshipped as God. Notice that the worship is only by those who are not saved and it will only be for 3½ years.

Rev. 13:9
If any man have an ear, let him hear.
Rev. 13:10
He that leadeth into captivity shall go into captivity: he that killeth with the sword must be killed with the sword. Here is the patience and the faith of the saints.

The patience and faith of the saints is that they will see many of their loved ones raped and killed. Their thoughts will surely be, "when will this carnage of God's saints end?" They will have to endure their afflictions based on their faith in Jesus Christ as Savior. When will it end? The answer is, 3½ years, when Jesus splits the Eastern sky and destroys the armies of the Antichrist at the Battle of Armageddon. At least the saints who are still alive at this time know that within 3½ years, Jesus will arrive to save them from further destruction. However, many will die for their faith before that happens.

Is. 13:15-16
¹⁵Every one that is found shall be thrust through; and every one that is joined *unto them* shall fall by the sword.
¹⁶Their children also shall be dashed to pieces before their eyes; their houses shall be spoiled, and their wives ravished.

The False Prophet and 666

As I stated at the beginning of this chapter, many events will happen in quick succession and many within a period of one day. We now see a new figurehead arise into prominence. He is called "another beast" and he will become known as the "False Prophet." He will become the third person of the "Unholy Trinity." His duties are to mimic the Holy Spirit as his counter. As the Holy Spirit's role is to exalt Jesus Christ and to draw mankind to trust in Jesus Christ, the False Prophet's role is to exalt the Antichrist and bring mankind to trust in the Antichrist. This individual, very probably, has been a member of the Antichrist's advisory team from the beginning. However, he has not been in the limelight until now. It is obvious that he also receives power from Satan, although not personally possessed by Satan. Satan himself is not omnipresent and therefore can only possess one human being at a time. However, this does not eliminate the False Prophet from being possessed by one of Satan's high-ranking demon angels.

Rev. 13:11
And I beheld another beast coming up out of the earth; and he had two horns like a lamb, and he spake as a dragon.

Verse 11 says "he spake as a dragon" which means he spoke in the power of Satan. Either way, this False Prophet will have some of the same powers as the Antichrist, but his duty is to exalt the Antichrist and deceive the world into thinking that the Antichrist is God.

Rev. 13:12
And he exerciseth all the power of the first beast before him, and causeth the earth and them which dwell therein to worship the first beast, whose deadly wound was healed.

The False Prophet promotes the lie we discussed earlier, that the Antichrist was killed and resurrected. Is it any wonder that people will believe him? Even today, the world is deceived by the Theory of Evolution. Today, this is "the lie" that Satan has propagated and most of the world has believed it. Even some Christians believe God may have used some form of evolution in His creation. Absolutely not! Creation and Evolution are diametrically opposed! Millions of babies have been aborted because young women are told that we are mere animals or that the "fetus" is like another organ or part of her body. World wars have been fought because dictators have convinced their people that other races are inferior and they are nothing but lower forms of animals in the human race. NO, and a million times, NO! All of mankind was made in the image of God and are in need of His salvation. Every soul is precious in His sight including the babies in the womb. They are not a "fetus." They are human beings with emotions, feelings, a soul and anything else in which one could describe a human being. Even though millions of babies have been aborted, God can, and will forgive anyone who has ever had an abortion, if they will only ask Him for forgiveness.

Rev. 13:13
And he doeth great wonders, so that he maketh fire come down from heaven on the earth in the sight of men,
Rev. 13:14
And deceiveth them that dwell on the earth by *the means of* those miracles which he had power to do in the sight of the beast; saying to them that dwell on the earth, that they should make an image to the beast, which had the wound by a sword, and did live.

I have decided this would be a good place for Psalm 37 because it relates to these miracles the False Prophet performs and yet it tells the story of God's grace for His people and His judgment on the wicked. This Psalm could fit within virtually all of the Tribulation Period, along with all of time, because of the riches it portrays within its words, but it is especially fitting here.

Ps. 37:1-40

[1]Fret not thyself because of evildoers, neither be thou envious against the workers of iniquity.

[2]For they shall soon be cut down like the grass, and wither as the green herb.

[3]Trust in the LORD, and do good; *so* shalt thou dwell in the land, and verily thou shalt be fed.

[4]Delight thyself also in the LORD; and he shall give thee the desires of thine heart.

[5]Commit thy way unto the LORD; trust also in him; and he shall bring *it* to pass.

[6]And he shall bring forth thy righteousness as the light, and thy judgment as the noonday.

[7]Rest in the LORD, and wait patiently for him: fret not thyself because of him who prospereth in his way, because of the man who bringeth wicked devices to pass.

[8]Cease from anger, and forsake wrath: fret not thyself in any wise to do evil.

[9]For evildoers shall be cut off: but those that wait upon the LORD, they shall inherit the earth.

[10]For yet a little while, and the wicked *shall* not *be*: yea, thou shalt diligently consider his place, and it *shall* not *be*.

[11]But the meek shall inherit the earth; and shall delight themselves in the abundance of peace.

[12]The wicked plotteth against the just, and gnasheth upon him with his teeth.

[13]The Lord shall laugh at him: for he seeth that his day is coming.

[14]The wicked have drawn out the sword, and have bent their bow, to cast down the poor and needy, *and* to slay such as be of upright conversation.

[15]Their sword shall enter into their own heart, and their bows shall be broken.

[16]A little that a righteous man hath *is* better than the riches of many wicked.

[17]For the arms of the wicked shall be broken: but the LORD

upholdeth the righteous.

[18]The LORD knoweth the days of the upright: and their inheritance shall be for ever.

[19]They shall not be ashamed in the evil time: and in the days of famine they shall be satisfied.

[20]But the wicked shall perish, and the enemies of the LORD *shall be* as the fat of lambs: they shall consume; into smoke shall they consume away.

[21]The wicked borroweth, and payeth not again: but the righteous showeth mercy, and giveth.

[22]For *such as be* blessed of him shall inherit the earth; and *they that be* cursed of him shall be cut off.

[23]The steps of a *good* man are ordered by the LORD: and he delighteth in his way.

[24]Though he fall, he shall not be utterly cast down: for the LORD upholdeth *him with* his hand.

[25]I have been young, and *now* am old; yet have I not seen the righteous forsaken, nor his seed begging bread.

[26]*He is* ever merciful, and lendeth; and his seed *is* blessed.

[27]Depart from evil, and do good; and dwell for evermore.

[28]For the LORD loveth judgment, and forsaketh not his saints; they are preserved for ever: but the seed of the wicked shall be cut off.

[29]The righteous shall inherit the land, and dwell therein for ever.

[30]The mouth of the righteous speaketh wisdom, and his tongue talketh of judgment.

[31]The law of his God *is* in his heart; none of his steps shall slide.

[32]The wicked watcheth the righteous, and seeketh to slay him.

[33]The LORD will not leave him in his hand, nor condemn him when he is judged.

[34]Wait on the LORD, and keep his way, and he shall exalt thee to inherit the land: when the wicked are cut off, thou shalt see *it*.

[35]I have seen the wicked in great power, and spreading himself like a green bay tree.

[36]Yet he passed away, and, lo, he *was* not: yea, I sought him, but he could not be found.

[37]Mark the perfect *man*, and behold the upright: for the end of *that* man *is* peace.

[38]But the transgressors shall be destroyed together: the end of the wicked shall be cut off.

[39]But the salvation of the righteous *is* of the LORD: *he is* their strength in the time of trouble.

[40]And the LORD shall help them, and deliver them: he shall deliver them from the wicked, and save them, because they trust in him.

The False Prophet will convince millions with his wonders and so-called miracles to place their trust in the Antichrist. He makes fire come down from heaven. Some might not believe that mere humans could perform such miracles, that they must come from God. May I remind you that demonic forces have performed similar miracles in the past, which only God allowed. When Moses stood before Pharaoh and cast his staff to the ground, it turned into a snake. However, Pharaoh's magicians did the same and their staffs turned into snakes also. Moses' snake consumed the magicians' snakes. Moses turned water into blood and so did the magicians. Moses called for frogs to cover the land and so did the magicians. You will notice after the frogs, the magicians could not perform the other miracles that God performed through Moses. God limits demon forces from performing beyond what He has ordained.

As seen in the verses above, the False Prophet deceives millions with his demonic miracles. He also continues to preach the lie of the resurrection of the Antichrist from the dead and convinces the people to make an image or an idol in honor of the Antichrist. This image could be another image in addition to the one the Antichrist used to place in the Holy of Holies or it could be the same. If it were the same image, then the False Prophet would have appeared on the scene before the Abomination of Desolation and the Antichrist would have received his head wound just before this same event. As I stated earlier, so many events happened in brief succession and possibly the same day, that it is very difficult to arrange the scripture in the exact order in which these events occur. The order of these events do not take away from the fact that these events occur and do not create any contradictions within scripture. As we have seen throughout our study, many individual verses within scripture give us a view of several different eras of time, several different events occurring simultaneously and sometimes spans of thousands of years.

Rev. 13:15
And he had power to give life unto the image of the beast, that the image of the beast should both speak, and cause that as many as would not worship the image of the beast should be killed.

We see that the False Prophet seemingly brings the Antichrist's idol to life and has the statue speak. He is a master of delusion, since he receives his power from Satan also. Could he have caused this image to come to life and speak? It could be that God allowed him to perform this miracle, but I believe he performed another masterful trick.

Remember decades ago, the Jim Jones cult who drank poisoned Kool-Aid and died? Shortly before this suicide act, Jim Jones convinced his followers that he was God. In his church stood a regular water fountain as most churches have today. Jim Jones had his faithful few, rig the water fountain with a compressed container of wine, much like the compressed containers that are used in fountain coke machines. (If you are from the South, we say "Coke" even if it is a Pepsi, Dr. Pepper or whatever. It carries the same meaning as soda, pop or soft drink). He then had a switch run from the water fountain to his pulpit. When preaching one day, he told his congregation that he could prove that he is God. He told them to go to the water fountain and drink from the fountain. When they surrounded the water fountain and the water began to flow, Jim Jones flipped the switch, located in his pulpit, to the compressed container of wine and the water turned into wine before their very eyes. Was this a miracle? Not at all! This was a demented individual controlled by demonic forces who tricked a spiritually hungry group of people into believing that he was God. Hence, they followed him to their deaths.

The same will happen with millions of people during the last half of the Tribulation Period as they follow the Antichrist to their death.

Rev. 13:16
And he causeth all, both small and great, rich and poor, free and bond, to receive a mark in their right hand, or in their foreheads:

Rev. 13:17
And that no man might buy or sell, save he that had the mark, or the name of the beast, or the number of his name.
Rev. 13:18
Here is wisdom. Let him that hath understanding count the number of the beast: for it is the number of a man; and his number *is* Six hundred threescore *and* six.

As we see in the verses above, the False Prophet and the Antichrist are not satisfied with people saying they verbally believe in them, they want a physical mark to prove their loyalty. Of all scripture in the Bible, these verses have caused more controversy than any other. Speculations of the number 666 have run rampant. Some believe the number is that of the Pope. During World War II, some believed it was the number of Hitler. I do not believe it is the number of the Pope because, as we discussed earlier, I believe the Pope, Rome and the Harlot Religious System will be destroyed before this number is issued. Obviously, it was not Hitler because he is dead. Regardless, it will certainly be the number of the Antichrist during the last 3½ years of the Tribulation. No one will be able to buy or sell except those who have this mark.

The Food and Drug Administration on October 12, 2004, approved the use of a computer RFID chip to be inserted just under the skin of an individual to be used for medical identification purposes. Verichip, a product of Applied Digital Solutions of Delray Beach, Florida, is a small computer chip about the size of a grain of rice and can be inserted with a syringe under the skin. It can speed vital information about a patient's medical history to doctors and hospitals. The dormant chip stores a code that releases patient-specific information when a scanner passes over it. According to some sources, microchips have already been implanted in over one million pets for tracking and recovery purposes.

Beginning in October 2005, U.S. Passports were suppose to contain a radio frequency I.D. chip. According to the Bush administration, all U.S. passports will be implanted with remotely readable computer chips starting in October 2006.

Eventually the government contemplates adding addition information such a fingerprints or iris scans. As of the writing of this book, some in the U.S. Senate are proposing RFID tagging of legal immigrants and immigrant worker program related individuals, so there can be some control and identification of legal immigrants for companies and the government to use for identification.

As we see, the technology exists today that has not existed in the past. As with all technology, this technology although designed for good use, could be used for evil purposes later. Does this mean that Christians should protest the production of these devices? I do not believe we should, because the Antichrist will use whatever is at his disposal regardless of the original use of the device. If you are living during the Tribulation Period and reading this book, I would suggest that you do not allow this or a similar device to be inserted. If you are living before the Rapture of the Church and are a born again Christian, you do not have to worry about such matters, for you will not be on earth during the Tribulation.

What does this mean for those who, during this portion of the Tribulation Period, do not have the mark of the beast? They will have to go underground, scavenge for food and water, hide their foreheads and right hand when in public and pray that they are not exposed by others. Those who are saved, up to this point, will not, nor ever, take this mark. Revelation 19:20 states, "...which he deceived them that had received the mark of the beast, and them that worshipped his image..." According to this verse, those who obtain the mark of the beast will be deceived. It is as though they have stepped over that boundary and have become "reprobate" in spirit. Reprobate means one who is completely impure, immoral, has completely rejected God and is rejected by God. In other words, he has committed the "unpardonable sin" of rejecting Jesus Christ for the last time and therefore God "gave them over to a reprobate mind" as Romans 1:28 states.

Let me describe reprobate in terms of an illustration. Assume that someone takes a hot iron and places it on their arm and leaves it there until all the nerve endings have been destroyed. Sure, there will be a lot of pain during the process. Later, you could take needles and pins and prick this person's arm where the nerves have been destroyed and they will never feel the prick. This is similar to being reprobate. Their spiritual nerve endings have been seared by their continued rejection of Jesus as Savior. Regardless of the pricking that Jesus continues to perform on their spiritual heart, their conscious has become seared and can no longer feel the need for a Savior. Can someone cross over the line of no return or the line God has drawn where a person will never be saved? Yes! As we saw with Pharaoh, Pharaoh hardened his heart toward God so many times, that later we read in Exodus 9:12 where "the LORD hardened the heart of Pharaoh." Pharaoh crossed over the line to become reprobate.

Let us hope that no one, who has come this far in this study, continues to distrust Jesus Christ continually and become reprobate according to God's view. God is "not willing that any should perish," but that all could be saved. How is one to know if they have become reprobate? Actually, the individual that has become reprobate will never know that they are reprobate. It is like telling an alcoholic that he/she is an alcoholic. They do not believe they are an alcoholic. However, an alcoholic can come to the point in their life where they realize they need help. A reprobate person will never come to the point where they think they need help. Their continued rejection of Jesus Christ has seared their conscious to the point they do not believe there is a need for a Savior. If you still have a concern and are searching for answers, then you have not become reprobate, yet. However, do not put off your decision to trust Christ, as it could be that eventually the Holy Spirit of God may quit drawing you to Him, pricking your spiritual heart and turn you over to become reprobate. I believe today we see more reprobate individuals than ever in my lifetime. Can I know if someone is reprobate in mind? It is possible, but God is the only true judge. We look on the outward appearance, while God looks on the heart.

Someone may ask, "What if a Christian, living in this Tribulation time era, is drugged and forced to take the mark of the beast without his consent?" We are not told whether this could happen or not. However, I am sure if such an event could happen, God would control it so this Christian would not be considered reprobate but, as always, never be able to lose his or her salvation. Revelation states they must receive the mark "and" worship the image. In this situation, this individual would never worship the image of the beast even though he was given the mark while unconscious. Let us leave this in God's hands. The best way to ensure you would never fall into such a situation is to trust Christ before the Rapture and you will not be on earth to worry about the mark. If you are reading this book and are living during this Tribulation time era and have accepted Jesus Christ as your personal Savior, then Paul stated in Hebrews 13:5, speaking of Jesus, "...I will never leave thee, nor forsake thee..." Your salvation is secure in Jesus Christ, forever. No one can take that away from you.

The Antichrist Begins His Persecution of the Remnant Jews

Rev. 12:13
And when the dragon saw that he was cast unto the earth, he persecuted the woman which brought forth the man *child*.

Until this point in the Tribulation, the nation of Israel has enjoyed a peaceful existence under the treaty with the Antichrist and the world. As stated earlier, the Antichrist commits the abomination of desolation and the remnant Jews now know that he is not their Messiah. Persecution of the remnant Jews and Jerusalem will begin at a height never seen before in the history of the Jewish people. Not even the Babylonians, Romans, Hitler, Stalin and anyone else who have persecuted and killed Jews throughout history could compare to the death and persecution that will happen in this last half of the Tribulation called the "time of Jacob's trouble."

Jer. 30:6-7

[6]Ask ye now, and see whether a man doth travail with child? wherefore do I see every man with his hands on his loins, as a woman in travail, and all faces are turned into paleness? [7]Alas! for that day *is* great, so that none *is* like it: it *is* even the time of Jacob's trouble; but he shall be saved out of it.

The remnant Jews in Jerusalem will be encompassed about by the Antichrist and his armies who are ready to devour them. Satan is ready to destroy them as he has tried in the past. He thinks he has them where he wants them and then God steps in again and takes them to safety.

Mic. 5:7-8

[7]And the remnant of Jacob shall be in the midst of many people as a dew from the LORD, as the showers upon the grass, that tarrieth not for man, nor waiteth for the sons of men.
[8]And the remnant of Jacob shall be among the Gentiles in the midst of many people as a lion among the beasts of the forest, as a young lion among the flocks of sheep: who, if he go through, both treadeth down, and teareth in pieces, and none can deliver.

I believe the scriptures, in Romans and Hosea seen below, teach us that there will be an unprecedented number of Jews come to trust Jesus as their personal Savior at this time. This does not mean that at this point in the Tribulation all Jews will be saved. However, it does teach us that at Jesus' Second Coming to earth, those Jews who are left on the earth that are still alive will have trusted Him as Lord and Savior. During the last 3½ years of the Tribulation to come, many Jews and Gentiles, both saved and unsaved, will die. We can today thank God that the Jewish people turned away from Jesus for a while, so we Gentiles would have the opportunity to be saved. Even though the Jews turned from God and did not accept His Son Jesus, they are still God's chosen, "Elect" people. The scales will be removed from their eyes in great numbers at this point in the Tribulation and many will realize Jesus truly is the Messiah.

Rom. 11:25-28

[25]For I would not, brethren, that ye should be ignorant of this

mystery, lest ye should be wise in your own conceits; that blindness in part is happened to Israel, until the fulness of the Gentiles be come in.

[26]And so all Israel shall be saved: as it is written, There shall come out of Sion the Deliverer, and shall turn away ungodliness from Jacob:

[27]For this *is* my covenant unto them, when I shall take away their sins.

[28]As concerning the gospel, *they are* enemies for your sakes: but as touching the election, *they are* beloved for the fathers' sakes.

Hos. 3:5

[5]Afterward shall the children of Israel return, and seek the LORD their God, and David their king; and shall fear the LORD and his goodness in the latter days.

Hos. 5:15

[15]I will go *and* return to my place, till they acknowledge their offence, and seek my face: in their affliction they will seek me early.

Hos. 6:1-3

[1]Come, and let us return unto the LORD: for he hath torn, and he will heal us; he hath smitten, and he will bind us up.

[2]After two days will he revive us: in the third day he will raise us up, and we shall live in his sight.

[3]Then shall we know, *if* we follow on to know the LORD: his going forth is prepared as the morning; and he shall come unto us as the rain, as the latter *and* former rain unto the earth.

In Zechariah, we see that the plagues have had an effect upon the Jewish population.

Zech. 13:8-9

[8]And it shall come to pass, *that* in all the land, saith the LORD, two parts therein shall be cut off *and* die; but the third shall be left therein.

[9]And I will bring the third part through the fire, and will refine them as silver is refined, and will try them as gold is tried: they shall call on my name, and I will hear them: I will say, It *is* my people: and they shall say, The LORD *is* my God.

Very possibly, at this point, there is only a one-third Jewish population left on earth. There is estimated to be over 13 million Jews on earth today. If the phrase "in all the land" refers to the whole earth and only one-third of this total survived, that would equate to around

4 million Jews. This would mean that over 9 million Jewish people would lose their lives during the Tribulation. If the phrase refers to the land of Israel only, the estimated population of Jews in Israel today is over 5.3 million. This would mean that only 1.7 million would survive and over 3.6 million would lose their lives.

The Antichrist Tries to Destroy the Remnant Jews
The Remnant Jews Flee to Petra

Rev. 12:6
And the woman fled into the wilderness, where she hath a place prepared of God, that they should feed her there a thousand two hundred *and* threescore days.

Many Bible scholars believe the place in which these Jews flee is a mountainous place called Petra. Petra was first established sometime around the 6th century B.C. by the Nabataean Arabs, a nomadic tribe who settled in the area and built this fortress within the mountains. It is a mountainous city fortress located in Jordan. The city is surrounded by towering hills of sandstone, which gave the city some natural protection against invaders. The site is sandstone, which allowed the Nabataeans to carve their temples and tombs into the rock.

In 1994, Jordan and Israel signed a treaty, which included a tourism agreement allowing Jordanians to visit sites in Jerusalem and Israel and allowing Jews to visit sites in Jordan. Before this treaty, Israeli settlers could not visit Petra. It was reported that many Jews in the 1950's and 1960's were so intrigued with Petra, they would sneak into Petra just to view this site. Today, Jews can visit Petra because of the 1994 treaty with Jordan. It has become the most favored tourist site in Jordan for Jews.

Petra is about an eight-hour drive from Jerusalem. However, as we will see in Revelation 12:14, the remnant

Jews will probably go by air.

Mt. 24:16-22

[16]Then let them which be in Judaea flee into the mountains:

[17]Let him which is on the housetop not come down to take any thing out of his house:

[18]Neither let him which is in the field return back to take his clothes.

[19]And woe unto them that are with child, and to them that give suck in those days!

[20]But pray ye that your flight be not in the winter, neither on the sabbath day:

[21]For then shall be great tribulation, such as was not since the beginning of the world to this time, no, nor ever shall be.

[22]And except those days should be shortened, there should no flesh be saved: but for the elect's sake those days shall be shortened.

We are told in verse 21, that we are now in the "great tribulation" which is referring to the last half or 3½ years of the Tribulation.

Zech. 14:5

[5]And ye shall flee to the valley of the mountains; for the valley of the mountains shall reach unto Azal: yea, ye shall flee, like as ye fled from before the earthquake in the days of Uzziah king of Judah: and the LORD my God shall come, and all the saints with thee.

This verse prophesies a time when the Jewish remnant will flee to the mountains. I believe these mountains are the mountains where Petra is located. Once again, no one can be dogmatic that these mountains are the same as those of Petra, but the text of scripture speaks of a time when they will flee quickly and in fear. These are the same mountains mentioned in Matthew 24 above and the same time period. Notice at the end of verse 5, Zechariah states that after they flee, the Lord will come and "all the saints with thee." Therefore the remnant will flee and take abode in Petra for 3½ years and then the Second Coming to earth will occur.

Rev. 12:14
And to the woman were given two wings of a great eagle, that she might fly into the wilderness, into her place, where she is nourished for a time, and times, and half a time, from the face of the serpent.

The remnant Jews will probably be transported by air to Petra, which is an eight-hour drive from Jerusalem. I have to assume that there will be a lot of helicopters available at this time that could be used for this transport. This scenario fits well with the phrase "wings of a great eagle." God could miraculously translate them to Petra if He wishes. Whatever the transport, they will be transported very quickly, because the Antichrist, who is possessed by Satan, will try his best to destroy them after they arrive at Petra.

Rev. 12:15
And the serpent cast out of his mouth water as a flood after the woman, that he might cause her to be carried away of the flood.

At the entrance to Petra, the walls of sandstone rise steeply on the left and right, and a narrow cleft reveals the entrance to the Siq, the principal route into Petra. The walls of the Siq are lined with channels to carry drinking water to the city, while a dam to the right of the entrance diverts an adjoining stream through a tunnel to prevent it from flooding the Siq. Another reason I believe this city is Petra, is because of this dam and water supply. It supplies a perfect opportunity for the Antichrist to try to blow up the dam and flood the city and kill the remnant.

The Siq narrows to a little more than five yards in width, and the walls tower up hundreds of yards on either side.

The Siq (Photograph Courtesy of Shari and JoAnn Vickers)

At the end of the Siq appears the monument of *el Khazneh*, the Treasury. This is an enormous royal tomb, which was carved out of solid rock in the side of the mountain.

The Treasury (Photograph Courtesy of Jerry Johnston)

Beyond this, a stairway is cut in the rock to reveal rock-carved streets lined with hundreds of temples, royal tombs, large and small houses, banqueting halls, water channels and reservoirs, baths, monumental staircases, markets, arched gates, public buildings and paved streets. There is also a Roman amphitheater with seating for about 3,000.

The Roman Amphitheatre at Petra
(Photograph Courtesy of Jerry Johnston)

Rev. 12:16
And the earth helped the woman, and the earth opened her mouth, and swallowed up the flood which the dragon cast out of his mouth.

We are told that the "earth opened her mouth and swallowed up the flood." This suggests that God caused an earthquake to separate the earth and consume the waters. Satan continues to try his best to destroy God's people, but he loses more than he wins. He might cause many of God's people to be killed, but he will never rid the earth of God's remnant of believers. His time is short.

Rev. 12:17
And the dragon was wroth with the woman, and went to make war with the remnant of her seed, which keep the commandments of God, and have the testimony of Jesus Christ.

Because the Devil, who is in control of the Antichrist's body, cannot destroy God's remnant Jews again, he decides to go back to Jerusalem and make war with the other Jews and those other Christians left on earth. He is furious and the world will reap his fury for 3½ more years to come.

144,000 Are Now in Heaven at the Throne of God

The first five verses in Revelation 14 are difficult to discern as to whether this event takes place on earth or in heaven. Some believe this event takes place on earth at the end of the Tribulation Period at the Second Coming of Christ to earth. Others believe that these 144,000 Jews, who were saved at the beginning of the Tribulation, will survive the whole Tribulation Period unharmed. Their theory revolves around the phrase "a Lamb stood on the mount Sion," meaning the earthly site of Jerusalem at the Second Coming to earth. My theory is that this event takes place in heaven at the throne room of God.

Rev. 14:1
And I looked, and, lo, a Lamb stood on the mount Sion, and with him an hundred forty *and* four thousand, having his Father's name written in their foreheads.

We see "a Lamb stood on the mount Sion," or "Zion," but this could be the heavenly city as seen in the book of Hebrews below. I happen to believe that it is the heavenly city, because the next few verses in Revelation 14 take us to a heavenly scene.

Heb. 12:22
[22]But ye are come unto mount Sion, and unto the city of the living God, the heavenly Jerusalem, and to an innumerable company of angels,

"A Lamb" is without question, Jesus Christ. The 144,000 are seen standing "with him" which places them in this heavenly scene. Whether these 144,000 were martyred or were raptured, is not clear. Could there be another rapture in the middle of the Tribulation? The two witnesses were brought back to life and raptured, so why could there not be a rapture of this group? I do not have the answer shown clearly in scripture, but their preaching and witnessing were complete at this time. Whether through death or rapture, again no one can be dogmatic in their theory. Revelation 7:9-17, which are placed at the end of the Tribulation at the resurrection and Revelation 20:3, which is also at the end of the Tribulation, both could include these 144,000 as martyred saints of the Tribulation. These references speak of the saints who were martyred for their faith during the Tribulation. All Tribulation Saints who die during the Tribulation will be resurrected just before the Millennial Reign of Christ on earth, which is just after the Tribulation Period. The fact remains that these 144,000 are no longer on earth. As I stated before in Matthew 24, the gospel has now been preached to the whole world as a result of this group of 144,000 evangelists. Their mission complete, the Lord sees fit to take them out of the scene and bring them to heaven.

Rev. 14:2
And I heard a voice from heaven, as the voice of many waters, and as the voice of a great thunder: and I heard the voice of harpers harping with their harps:

Rev. 14:3
And they sung as it were a new song before the throne, and before the four beasts, and the elders: and no man could learn that song but the hundred *and* forty *and* four thousand, which were redeemed from the earth.

Once again, verses 2-3 are a scene in heaven and therefore, I believe that these 144,000 are in heaven at this time. One might say, how can they be in heaven if the resurrection has not occurred? All the souls and spirits of saints at death immediately go to be with Christ in heaven. II Cor. 5:8 states, "We are confident, *I say*, and willing rather to be absent from the body, and to be present with the Lord." The term resurrection always refers to the body, not the soul and spirit. Therefore, the resurrection of the body to join the soul and spirit will happen later after the Tribulation for these saints.

The four beasts and the elders are also in heaven and are located around the throne of God. Only the 144,000 could learn this particular "new song." Could it be that they were the elite group of Christians who braved the first half of the Tribulation without fear and carried the Gospel to the whole world, and therefore, no one else could boast of completing this task? We are told the heavenly angels cannot sing the praises of the gospel of salvation of man because they have not experienced the personal redemption that saved mankind has experienced.

1 Pet. 1:12
[12]Unto whom it was revealed, that not unto themselves, but unto us they did minister the things, which are now reported unto you by them that have preached the gospel unto you with the Holy Ghost sent down from heaven; which things the angels desire to look into.

Therefore, these 144,000 could be the only ones to learn and sing this new song because they alone experienced something no other person on earth has experienced.

Rev. 14:4
These are they which were not defiled with women; for they are virgins. These are they which follow the Lamb whithersoever he goeth. These were redeemed from among men, *being* the firstfruits unto God and to the Lamb.
Rev. 14:5
And in their mouth was found no guile: for they are without fault before the throne of God.

The character of these men was impeccable. The phrase "not defiled with women" could mean "they were virgins." It is not a sin to marry and, as a matter of fact, Paul states that it is a good thing to find a wife. However, if you feel led of God not to marry, then it is good to be as Paul was, a virgin eunuch. A eunuch simply meant one who could control his or her thought life and one who abstains from sex. Today, at home and in our public schools, we could do with more teaching of abstaining. I do not mean that we should abstain from marrying, but abstain from having sex until after marriage and only with our wife or husband.

These men were completely dedicated to following Jesus at all times. Their heart, mind, soul and spirit were brought to the understanding of preaching Christ and Christ crucified, buried and risen.

We are also told they were "redeemed from among men" which means they were purchased by Christ in a similar way that Paul was redeemed or purchased by Jesus Christ. All the saved from all ages are "redeemed" or purchased by the shed blood of Jesus Christ. In this same verse, we see that these men were also called the "firstfruits." This could mean that they were the first to be saved after the Tribulation began. As you recall, their salvation came just before the Trumpet Judgments were sounded. It could also mean they were considered part of the "firstfruits" of the first resurrection. The subject of when and where this event takes place will be up for debate until we see Jesus.

We see that in these men "was found no guile." This means there was found no deceit. They practiced what they preached and preached the truth regardless of the outcome. John the Baptist was like that in that he told it like it was and eventually he lost his head over his truthful preaching. These men did not water down the gospel or perform tricks to entice anyone. They told it like it is. Standing "without fault before the throne of God" does not mean these men were sinless. It simply means that they could stand before the throne of God and claim the blood of Jesus Christ who washed away their sins. Therefore God sees them, as he sees all Christians, through the blood of Jesus who presents us to the Father without fault, spot, or blemish.

An Angel Preaches the Gospel for the First Time and the Gospel Has Now Been Preached to All Mankind – The Great Commission is Fulfilled

Rev. 14:6
And I saw another angel fly in the midst of heaven, having the everlasting gospel to preach unto them that dwell on the earth, and to every nation, and kindred, and tongue, and people,
Rev. 14:7
Saying with a loud voice, Fear God, and give glory to him; for the hour of his judgment is come: and worship him that made heaven, and earth, and the sea, and the fountains of waters.

This is the first time in the history of man that an angel preaches the gospel. Before this event, the gospel has been preached by mankind alone. As I stated earlier, the middle of the Tribulation denotes a huge milestone in time. So much has happened in such a very short time and possibly within one to four days. Here we see that the gospel is preached for the last time to unsaved mankind. The 144,000 are no longer preaching the gospel to the unsaved, either. This is the fulfillment of commandment to preach the gospel throughout the world.

Mt. 24:14-16
[14]And this gospel of the kingdom shall be preached in all the world for a witness unto all nations; and then shall the end come.
[15]When ye therefore shall see the abomination of desolation, spoken of by Daniel the prophet, stand in the holy place, (whoso readeth, let him understand:)
[16]Then let them which be in Judaea flee into the mountains:

I have included verses 15-16 in the above group to show that the middle of the Tribulation is the timing of the end of preaching the gospel to unsaved man. As you see, the abomination of desolation and the fleeing of the remnant Jews to the mountains takes place in the same time period. Does this mean that because the gospel is no longer preached to the unsaved, that no one else will be saved. It absolutely does not mean that! The Word of God will not return void. The fact that everyone has heard the gospel means that the seed has been planted into every soul on earth. This seed, if it finds a fertile soul who later allows the seed to grow in his or her heart, could yield to the Word and trust Christ as their personal Savior. Scripture tells us in the parable of the sowing of the seed in Matthew 13 and Luke 8, that some will fall by the wayside, some on thorny ground, some on stony ground and some on fertile ground. In other words, the Word continues to grow in the heart of a willing person until it springs forth unto salvation.

Because the gospel has been preached throughout the world does not limit Christians from teaching and exhorting each other or other unsaved people with the gospel message. There has never in the past, nor will there ever be in the future, a time when the gospel is not preached or taught. The whole meaning of scripture is the gospel of Jesus Christ's death, burial and resurrection. This verse simply means that it has been fulfilled to preach the gospel throughout the world. Even during the Millennium and new heaven and new earth, we will continue to hear the gospel message, because that is why God made mankind. Jesus Christ is the gospel. We saw in the beginning of the book of Revelation that Jesus is the Alpha and Omega, the beginning and the end. Therefore, His message will always exist as long as Jesus exists, which is forever.

Warnings to Those Who Receive the Mark of the Beast and Who Worship the Beast

Rev. 14:9
And the third angel followed them, saying with a loud voice, If any man worship the beast and his image, and receive *his* mark in his forehead, or in his hand,
Rev. 14:10
The same shall drink of the wine of the wrath of God, which is poured out without mixture into the cup of his indignation; and he shall be tormented with fire and brimstone in the presence of the

holy angels, and in the presence of the Lamb:

We now see the warning to those who worship the beast and receive his mark of 666. These verses introduce us to the Vial Judgments and the next period of time. It will be the last half of the Tribulation, known as the wrath of God's cup of indignation. There is no hope for those who have received the mark of the beast and worship him as their savior. They are reprobate and will never be able to be saved and their final doom will be the Lake of Fire. This is God's warning to unsaved mankind of what will happen to them. At the Second Coming these will be cast into Hell (Hades) and at the end of the Millennium all that are in Hell will be cast into the Lake of Fire by the angels of God.

We are told that God's cup of indignation is "without mixture," meaning that it is not watered down. It is pure and just and He will not hold back his just and exact judgments on unsaved mankind in the next 3½ years.

Rev. 14:11
And the smoke of their torment ascendeth up for ever and ever: and they have no rest day nor night, who worship the beast and his image, and whosoever receiveth the mark of his name.

This is the forewarning to those mentioned in Verse 9, that the Lake of Fire is not a place of annihilation, but a place of everlasting torment. There will be no rest at any time and their torment will be forever. Some people have made joking comments about Hell and the Lake of Fire as though it will be a place where sin is always on the mind and everyone could join in on a big orgy. I have news for you, Verse 11 specifically warns us that it is not a place of everlasting sinful pleasures, but a place of everlasting torment. People will be in the worst pain known to man forever and will not find relief. This place will not only be for those of the Tribulation Period who never trust Christ as their Savior, but for those from all the ages past, present and future who do not trust Him. This alone should have Christians everywhere, trying their best to win the lost so they do not have to go to this awful place.

The Foretelling of the Death of Many Saints in the Last Half of the Tribulation

Rev. 14:12
Here is the patience of the saints: here *are* they that keep the commandments of God, and the faith of Jesus.
Rev. 14:13
And I heard a voice from heaven saying unto me, Write, Blessed *are* the dead which die in the Lord from henceforth: Yea, saith the Spirit, that they may rest from their labours; and their works do follow them.

Once again, the saints, the saved of this Tribulation period that are still alive, are told to be patient and continue to put their faith and trust in Jesus. They have gone through many trials and tribulations because of their faith and endured hardship that few Christians in the past have experienced. Many of them will experience physical death for their faith. However, God tells them that this death will be considered "rest from their labours." We, in our fleshly nature, many times think of death as a horrible experience. However, God sees the death of a Christian as a restful experience. If you have read Foxes Book of Martyrs, you will see many have been tortured for their faith and yet their death seemed peaceful. In the Book of Acts Chapter 7, when Stephen was being stoned to death, he looked up into heaven and saw Jesus "standing" at the right hand of the Father. To Stephen it was time to rest from his labors. This same chapter states that Stephen "fell asleep," meaning that he went to rest with Jesus and the sting of death had no affect on him.

Verse 13 also tells us that even after the death of these believers, "their works do follow them." What a testimony they leave behind! People will see their deaths and be astonished that they looked so peaceful. I am sure many unsaved who witness the deaths of these Christians come to accept Christ themselves just because of what they witnessed.

This is the meaning of the phrase "their works do follow them." I wonder if our works will follow us in similar manner or will our works as a Christian be considered a stumbling block to the unsaved? What about you dear reader? If you are a Christian, do your works represent Christ or do they cause others to say, "If that is the way a Christian is suppose to be, then I do not want to have anything to do with Christianity?" You may be surprised to know how many people may have said that about you or me. I hid behind hypocrites in the church for many years before I trusted Christ as my personal Savior. One day I heard a statement "you must be smaller than what you hide behind." I got saved after hearing a message on the Second Coming of Jesus Christ. Do not let hypocrites who claim to be saved cause you to not be saved. If you are saved, do not become someone that would cause others to stumble. It is best to not tell the world you are saved than to show the world how a Christian should not act.

11

The Seven Vials Poured Out

This chapter introduces us to the worst judgments to ever have inflicted the earth since the flood. We will see that these Vial Judgments are truly the last judgments and if time had not been shortened, all of mankind would have been destroyed. God is a loving and merciful God, but He is also the God of Judgment who has to judge sin. No one wants to think of God in any other way than the God of Love. He certainly is the God of Love, but He is also the God of Judgment and all His judgments are true and just. We have come to a time in the future where God is about to judge those who are not saved with the fierceness of His wrath. Millions, even billions, will die during this last half of the Tribulation Period or 3½ years. The vials, spoken of in Revelation, are not to be confused with the vials in a chemistry lab today. These are more accurately called "bowls" today. Therefore, I will use the word "bowl" or "bowls" when referring to vials within our commentary.

Scene in Heaven of Many Saints Who Were Murdered by the Antichrist

---

Rev. 15:1
And I saw another sign in heaven, great and marvellous, seven angels having the seven last plagues; for in them is filled up the wrath of God.

Rev. 15:2
And I saw as it were a sea of glass mingled with fire: and them that had gotten the victory over the beast, and over his image, and over his mark, *and* over the number of his name, stand on the sea of

glass, having the harps of God.
Rev. 15:3
And they sing the song of Moses the servant of God, and the song of the Lamb, saying, Great and marvellous *are* thy works, Lord God Almighty; just and true *are* thy ways, thou King of saints.
Rev. 15:4
Who shall not fear thee, O Lord, and glorify thy name? for *thou* only *art* holy: for all nations shall come and worship before thee; for thy judgments are made manifest.

The seven angels with the last seven plagues are introduced having bowls filled to the brim with the wrath of God. These verses show us that many Christians during this last half of the Tribulation will be martyred for their faith in Jesus and overcome the Antichrist and his idolatrous teachings. They are seen in heaven with God. They "sing the song of Moses and the song of the Lamb." The song that Moses sang is found in Exodus 15. The summary of Moses' song is found in Revelation 15:3-4 where he sings about God's greatness and works which are just and true. Moses has just led the children of Israel out of Egypt and the Lord has just drowned Pharaoh and his army in the Red Sea, saving the children of Israel from certain destruction. These Christian martyrs of the last half of the Tribulation sing the same song of God's salvation through the Lord Jesus Christ. It is the same song, because as God saved Moses and Israel from Pharaoh, so God saves these Tribulation Saints from the Antichrist. Their salvation may not have been from physical death, but they were certainly saved from the Second Death, which is separation from God forever. Those who worship the Antichrist will experience the separation from God forever in the Lake of Fire.

Seven Angels with the Seven Golden Bowls Filled With God's Wrath

---

Rev. 15:5
And after that I looked, and, behold, the temple of the tabernacle of the testimony in heaven was opened:

Rev. 15:6
And the seven angels came out of the temple, having the seven plagues, clothed in pure and white linen, and having their breasts girded with golden girdles.
Rev. 15:7
And one of the four beasts gave unto the seven angels seven golden vials full of the wrath of God, who liveth for ever and ever.

What an amazing scene in heaven as these seven angels come out of the temple in heaven! They come over to one of the four beasts, living creatures that are usually always seen around the throne of God saying "Holy, Holy." One of the beasts gives each of them a golden bowl filled with the wrath of God. Once again, we are told that God will never have an ending. He lives forever. The pure linen and the golden girdles represent the just judgments of God. God's wrath is true and just and His judgments of sin are pure and without explanation. God has to judge sin and the Father of Sin. Satan and his cronies must be judged. These vials or bowls of wrath are huge in their effect on the earth. The seal and trumpet judgments may have been blamed on the two witnesses, but they were from God as are the bowl judgments. We will see that unsaved man will still continue to curse God even after these judgments are executed upon them.

Rev. 15:8
And the temple was filled with smoke from the glory of God, and from his power; and no man was able to enter into the temple, till the seven plagues of the seven angels were fulfilled.

The verses previous to this were talking about the temple in heaven. This verse could be referring to the same heavenly temple. However, the statement "no man was able to enter into the temple" leads me to believe that this is the earthly temple in Jerusalem. It would stand to reason that this would be true, because most of the remnant Jews have fled to Petra and those who are left are hiding for their lives or serving the Antichrist if they took his mark. It could mean both the earthly and the heavenly temple. Whether this is the heavenly temple or the earthly temple, no "man" will enter into it until all the bowl judgments have been poured out into the earth. It will be "filled with the smoke from the glory of God, and his power." God did this when the tabernacle was in the wilderness with Moses.

Ex. 40:34-35
[34]Then a cloud covered the tent of the congregation, and the glory of the LORD filled the tabernacle.
[35]And Moses was not able to enter into the tent of the congregation, because the cloud abode thereon, and the glory of the LORD filled the tabernacle.

Rev. 16:1
And I heard a great voice out of the temple saying to the seven angels, Go your ways, and pour out the vials of the wrath of God upon the earth.

No more delay, as the "great voice out of the temple" tells the angels to pour out the bowls upon the earth. This voice is none other than God Himself, since no one else could be in the temple when God's glory filled it. God ordained these judgments. The last 3½ years of the Tribulation, known as the Great Tribulation or Jacob's Trouble, will see unprecedented judgment and pain. Notice the parallel of the bowl judgments two, three, four and six to the trumpet judgments two, three, four and six. The trumpet judgments only affected one-third of its prey, while the bowl judgments will affect the other two-thirds or all that is left.

The First Bowl is Poured Out and Causes Sores on Them Who Have the Mark of the Beast

Rev. 16:2
And the first went, and poured out his vial upon the earth; and there fell a noisome and grievous sore upon the men which had the mark of the beast, and *upon* them which worshipped his image.

Notice in Exodus below, where Moses calls for the plague

of boils on the Egyptians. These sores were so grievous that even the magicians could not stand before Moses to try to contradict him. It is unusual to have a righteous man stand and speak and no one to contradict him. We could use a few boils like that today. With all kidding aside, notice "the Lord hardened the heart of Pharaoh." Once again, we will see in Revelation 16:11 that the men have become reprobate, as we discussed earlier, like Pharaoh and have hardened their heart to the point that God turns from them and begins to harden their hearts Himself.

Ex. 9:8-12

[8]And the LORD said unto Moses and unto Aaron, Take to you handfuls of ashes of the furnace, and let Moses sprinkle it toward the heaven in the sight of Pharaoh

[9]And it shall become small dust in all the land of Egypt, and shall be a boil breaking forth *with* blains upon man, and upon beast, throughout all the land of Egypt.

[10]And they took ashes of the furnace, and stood before Pharaoh; and Moses sprinkled it up toward heaven; and it became a boil breaking forth *with* blains upon man, and upon beast.

[11]And the magicians could not stand before Moses because of the boils; for the boil was upon the magicians, and upon all the Egyptians.

[12]And the LORD hardened the heart of Pharaoh, and he hearkened not unto them; as the LORD had spoken unto Moses.

The plague of Moses' day only affected the Egyptians, and in a similar way, this first bowl judgment only affects those who have the 666 mark of the beast and who worship the Antichrist throughout the world. The word "noisome and grievous sore" means, in the Greek, "an ulcerated-sore, bad, an evil." This would be a pandemic plague of sores and will probably plunge the world into further chaos. The word "men" refers to mankind, both male and female.

Today, the world is concerned about the "bird flu" that has begun to affect places in Africa, China and the Far East. There are scientists and doctors who state this could, and probably will, become pandemic at some point throughout the world very soon. Vaccines are being developed today to help reduce its affect on the world. However, there will only be enough vaccine to cover those in the medical field and the higher end of governments, so cities and counties would not be shut down or destroyed by this disease.

This particular disease from this first bowl judgment will not have the warning the bird flu has today. It will happen all of a sudden and there will be no time to produce vaccine to fight off this disease. Many will die from these sores. I am sure there will be jealousy and wonder as to why the sores did not affect the Christians. This will probably cause many Christians to be killed by those who contract the disease of sores because of the jealously and hatred for God.

The Second Bowl is Poured Out Upon the Sea and the Sea Becomes Blood

Rev. 16:3
And the second angel poured out his vial upon the sea; and it became as the blood of a dead *man*: and every living soul died in the sea.

During the second trumpet judgment, one-third of the sea turned to blood and one-third of the life in the sea died. Here we see the sea became as blood and everything living in it died. This means that the other two-thirds of the sea and everything living in the sea are now destroyed. Did the sea literally turn to blood? Why is that hard for us to believe? God created this world and He certainly is not limited in what He can do to it. Whether it was actual blood or something that appeared to be blood is not the essence of the verse. The essence of the verse is that "every" living creature in the sea died and that God has complete control over His universe. As I have stated, some groups of "so-called" Christians, believe that God lost control of the universe when Adam sinned in the garden and will not get it back until Jesus returns. Tell that to the Egyptians of Moses' day and those living during the Tribulation. Any blind man can see God is in control and has NEVER lost control. If He had ever lost control, He would not be God and the writing of this book could be considered a fairy-tale.

The Third Bowl is Poured Out Upon the Fresh Waters and They Became Blood

Rev. 16:4
And the third angel poured out his vial upon the rivers and fountains of waters; and they became blood.
Rev. 16:5
And I heard the angel of the waters say, Thou art righteous, O Lord, which art, and wast, and shalt be, because thou hast judged thus.
Rev. 16:6
For they have shed the blood of saints and prophets, and thou hast given them blood to drink; for they are worthy.

The third bowl is poured out and the fresh water sources are all now turned to blood. At the third trumpet judgment, in the first half of the Tribulation, we saw one-third of the fresh water sources became bitter and men died because of the water. Here we see the other two-thirds or all of the earth's water sources are destroyed and become blood. It is hard to imagine how anyone could survive without water. I have to assume that the only source of water for people to drink is the water that was bottled prior to this judgment. Remember earlier, the statement that people will not be able to buy nor sell without the mark of the beast. Bottled water, soft drinks, milk and any other drinks will become worth more than gold or the lives of others. People will kill to obtain a bottle of water or soft drink.

God's Judgments are Righteous

Rev. 16:7
And I heard another out of the altar say, Even so, Lord God Almighty, true and righteous *are* thy judgments.

We are reminded even during these disastrous plagues that these judgments are valid, right, true and just. I am sure God wanted to remind the reader that may have begun to think, "how could God be so cruel?" that God has been very patient with man for thousands of years. He has allowed man to sin, blaspheme Him, kill His prophets and saints and it is the time to judge an earth that has become like it was during Noah's day. The world is full of corruption, sin, violence, drunkenness, people without natural affection (homosexuality), murderers and the list is too long to continue. You name a sin and it is open and prevalent during this age and the people are proud of it. Do not even begin to think, "He's a cruel God." He is Just and has tried every way possible to save those who are willing.

The Fourth Bowl is Poured Out Upon the Sun and Men are Scorched with Fire

Rev. 16:8
And the fourth angel poured out his vial upon the sun; and power was given unto him to scorch men with fire.
Rev. 16:9
And men were scorched with great heat, and blasphemed the name of God, which hath power over these plagues: and they repented not to give him glory.

We saw in the fourth trumpet judgment, one-third of the sun, moon and stars were darkened. You would think that this would cool the earth down. Now we see that the sun's heat will intensify to the point of actually causing men to be scorched with fire. One might suggest: "the ozone layer must be almost completely gone at this point and therefore there is no protection for mankind from the sun." Remember, God does not have to wait for the ozone layer to deplete to have the sun scorch men. He created the sun and can perform any miracle He wishes and at the time He chooses. God sets the boundaries, not man.

Notice as I stated earlier, these judgments seem to be directed towards man's idols. Throughout the history of man, man has worshiped the sun, moon and stars along with other idolatrous items. We see that God is showing them that these are mere idols and He does not like the fact that mankind continues to push Him aside to worship some ridiculous idol. It is almost like He is saying "OK, you want to worship the sun, then reap the results of your idolatrous worship." I am constantly frustrated with man today in their unwillingness to accept the fact that there is a Supreme Being and His name is Jesus Christ! It is certainly a good thing that I am not God or else these plagues would have already been fulfilled long ago. Thank God I am not God!

We see that unsaved man at this point of the Tribulation Period will still not repent and give God the glory. Talk about "mule-headed!" Please allow me this crude illustration. A person curses someone to their face who is standing in front of him with a gun. This person with the gun proceeds to shoot him in the arm. That same person stands back to his feet and curses him again. The gunman shoots him in the leg and this continues. Would you not counsel the first person that is being shot, to keep his mouth shut and ask the gunman to forgive him? The idea is almost the same. These people continue to curse God and God brings on the next plague. Once again, please do not think I am attempting to compare God to a heartless gunman.

The Fifth Bowl is Poured Out Upon the Antichrist Headquarters and His Kingdom

Rev. 16:10
And the fifth angel poured out his vial upon the seat of the beast; and his kingdom was full of darkness; and they gnawed their tongues for pain,
Rev. 16:11
And blasphemed the God of heaven because of their pains and their sores, and repented not of their deeds.

The Fifth Bowl is directed toward the Antichrist's headquarters and his kingdom. Total darkness is so dark that it is as though you could cut it with a knife. One weekend my wife, daughter and I took a trip to Ruby Falls in Chattanooga, Tennessee. We went deep into a large cavern in the ground. There was a light shining on the falls. Then we were told they were about to turn out all the lights and close the door to the cave and for us not to be alarmed. Also, we were told we could go blind after too much time in total darkness. When the lights went out and the door was blocked so light could not enter, it was total darkness. It was frightening to say the least and you could not see your hand in front of your face, literally. Fear gripped everyone, even though the lights were only out for seconds. I suspect the darkness, which is mentioned in Verse 10, will be even darker than what we experienced that day. Or was it night? That is right, the unsaved living during this time period, will not know whether it is day or night. You may as well take a seat where you are or else you will surely stumble over everything.

The Greek word for "kingdom" is "basileia" which means "the territory subject to the rule of a king." Because the Antichrist is ruler of the ten nations mentioned earlier, this could mean that all of these nations will be affected by this plague. It could also be said that he seems to be ruler of the whole world and therefore the whole world will be cast into darkness. Either interpretation could be correct and neither would take away from the text of the scripture. Since I believe that Babylon will be rebuilt in close proximity of where old Babylon existed, this would mean that this particular plague also affects this area. As we will see later in this study, Babylon, which is located in modern day Iraq, will have been rebuilt, probably early in the Tribulation Period or before the Tribulation, and will become the headquarters of the Antichrist. We will discuss this in more detail when we reach Revelation 18.

Therefore, his headquarters area and the rest of the Antichrist's kingdom will be thrust into total darkness. Verse 11 states they blasphemed God and repented not of their deeds. This plague will not affect those who are saved, for those who are saved would never blaspheme God. Those who are saved will be able to go about and not be seen by the unsaved in these areas. This will be an opportunity to gather food, drink and vital necessities they will need to survive. They will see the pain and hear the cries of these unsaved people who are in excruciating pain from the total darkness and sores. If you are saved and reading this book during this Tribulation time period, make your plans for this plague and gather all the food, drink and necessities you can and take them back to your hiding place. We are not told how long this plague of darkness will continue. It could be hours or days or months.

The Sixth Bowl is Poured Out and the Euphrates River is Dried Up

Rev. 16:12
And the sixth angel poured out his vial upon the great river Euphrates; and the water thereof was dried up, that the way of the kings of the east might be prepared.

The Sixth Bowl is poured out and we see the Euphrates River is dried up and the reason is to make a way for the kings of the east to come to the upcoming Battle of Armageddon. The Fifth and Sixth Bowl Judgments seem to be localized around the Antichrist's headquarters and kingdom. The Euphrates River is located in Iraq and the city of Babylon is located on the Euphrates River southwest of today's city of Baghdad.

The Euphrates River begins in Southeastern Turkey and flows through Syria and then through Iraq. Other than the two rivers in Turkey which form the Euphrates, the Western and Eastern Euphrates, there are no other sources of water that make up the Euphrates River for its almost 1800 mile journey. On the Euphrates River, there have been construction projects for over 22 dams and 19 power plants in Turkey to be completed in 2005. One dam was completed in 1973 and one dam is under construction in Syria and seven dams are completed in Iraq.

It would seem to be an easy task to stop the flow of this river, humanly speaking, if God chose to use this method. However, as I have stated before, God does not have to have manmade concoctions to perform His miracles. He did not use manmade concoctions to dry up the Rea Sea for millions of Jews to cross on dry land or to dry up the Jordan River for the Jews to cross. The Euphrates River will be dried up regardless of the method He chooses.

It is ironic that even some Islamic teachings teach that the Euphrates River will be dried up and reveal an abundance of gold. They go on to say that people will fight over the gold and 99 out of 100 will die *(Sahih Bukhari, Sahih Muslim)*. One of these teachings will definitely come to pass, the drying up of the Euphrates River. However, the killing portion will probably take place in Israel at the Battle of Armageddon. It will be likely that 100% of these will be killed, because I doubt that any of them would have trusted Jesus Christ as their Savior at that point.

The sixth trumpet also affected something relating to the Euphrates River. Four angels were loosed and headed up a demonic army of 200 million to slay a third of mankind close to the end of the first half of the Tribulation. Some scholars believe the Sixth Trumpet and the Sixth Bowl Judgments correlate to fulfill the same prophecy. I do not believe these are one in the same. As mentioned earlier, the 200 million army of the Sixth Trumpet Judgment is a demonic army who slay men during the 1st half of the Tribulation. The Sixth Bowl Judgment is a separate event and is specifically used to dry up the Euphrates River to prepare the armies of the east to bring their millions to the Battle of Armageddon against the Lord of Hosts.

Dr. Harold Willmington notes:

"Here the God of heaven employs psychological warfare upon his enemies, conditioning them to gather themselves together in the near future at Armageddon."

"The Euphrates River is 1800 miles long and in some places 3600 feet wide. It is thirty feet deep. This river has been the dividing line between western and eastern civilization since the dawn of history. It served as the eastern border of the Old Roman Empire. Thus, the Euphrates becomes both the cradle and grave of man's civilization. Here the first godless city (Enoch, built by Cain; see Gen. 4: 16-17) went up, and here the last rebellious city will be constructed (Babylon, built by the Antichrist; see Rev. 18)." (*Willmington's Guide to the Bible, Tyndale House Publishers Inc., page 570)*

Gen. 4:16-17

[16]And Cain went out from the presence of the LORD, and dwelt in the land of Nod, on the east of Eden.

[17]And Cain knew his wife; and she conceived, and bare Enoch: and he builded a city, and called the name of the city, after the name of his son, Enoch.

The Seventh Bowl is Poured Out Into the Air and All the Earth is Thrust Into Imbalance

Rev. 16:17

And the seventh angel poured out his vial into the air; and there came a great voice out of the temple of heaven, from the throne, saying, It is done.

The Seventh Bowl is poured out into the atmosphere and God says "It is done." Remember in Revelation 15:8 that no man was allowed to enter into the temple until all the bowls are poured out onto earth. Well, this is God stating that all the judgments of wrath are completed and He is now ready for His Son Jesus to come back to earth in His Second Coming. However, just prior to this and also setting the stage, we will see several events take place in a very short time frame.

Rev. 16:18

And there were voices, and thunders, and lightnings; and there was a great earthquake, such as was not since men were upon the earth, so mighty an earthquake, *and* so great.

The storm of the ages is about to take place. "Thunders and lightnings" and then the greatest earthquake known to man is unleashed upon the earth. I do not believe we have developed a device to measure this earthquake.

Rev. 16:19
And the great city was divided into three parts, and the cities of the nations fell: and great Babylon came in remembrance before God, to give unto her the cup of the wine of the fierceness of his wrath.

Jerusalem is divided into three parts and many cities throughout the world are leveled. We also see that God is now eyeing the Antichrist's headquarters again and He is about to unleash the "fierceness of his wrath" upon it. We will see this shortly.

Rev. 16:20
And every island fled away, and the mountains were not found.

Recently on television, there was a documentary about the Island of Krakatoa located in Indonesia near the island of Java. This island was a volcanic island which exploded in 1883. Two-thirds of the island completely disappeared, causing shock waves and huge tsunamis to hit many islands and cause death and devastation everywhere. Over 165 villages were completely destroyed, 132 villages were seriously damaged, over 36,000 people were killed and the blast was heard over 3,000 miles away. The atmospheric shock waves reverberated around the world for five days. However, this will be considered a Sunday School picnic compared to the earthquake and disasters found in Verse 20.

The earthquake in Verse 20 will cause unbelievable disasters that have never been known to man, even far beyond the disaster of Krakatoa. Islands will be leveled or completely submerged under water, mountains will be thrown down and tsunamis will probably happen throughout the world.

Rev. 16:21
And there fell upon men a great hail out of heaven, *every stone* about the weight of a talent: and men blasphemed God because of

the plague of the hail; for the plague thereof was exceeding great.

Mt. 24:29

[29]Immediately after the tribulation of those days shall the sun be darkened, and the moon shall not give her light, and the stars shall fall from heaven, and the powers of the heavens shall be shaken:

This huge earthquake likely causes volcanoes to erupt throughout the world. Huge rocks are thrust high into the air and form 100-pound hailstones as they fall to earth. The largest recorded hailstone found in the U.S. was back in June 2003 in Aurora, Nebraska. According to an article in the National Geographic News dated August 4, 2003, this hailstone was about the size of a soccer ball. Because 40% of the hailstone broke off on contact and could not be found, it did not surpass the weight of the previous heaviest hailstone that weighed in at 1.5 pounds. The article goes on to say that according to NOAA, large hailstones can reach speeds of over 100 miles per hour as they fall.

Let me make some size estimates. We will assume that hailstones are similar in weight to crushed ice, since both contain air. Hailstones weigh less than crushed ice, but we will err on the conservative side. One cubic foot of crushed ice weighs around 37 pounds, so one hundred pounds would be equivalent to 2.7 cubic feet. This would be about the size of one and one-half basketballs. These would literally crush huge holes in houses, cars, planes, ships, people and anything in their paths. They could reach speeds surpassing 100-200 miles per hour. It would certainly cause death and destruction!

12

City of Babylon and Its World Economic System are Destroyed

As I have mentioned previously, Babylon had to be rebuilt sometime prior to its upcoming destruction, which we will see shortly. This would mean that Babylon would have had to have been rebuilt probably years before this destruction and possibly before the Tribulation Period begins. Since the Antichrist comes on the scene in the beginning of the Tribulation Period and probably ran the European Union from Rome, then had Rome destroyed, he will probably move his main headquarters, in the middle of the Tribulation Period, to the newly reconstructed city of Babylon.

As of the writing of this book, the United States coalition is in the process of converting Iraq into a democracy. Saddam Hussein has been captured, removed from power by the coalition's Liberation Invasion of Iraq and has been hanged for his atrocities. I have recently retrieved an article from the Internet, dated November 21, 2005, by Chris Tomlinson, an Associated Press writer. The title of the article is "Reconstruction Team Launched in Babylon." There is a photo of the U.S. Ambassador to Iraq, Zalmay Khalilzad, with the ruins of old Babylon in the background. The article states "the U.S. ambassador inaugurated a provincial reconstruction team in central Iraq." It goes on to say, " Khalilzad said the new teams, known as PRTs, will focus on developing the ability of Iraqi provincial officials to take the lead in rebuilding Iraq." Further into the article we find "While Secretary of State Condoleezza Rice launched the first two

PRTs in the northern city of Mosul during a visit Nov. 11, none of the teams will begin work in earnest until Dec. 15 election, officials said. The teams for Babil, Ninevah and Tamim will serve as a test for the rest, which will start work early next year." "Babil," or "Babel," is the province in which the city of Babylon is located.

The elections are now over and I assume these PRTs are under way. Saddam had already begun the reconstruction of Babylon years ago. He had completed Nebuchadnezzar's Palace, which he also called his palace, the Istar Gate, the Processional Street, the Istar Temple, Nebuchadnezzar's Museum, Marduk Gate, Nabu Temple and a Greek Theater. It could be these PRTs will complete the rest of the new city of Babylon within a few years.

The irony of all of this is that the Antichrist will make Babylon his headquarters and it will become the headquarters of the economic system for the whole world for 3½ years. No one would humanly predict such an event in the past, because Iraq in the past 2000 years has not been free enough or profitable enough to allow such an event to take place. The times in which we currently live are exciting times, knowing that God is arranging everything in His order so His scripture will be fulfilled 100%.

As I mentioned in the last chapter, in Revelation 16:19, "great Babylon came in remembrance before God." God is about to deal with the destruction of Babylon and its world economic system. We saw in the last chapter that several judgments came directly against the Antichrist's headquarters, the city of Babylon and his kingdom. Now we are about to see God destroy this city in the matter of one hour. It is obvious that the Antichrist has left this city by this time because he will appear later at the Battle of Armageddon. God has planned everything in beautiful perfection. There are no accidents with God.

Now we are about to embark on a Bible study that will encompass many different scripture references to show how beautifully the Bible interprets itself. If you are serious about the study of end-times, please read all the scripture references that will be supplied from here until the end of our study.

We are now closing in on the end of the last 3½ years of the Seven-Year Tribulation. The Seven Bowls of the last plagues have been poured out onto mankind.

Rev. 18:1
And after these things I saw another angel come down from heaven, having great power; and the earth was lightened with his glory.
Rev. 18:2
And he cried mightily with a strong voice, saying, Babylon the great is fallen, is fallen, and is become the habitation of devils, and the hold of every foul spirit, and a cage of every unclean and hateful bird.

These are the preface verses for the next 22 verses that speak about the fall of Babylon. We see that Babylon is fallen and devils and foul spirits now inhabit it along with birds of prey. This is a summary of the results of the next 22 verses. Babylon is the headquarters of the Antichrist and his cronies. From our previous study, we know the Antichrist is possessed by Satan. Verse 2 informs us that probably most of the inhabitants of Babylon are also possessed with demons. It stands to reason that Satan will make sure that his demons who surround him possess those individual humans who are yielded to the Antichrist. I believe that because of the destruction of this city and its inhabitants, who are demon possessed, that these demons are left to inhabit the city in a non-human form. It could be that they possess the birds and beasts in the area. They are considered evil spirits and certainly go to and fro on this earth. Just before Jesus cast the demons out of the maniac of the country of the Gadarenes, the demons requested that they be allowed to possess the herd of pigs instead of being cast into the bottomless pit. Jesus granted their request and the pigs ran down a hill and off a cliff to their destruction. These same demons later could also possess unsaved humans again. Demons cannot possess someone who is a child of God. As relates to humans, only the unsaved can be possessed by demons.

Jer. 50:39

[39]Therefore the wild beasts of the desert with the wild beasts of the islands shall dwell *there*, and the owls shall dwell therein: and it shall be no more inhabited for ever; neither shall it be dwelt in from generation to generation.

Jer. 51:37

[37]And Babylon shall become heaps, a dwellingplace for dragons, an astonishment, and an hissing, without an inhabitant.

Babylon will never be inhabited again by human beings. These are possibly the beasts that become possessed by the evil demonic spirits.

Jer. 51:17-18

[17]Every man is brutish by *his* knowledge; every founder is confounded by the graven image: for his molten image *is* falsehood, and *there is* no breath in them.
[18]They *are* vanity, the work of errors: in the time of their visitation they shall perish.

Everything in Babylon is related to idol worship and falsehood. This is one of the reasons for its destruction.

Rev. 18:3

For all nations have drunk of the wine of the wrath of her fornication, and the kings of the earth have committed fornication with her, and the merchants of the earth are waxed rich through the abundance of her delicacies.

Jer. 50:23

[23]How is the hammer of the whole earth cut asunder and broken! how is Babylon become a desolation among the nations!

"Hammer" here means a device that an artist used to form gold around its object to be covered. This hammer was used to beat the gold and mold it into exactly what the artist desired. "Hammer" then is metaphorically Babylon, who has formed and fashioned the world exactly how it wanted the world to look.

Jer. 51:7

[7]Babylon *hath been* a golden cup in the LORD'S hand, that made all the earth drunken: the nations have drunken of her wine; therefore the nations are mad.

In this case, it was the gold cup in which the world drank of Babylon's lies and fornications.

Is. 14:18

[18]All the kings of the nations, *even* all of them, lie in glory, every one in his own house.

The Antichrist has done an amazing job of lying to the whole world and convincing them that his way is the only way. Notice Verse 3 states that virtually everyone who follows the Antichrist's idea of economics become rich. They also believe that he is God and bought into every form of his worship.

This is a lesson to each of us. Just because someone is rich in this world's goods, does not mean that God has blessed them with these riches. I do not mean to suggest that everyone who is rich is not of God. I simply mean that success in the eyes of God is not measured in material riches, but in spiritual riches. You can only have spiritual riches if you have trusted His Son Jesus Christ as your personal Savior. Trusting Jesus does not guarantee material riches, as some so-called preachers preach today. As a matter of fact, many Christians will never see this world's riches, but will inherit the riches of God forever. Beware of any preacher or teacher that states when you get saved, God will bless you with material riches, increase your pocketbook, increase your bank account, etc. When you hear this, run and flee from this person with all your might. This is a liar and deceiver and you best not listen to his/her lies. You will notice this particular preacher or teacher is the one who becomes rich, because he or she preys on your finances with the same deception that the Antichrist deceives the nations.

Rev. 18:4
And I heard another voice from heaven, saying, Come out of her, my people, that ye be not partakers of her sins, and that ye receive not of her plagues.
Rev. 18:5
For her sins have reached unto heaven, and God hath remembered her iniquities.

Jer. 50:8

[8]Remove out of the midst of Babylon, and go forth out of the land of the Chaldeans, and be as the he goats before the flocks.

It is said that the male goats, as soon as the gate is opened, will be the first ones out the gate and without hesitation. This sounds like good advice, seeing what is about to happen to this city.

Jer. 51:6

[6]Flee out of the midst of Babylon, and deliver every man his soul: be not cut off in her iniquity; for this *is* the time of the LORD'S vengeance; he will render unto her a recompense.

Jer. 51:45

[45]My people, go ye out of the midst of her, and deliver ye every man his soul from the fierce anger of the LORD.

Just before the destruction of Babylon, those who are saved that still may be in Babylon, are told to leave the city immediately, so they will not be harmed by the upcoming judgment.

Verse 5 states that "God hath remembered her iniquities." It is so nice to know that for those of us who are saved, regardless of the time era, our sins will never be remembered. God states in Hebrews 10:17 "And their sins and iniquities will I remember no more." However, those who are not saved, God will remember their sins and iniquities.

Rev. 18:6
Reward her even as she rewarded you, and double unto her double according to her works: in the cup which she hath filled fill to her double.

Jer. 50:14-15, 21, 29

[14]Put yourselves in array against Babylon round about: all ye that bend the bow, shoot at her, spare no arrows: for she hath sinned

against the LORD.

[15]Shout against her round about: she hath given her hand: her foundations are fallen, her walls are thrown down: for it *is* the vengeance of the LORD: take vengeance upon her; as she hath done, do unto her.

[21]Go up against the land of Merathaim, *even* against it, and against the inhabitants of Pekod: waste and utterly destroy after them, saith the LORD, and do according to all that I have commanded thee.

[29]Call together the archers against Babylon: all ye that bend the bow, camp against it round about; let none thereof escape: recompense her according to her work; according to all that she hath done, do unto her: for she hath been proud against the LORD, against the Holy One of Israel.

Jer. 51:24

[24]And I will render unto Babylon and to all the inhabitants of Chaldea all their evil that they have done in Zion in your sight, saith the LORD.

This is one soup in which no one would want seconds. Have you ever wished that some wicked murdering ruler or some wicked murderer would reap double of what he has sown? Well, God is going to cause Babylon to reap at least double of what she has sown on earth. As a result of Babylon's rule over the world, millions of people, both saved and unsaved, have been brutally tortured and murdered. They have ravaged homes and lands, destroyed cities, raped and murdered, worshipped idols, and the list would be too long to continue.

Rev. 18:7
How much she hath glorified herself, and lived deliciously, so much torment and sorrow give her: for she saith in her heart, I sit a queen, and am no widow, and shall see no sorrow.

Notice the boasting and foolish pride of this city. They have come to the point in their mind that nothing could stop them, nothing is better than them and nothing can harm them. As you will see in the supporting verses below, reconstructed Babylon of the Tribulation is the "daughter of Babylon" or daughter of the ancient city. Scripture tells us in Proverbs

16:18, "Pride *goeth* before destruction, and an haughty spirit before a fall." I believe Babylon falls into this category.

Jer. 50:35-38

[35]A sword *is* upon the Chaldeans, saith the LORD, and upon the inhabitants of Babylon, and upon her princes, and upon her wise *men*.

[36]A sword *is* upon the liars; and they shall dote: a sword *is* upon her mighty men; and they shall be dismayed.

[37]A sword *is* upon their horses, and upon their chariots, and upon all the mingled people that *are* in the midst of her; and they shall become as women: a sword *is* upon her treasures; and they shall be robbed.

[38]A drought *is* upon her waters; and they shall be dried up: for it *is* the land of graven images, and they are mad upon *their* idols.

Is. 47:1-8

[1]Come down, and sit in the dust, O virgin daughter of Babylon, sit on the ground: *there is* no throne, O daughter of the Chaldeans: for thou shalt no more be called tender and delicate.

[2]Take the millstones, and grind meal: uncover thy locks, make bare the leg, uncover the thigh, pass over the rivers.

[3]Thy nakedness shall be uncovered, yea, thy shame shall be seen: I will take vengeance, and I will not meet *thee as* a man.

[4]*As for* our redeemer, the LORD of hosts *is* his name, the Holy One of Israel.

[5]Sit thou silent, and get thee into darkness, O daughter of the Chaldeans: for thou shalt no more be called, The lady of kingdoms.

[6]I was wroth with my people, I have polluted mine inheritance, and given them into thine hand: thou didst show them no mercy; upon the ancient hast thou very heavily laid thy yoke.

[7]And thou saidst, I shall be a lady for ever: *so* that thou didst not lay these *things* to thy heart, neither didst remember the latter end of it.

[8]Therefore hear now this, *thou that art* given to pleasures, that dwellest carelessly, that sayest in thine heart, I *am*, and none else beside me; I shall not sit *as* a widow, neither shall I know the loss of children:

Rev. 18:8

Therefore shall her plagues come in one day, death, and mourning, and famine; and she shall be utterly burned with fire: for strong *is* the Lord God who judgeth her.

Is. 47:9-10, 14

[9]But these two *things* shall come to thee in a moment in one day,

the loss of children, and widowhood: they shall come upon thee in their perfection for the multitude of thy sorceries, *and* for the great abundance of thine enchantments.

[10]For thou hast trusted in thy wickedness: thou hast said, None seeth me. Thy wisdom and thy knowledge, it hath perverted thee; and thou hast said in thine heart, I *am*, and none else beside me.

[14]Behold, they shall be as stubble; the fire shall burn them; they shall not deliver themselves from the power of the flame: *there shall* not *be* a coal to warm at, *nor* fire to sit before it.

Jer. 50:25, 32

[25]The LORD hath opened his armoury, and hath brought forth the weapons of his indignation: for this *is* the work of the Lord GOD of hosts in the land of the Chaldeans.

[32]And the most proud shall stumble and fall, and none shall raise him up: and I will kindle a fire in his cities, and it shall devour all round about him.

Jer. 51:25, 30, 32, 47

[25]Behold, I *am* against thee, O destroying mountain, saith the LORD, which destroyest all the earth: and I will stretch out mine hand upon thee, and roll thee down from the rocks, and will make thee a burnt mountain.

[30]The mighty men of Babylon have forborn to fight, they have remained in *their* holds: their might hath failed; they became as women: they have burned her dwellingplaces; her bars are broken.

[32]And that the passages are stopped, and the reeds they have burned with fire, and the men of war are affrighted.

[47]Therefore, behold, the days come, that I will do judgment upon the graven images of Babylon: and her whole land shall be confounded, and all her slain shall fall in the midst of her.

The judgment will fall and Babylon will be destroyed in one day. There will be death, famine, fire and mourning by those who see this destruction. How many of us remember September 11, 2001, when the terrorists flew the planes into New York's Twin Towers and the Pentagon? Horror gripped the world and prayers and mourning went throughout the world for those affected and for America. We were all shocked and dismayed. How could this happen to America, the land of the free and home of the brave? In America, we had almost become like the new Babylon in that we thought we could not be attacked. Obviously, the attack on the Twin Towers and the Pentagon have no relation to the destruction of

Babylon. However, the world will be shocked again to see this great city completely destroyed.

Rev. 18:9
And the kings of the earth, who have committed fornication and lived deliciously with her, shall bewail her, and lament for her, when they shall see the smoke of her burning,

Jer. 50:46
[46]At the noise of the taking of Babylon the earth is moved, and the cry is heard among the nations.

Once again we see that kings and nations will cry over the destruction of Babylon. I am sure many of these kings cry because they had so much money invested in Babylon. It may be possible that all the stock exchanges from all over the world decided to move their headquarters to Babylon. I am told that as a result of the crash of the New York Stock Exchange in 1929, many people committed suicide and some even jumped out of buildings. This will surely happen throughout the world when Babylon is destroyed.

Rev. 18:10
Standing afar off for the fear of her torment, saying, Alas, alas that great city Babylon, that mighty city! for in one hour is thy judgment come.

Is. 47:11
[11]Therefore shall evil come upon thee; thou shalt not know from whence it riseth: and mischief shall fall upon thee; thou shalt not be able to put it off: and desolation shall come upon thee suddenly, *which* thou shalt not know.

Jer. 50:27
[27]Slay all her bullocks; let them go down to the slaughter: woe unto them! for their day is come, the time of their visitation.

Jer. 51:55
[55]Because the LORD hath spoiled Babylon, and destroyed out of her the great voice; when her waves do roar like great waters, a noise of their voice is uttered:

Fear will continue to grip those who see this destruction. Their cry will be huge. Now the reality of the actual time frame of destruction is revealed. Babylon will be destroyed in one hour. Earlier we were told it would be destroyed in one day and now we see that within that one day, it will only take one hour for its destruction. As Verse 8 told us "… for strong is the Lord God who judgeth her." God's judgment is surely strong and quick. The judgment will be so fast that the inhabitants will not even know from which direction it comes. I have a hint: Look up!

Rev. 18:11
And the merchants of the earth shall weep and mourn over her; for no man buyeth their merchandise any more:
Rev. 18:12
The merchandise of gold, and silver, and precious stones, and of pearls, and fine linen, and purple, and silk, and scarlet, and all thyine wood, and all manner vessels of ivory, and all manner vessels of most precious wood, and of brass, and iron, and marble,
Rev. 18:13
And cinnamon, and odours, and ointments, and frankincense, and wine, and oil, and fine flour, and wheat, and beasts, and sheep, and horses, and chariots, and slaves, and souls of men.
Rev. 18:14
And the fruits that thy soul lusted after are departed from thee, and all things which were dainty and goodly are departed from thee, and thou shalt find them no more at all.
Rev. 18:15
The merchants of these things, which were made rich by her, shall stand afar off for the fear of her torment, weeping and wailing,
Rev. 18:16
And saying, Alas, alas that great city, that was clothed in fine linen, and purple, and scarlet, and decked with gold, and precious stones, and pearls!

Is. 47:12-13, 15
[12]Stand now with thine enchantments, and with the multitude of thy sorceries, wherein thou hast laboured from thy youth; if so be thou shalt be able to profit, if so be thou mayest prevail.
[13]Thou art wearied in the multitude of thy counsels. Let now the astrologers, the stargazers, the monthly prognosticators, stand up, and save thee from *these things* that shall come upon thee.
[15]Thus shall they be unto thee with whom thou hast laboured, *even* thy merchants, from thy youth: they shall wander every one to his quarter; none shall save thee.

Jer. 50:13

[13]Because of the wrath of the LORD it shall not be inhabited, but it shall be wholly desolate: every one that goeth by Babylon shall be astonished, and hiss at all her plagues.

Jer. 51:8,13

[8]Babylon is suddenly fallen and destroyed: howl for her; take balm for her pain, if so be she may be healed.

[13]O thou that dwellest upon many waters, abundant in treasures, thine end is come, *and* the measure of thy covetousness.

The verses above tell us of the material riches that have encompassed Babylon. It is a city full of riches and probably the richest city ever to have existed on earth at any time in history. Its wealth is indescribable. We see that Babylon also recreated the slave trade, as slavery was a part of the description of this city. Sorcery, witchcraft and stargazing are the height of their religious acts. Part of the reason for their judgment is their occult worship and fornication with these lying prophets. Can soothsayers and sorcerers today inform law enforcement what may have happened at murder scenes through their divinations? I think they can, because they are delving into the world of the occult where demonic forces are prevalent. Do the demons know who committed murders and violent acts? They certainly do and were probably there coaching it on through lies to the ones committing these acts. Are all murderers demon possessed? I do not know, but there are certainly demons present in such godless acts. Is it wrong to seek advice from soothsayers and sorcerers? The Bible clearly states it is wrong and here we see a city being destroyed because of their fornications with demonic forces.

It amazes me today how Hollywood has desensitized the world with its movies about sorceries and witchcraft. Hollywood promotes them as though they are heroes of the world and out to promote good and unity. According to the Bible, they are evil and their final goal will be to promote confusion and anarchy. I Corinthians 5:6 tells us that, "...a little leaven leaveneth the whole lump." Do not be fooled by these so-called prophets.

Rev. 18:17
For in one hour so great riches is come to nought. And every shipmaster, and all the company in ships, and sailors, and as many as trade by sea, stood afar off,

These seamen see the destruction, but since shipping was destroyed a while back, they are on land viewing this destruction. They probably watch the destruction unfold via television or Internet or some saw it from a distance. Notice "stood afar off" and then in Verse 19 "they cast dust on their heads." These phrases suggest that they are on land.

Rev. 18:18
And cried when they saw the smoke of her burning, saying, What *city is* like unto this great city!
Rev. 18:19
And they cast dust on their heads, and cried, weeping and wailing, saying, Alas, alas that great city, wherein were made rich all that had ships in the sea by reason of her costliness! for in one hour is she made desolate.

Jer. 50:30-31
[30]Therefore shall her young men fall in the streets, and all her men of war shall be cut off in that day, saith the LORD.
[31]Behold, I *am* against thee, *O thou* most proud, saith the Lord GOD of hosts: for thy day is come, the time *that* I will visit thee.

As we saw earlier, Babylon will be destroyed in one hour. This great city, possibly the greatest city the world has ever known, will be destroyed in one hour.

Rev. 14:8
And there followed another angel, saying, Babylon is fallen, is fallen, that great city, because she made all nations drink of the wine of the wrath of her fornication.

I have placed this verse at this location of our study because it relates directly to the final destruction of Babylon. Babylon is destroyed, never to be inhabited again.

Rev. 18:20
Rejoice over her, *thou* heaven, and *ye* holy apostles and prophets; for God hath avenged you on her.

> Jer. 51:10, 48-49
> [10]The LORD hath brought forth our righteousness: come, and let us declare in Zion the work of the LORD our God.
> [48]Then the heaven and the earth, and all that *is* therein, shall sing for Babylon: for the spoilers shall come unto her from the north, saith the LORD.
> [49]As Babylon *hath caused* the slain of Israel to fall, so at Babylon shall fall the slain of all the earth.

All in heaven are told to rejoice over Babylon's destruction and that God has answered the prayers of the saints in judgment upon this godless city.

Rev. 18:21
And a mighty angel took up a stone like a great millstone, and cast *it* into the sea, saying, Thus with violence shall that great city Babylon be thrown down, and shall be found no more at all.

The casting of the "great millstone" into the sea is a symbolism of how quick Babylon will be destroyed. The violence associated with the millstone thrusting through the calm waters is symbolic of the destruction that will be thrust upon Babylon and the fact that Babylon will never rise again. Have you ever stood by the side of a calm lake and one of your "faithful buddies" throws a huge stone into the lake where you seem to be meditating? It will scare you to death and get you wet! This is similar to the symbolism used by the angel.

> Jer. 50:26
> [26]Come against her from the utmost border, open her storehouses: cast her up as heaps, and destroy her utterly: let nothing of her be left.

> Jer. 51:63-64
> [63]And it shall be, when thou hast made an end of reading this book, *that* thou shalt bind a stone to it, and cast it into the midst of Euphrates:
> [64]And thou shalt say, Thus shall Babylon sink, and shall not rise from the evil that I will bring upon her: and they shall be weary.

Thus far *are* the words of Jeremiah.

Do not become confused about what Jeremiah is told to do by casting a millstone into the Euphrates to show the example and quickness by which Babylon will be destroyed. This is not the same millstone nor "sea" mentioned above. The Euphrates during Jeremiah's time was still running and not dry. The symbolism is the same as the angel's symbolism. Babylon will be destroyed instantly.

Rev. 18:22
And the voice of harpers, and musicians, and of pipers, and trumpeters, shall be heard no more at all in thee; and no craftsman, of whatsoever craft *he be*, shall be found any more in thee; and the sound of a millstone shall be heard no more at all in thee;

Jer. 50:12-13, 39-40

[12]Your mother shall be sore confounded; she that bare you shall be ashamed: behold, the hindermost of the nations *shall be* a wilderness, a dry land, and a desert.
[13]Because of the wrath of the LORD it shall not be inhabited, but it shall be wholly desolate: every one that goeth by Babylon shall be astonished, and hiss at all her plagues.
[39]Therefore the wild beasts of the desert with the wild beasts of the islands shall dwell *there*, and the owls shall dwell therein: and it shall be no more inhabited for ever; neither shall it be dwelt in from generation to generation.
[40]As God overthrew Sodom and Gomorrah and the neighbour *cities* thereof, saith the LORD; *so* shall no man abide there, neither shall any son of man dwell therein.

Jer. 51:26, 29, 43

[26]And they shall not take of thee a stone for a corner, nor a stone for foundations; but thou shalt be desolate for ever, saith the LORD.
[29]And the land shall tremble and sorrow: for every purpose of the LORD shall be performed against Babylon, to make the land of Babylon a desolation without an inhabitant.
[43]Her cities are a desolation, a dry land, and a wilderness, a land wherein no man dwelleth, neither doth *any* son of man pass thereby.

Is. 13:19-22

[19]And Babylon, the glory of kingdoms, the beauty of the Chaldees' excellency, shall be as when God overthrew Sodom

and Gomorrah.

[20]It shall never be inhabited, neither shall it be dwelt in from generation to generation: neither shall the Arabian pitch tent there; neither shall the shepherds make their fold there.

[21]But wild beasts of the desert shall lie there; and their houses shall be full of doleful creatures; and owls shall dwell there, and satyrs shall dance there.

[22]And the wild beasts of the islands shall cry in their desolate houses, and dragons in *their* pleasant palaces: and her time *is* near to come, and her days shall not be prolonged.

As seen in verse 21 and the supporting scriptures, Babylon will never be inhabited again. Even the stones that built up the city will never be used again for building. God will destroy Babylon in a similar fashion as He did Sodom and Gomorrah with fire and brimstone.

Rev. 18:23
And the light of a candle shall shine no more at all in thee; and the voice of the bridegroom and of the bride shall be heard no more at all in thee: for thy merchants were the great men of the earth; for by thy sorceries were all nations deceived.

Rev. 18:24
And in her was found the blood of prophets, and of saints, and of all that were slain upon the earth.

Verses 23 and 24 end the comments on the destruction of Babylon. We see at least two of the main reasons for its destruction: 1) sorceries, in which they deceived all the nations and 2) killing of the prophets and saints of God. This city is now gone from the history books forever. It was full of evil.

As I have stated in previous chapters, the ancient city of Babylon was the beginning of the occult and devil worship. Its influence and paganism have flourished even up to the time of this New Babylon. However, Babylon, both ancient and new, have come to an end. It is now time for the Lord of Hosts, the Lord Jesus Christ, to return in His Second Coming and the battle of all battles will begin, The Battle of Armageddon!

13

The Second Coming and the Battle of Armageddon

Remember in the Introduction to this book, I posed several questions about end-times? This chapter will supply answers to many of those questions. Will there be a battle known as Armageddon? Yes, there certainly will be such a battle and it is about to take place. Will there be a judgment day? We will see at the end of the Battle of Armageddon, there will be a judgment. However, the last judgment will be seen later in the Revelation at what is called the Great White Throne of Judgment. The judgment day nightmares about which many people today have concern was seen throughout the Tribulation Period.

Will there be a battle of holy angels versus evil angels? The Battle of Armageddon will also be a battle of the holy angels versus the evil angels. Who will win this battle? Stay tuned and you will see. Will there be a nuclear holocaust? Some scholars believe that the description of the end of the Battle of Armageddon describe the effects of a nuclear war. Will this world, as we know it today, come to an end? At the end of the Battle of Armageddon, this world will not come to an end. As a matter of fact, just after this war there will be judgment of the evil angels, the Antichrist, the False Prophet, Satan and those who are still living that have the mark of the beast. Then, there will be a period of one thousand years of bliss that will take place on earth. We will see the answer to the "end of the world" question further on in this book in later chapters.

We are now approaching the end of the Tribulation which

will culminate with the Second Coming of Christ to earth. We will see in this chapter, the final battle of the Tribulation Period, known as the Battle of Armageddon. This will be a battle between the Antichrist, his demons and all his armies of the world against Jesus Christ and His host from heaven. His host from heaven will be all the saints that have been resurrected at the Rapture and all the holy angels. We have already seen where the Antichrist was possessed by Satan. It stands to reason that most of his armies are probably possessed by the demons that were cast out of heaven along with Satan. Satan always has his unholy imitation to match God. Therefore, the Antichrist has his evil followers and his demon cohorts.

The Great Multitude in Heaven Just Before the Second Coming to Earth

Rev. 19:1
And after these things I heard a great voice of much people in heaven, saying, Alleluia; Salvation, and glory, and honour, and power, unto the Lord our God:
Rev. 19:2
For true and righteous *are* his judgments: for he hath judged the great whore, which did corrupt the earth with her fornication, and hath avenged the blood of his servants at her hand.
Rev. 19:3
And again they said, Alleluia And her smoke rose up for ever and ever.
Rev. 19:4
And the four and twenty elders and the four beasts fell down and worshipped God that sat on the throne, saying, Amen; Alleluia.
Rev. 19:5
And a voice came out of the throne, saying, Praise our God, all ye his servants, and ye that fear him, both small and great.
Rev. 19:6
And I heard as it were the voice of a great multitude, and as the voice of many waters, and as the voice of mighty thunderings, saying, Alleluia: for the Lord God omnipotent reigneth.

Dan. 7:9-10

[9] I beheld till the thrones were cast down, and the Ancient of days did sit, whose garment *was* white as snow, and the hair of his head like the pure wool: his throne *was like* the fiery flame, *and* his wheels *as* burning fire.

[10] A fiery stream issued and came forth from before him: thousand thousands ministered unto him, and ten thousand times ten thousand stood before him: the judgment was set, and the books were opened.

The scene in the previous verses is in heaven and an untold number of people are praising God and giving glory to God for all that He has done. Once again, we are told that His judgments are true and righteous. We see that the multitudes in heaven include those who are saved, the twenty-four elders, the four beasts and the holy angels. They have witnessed from heaven what has happened on earth during the Tribulation Period. This tells us that those in heaven are allowed to see at least some of the events that occur on earth when they go to heaven through death or the Rapture. Hebrews 12:1 states "Wherefore seeing we also are compassed about with so great a cloud of witnesses, let us lay aside every weight, and the sin which doth so easily beset *us*, and let us run with patience the race that is set before us."

We are also told that "the Lord God omnipotent reigneth," which is the announcement prelude to the Second Coming to earth. The time of the Gentiles is now fulfilled and time has come to judge the Antichrist and the earth for their evil deeds and fornications against God and His people. Jesus is ready to appear and stop this carnage by the Antichrist and to ensure His remnant is protected to go forth into His upcoming Millennial Reign on earth.

The Wedding in Heaven and the Marriage of the Lamb

Rev. 19:7

Let us be glad and rejoice, and give honour to him: for the marriage of the Lamb is come, and his wife hath made herself ready.

The wedding, or marriage of the Lamb, will take place in heaven before the Second Coming to earth.

Lk. 12:35-37

[35]Let your loins be girded about, and *your* lights burning;

[36]And ye yourselves like unto men that wait for their lord, when he will return from the wedding; that when he cometh and knocketh, they may open unto him immediately.

[37]Blessed *are* those servants, whom the lord when he cometh shall find watching: verily I say unto you, that he shall gird himself, and make them to sit down to meat, and will come forth and serve them.

Here we see that the wedding has already taken place before the marriage supper of the Lamb, because it is said that when He comes, He will serve them. The wedding takes place in heaven.

We have already concluded that the Judgment Seat of Christ took place during the Tribulation Period in heaven. This meant that the Church had already been made pure and holy before God the Father. She has prepared herself for the wedding ceremony. We also saw at the Judgment Seat, the Church, or Bride of Christ, was given crowns and clothed in fine linen.

Rev. 19:8

And to her was granted that she should be arrayed in fine linen, clean and white: for the fine linen is the righteousness of saints.

Here we are told that the bride is "arrayed in fine linen, clean and white" and that the linen represents the "righteousness of saints." This means that at the Judgment Seat, the saints' robes, or linens, represented their works or deeds of righteousness. Therefore, the Christian's wedding wardrobe could be determined by the amount of righteous deeds we perform on earth, as we discussed in the chapter about the Judgment Seat of Christ. Regardless of the length of the robe, the jewels that could be attached to the robe or the crowns given to the believers, the fact is that Jesus is the Bridegroom and we, the Church, are His Bride. You do not have to have fancy clothing to be in love or prove your love to someone. You do not have to have a fancy wedding to boast of your love for the other. However, God the Father is proud to show this union of His Son Jesus to His Bride the Church. It will be a wedding in the greatest chapel of all, heaven. The clothing is simple when looking from the outside, however the clothing's representation is everlasting when viewed from the inside or spiritual side. This righteousness also represents the righteousness of Jesus Christ and His sacrifice for all believers on the cross. He imputes His righteousness to every believer's account at the time of their salvation. What a gift, the gift of eternal life! No greater gift, no greater place, no greater family could one expect to be a part, than to be a part of the family of God. You cannot buy this gift and you cannot earn this gift. It is offered by the Son, free to anyone who accepts His offer.

Rev. 19:9
And he saith unto me, Write, Blessed *are* they which are called unto the marriage supper of the Lamb. And he saith unto me, These are the true sayings of God.

After the wedding, a great supper is provided by God the Father for His Son and His new Bride and the friends of the Bridegroom. I will leave this verse in this spot for continuity purposes. However, understand that the actual supper will not take place until after the Second Coming to earth, the judgment of nations and the judgment of the Antichrist and the False Prophet. I will repeat this verse again at that time.

Rev. 19:10
And I fell at his feet to worship him. And he said unto me, See *thou do it* not: I am thy fellowservant, and of thy brethren that have the testimony of Jesus: worship God: for the testimony of Jesus is the spirit of prophecy.

John is so awed at the fact of the marriage and marriage supper that he "fell at his feet to worship" the one who is telling him the story. This person immediately tells John not to worship him because he is a "fellowservant" just like John. Who is this "fellowservant?"

Rev. 22:8-9

[8] And I John saw these things, and heard *them*. And when I had heard and seen, I fell down to worship before the feet of the angel which showed me these things.

[9] Then saith he unto me, See *thou do it* not: for I am thy fellowservant, and of thy brethren the prophets, and of them which keep the sayings of this book: worship God.

As you can see, Revelation 19:10 and 22:8-9 are almost identical, except they are two different occasions. Both instances seem to suggest the same person. The name of this person is not given, but I believe that it is a human and not an angel. How, you might ask? He states that he is a worshiper of Jesus just like John. So are the angels. He also stated "and of thy brethren that have the testimony of Jesus." This gives us the clue that he is a saved human being who has already died, because he is in heaven during John's trip there to record the Revelation. John does not recognize him, whoever he may be. But remember, neither did the ladies who came to the tomb after Jesus' burial and ran into Jesus after He rose from the grave. God did not allow John to recognize this person at this time for a reason only God knows. John referred to the person as an angel in Revelation 22. Holy angels almost always took the form of men, so John was not in error assuming this was an angel. Also, the word "angel" in the original means "messenger."

At this time he has seen a number of angels performing God's work in heaven and on earth. However, this person corrects him and tells him again that he is "one of his fellowservants." Here we see a further qualification in that he is "of thy brethren the prophets." Does this mean he is an Old Testament prophet? Not necessarily, because there were New Testament prophets also. Could it be Daniel, Isaiah, Ezekiel, Jeremiah, Joel, Peter, James, etc? I happen to believe it is Daniel. We saw earlier in Chapter 9 of our book, that Daniel saw the vision of John and Jesus standing by the banks of the river and was told to "shut up the words and seal the book, even to the time of the end." I think Daniel has been given the privilege of telling the story to John, which Daniel was earlier told not to tell until the time of the end. The phrase "keep the sayings of this book" means he was told "not to reveal" or to "seal the book."

Regardless, the context seems to suggest this is a human being who has already died and gone to heaven. I realize the theory above will bring disagreement among some scholars, but since this is an area of scripture that can be debated, we can agree to disagree.

The Unholy Trinity and the Gathering of the Armies of the World to Israel

---

Rev. 16:13
And I saw three unclean spirits like frogs *come* out of the mouth of the dragon, and out of the mouth of the beast, and out of the mouth of the false prophet.

These "three unclean spirits like frogs" are difficult to comprehend. However, we are told in Verse 14 they are demonic spirits. They are evil spirits and they may be compared to frogs because they seem to jump to and fro throughout the earth. Frogs are also considered the symbol of "sin" in the Bible. This could be a picture of the sinful message that is sent by the unholy trinity to the world leaders and how it rebounds around the world, as we will see in the verses to come. Frogs are amphibious nocturnal creatures. They usually come out when it starts to become dark and can live on land and in water. The reptile that dwells in darkness is a good way to describe the unholy trinity. Their works are of darkness. We have seen in previous chapters that the identity of the dragon, beast and false prophet are: Satan, Antichrist and the False Prophet, respectively. These evil spirits could represent the lies of Satan (who is the father of lies), the blasphemy of the Antichrist (who is the king of blasphemy towards God) and the false spiritualism of the False Prophet (who teaches the false religion and worship of the Antichrist).

Rev. 16:14
For they are the spirits of devils, working miracles, *which* go forth unto the kings of the earth and of the whole world, to gather them to the battle of that great day of God Almighty.

The purpose of these evil spirits is to spread the word to the whole earth to come to the Battle of Armageddon to fight against Jesus and His host from heaven. Does Satan and his cohorts know when Jesus is coming? The answer is no, but you can be sure he knows something is about to take place. The Devil has known that this battle will take place at some point in time. He has not known when it would take place, but that this would be a battle of the host of heaven against Satan and his unholy angels. There will be those earthly humans whom the Devil has deceived who will be drawn to this battle.

Rev. 16:15
Behold, I come as a thief. Blessed is he that watcheth, and keepeth his garments, lest he walk naked, and they see his shame.

The Bible tells us that Jesus comes as a "thief." This does not mean that Jesus is a thief. It simply means that His coming will not be broadcast before the unsaved world. A thief does not announce his coming in advance or else he will be caught. The thief usually surprises his victims or comes totally unexpectedly. By the way, when He does come in the clouds, it will be abrupt and it will be loud. The Antichrist and his armies may be looking on earth, but the surprise will come from above. This verse is speaking to those who are saved that are still on the earth at this time. They are told to watch and be ready.

We were told in the scripture, speaking about the Rapture, that we were not in darkness that we should be overtaken by a thief. The reason is that those saved before the Rapture would expect his coming and welcome it. Here, He is coming and this coming means the destruction of the Antichrist, the False

Prophet and the chaining of Satan. Christians who are still alive will know by reading the Bible, see from the signs and judgments of the Tribulation and the time in days (7 Years or 1260 days + 1260 days) foretold in scripture   during the Tribulation when Jesus will come. Christians are admonished to be ready and have their garments close by them towards the end. We will see later where His coming will be to gather those saved who are left on earth and are watching for His coming.

Again, Christians will not be overtaken as a thief because of the Word of God that they have studied. The ones who will be overtaken as a thief will be the unsaved world. Someone might say, "the Devil and his cohorts can read also, why will they not know?" The Bible clearly states in I Corinthians 2:14 "But the natural man receiveth not the things of the Spirit of God: for they are foolishness unto him: neither can he know *them*, because they are spiritually discerned." "Natural man" is one who is not saved or one who is not regenerated. Therefore, the scriptures are spiritually discerned and Satan and his followers can read all they want, but never understand the true meaning behind scripture. Notice it says the scriptures are "foolishness" unto them and they cannot know them.

Rev. 16:16
And he gathered them together into a place called in the Hebrew tongue Armageddon.

The word "he" is God. God will actually gather all the horde of demonic possessed humans along with the Antichrist and the False Prophet to the place called Armageddon. God will draw them to this place. It could be that God puts in the minds of the unholy trinity and makes them think that something is going to take over their precious kingdom and therefore draws them to this area. Whatever the reason, they will come to this area fully armed and ready for battle. The Battle of Armageddon is about to take place.

Zech. 12:11

[11]In that day shall there be a great mourning in Jerusalem, as the mourning of Hadadrimmon in the valley of Megiddon.

Joel 3:2, 9-12

[2]I will also gather all nations, and will bring them down into the valley of Jehoshaphat, and will plead with them there for my people and *for* my heritage Israel, whom they have scattered among the nations, and parted my land.

[9]Proclaim ye this among the Gentiles; Prepare war, wake up the mighty men, let all the men of war draw near; let them come up:

[10]Beat your plowshares into swords, and your pruninghooks into spears: let the weak say, I *am* strong.

[11]Assemble yourselves, and come, all ye heathen, and gather yourselves together round about: thither cause thy mighty ones to come down, O LORD.

[12]Let the heathen be wakened, and come up to the valley of Jehoshaphat: for there will I sit to judge all the heathen round about.

(Photograph Courtesy of Shari and JoAnn Vickers)

The picture above is of the Valley of Megiddo. Further to the south is the Plain of Esdraelon, as it is known in the Greek, or the Jezreel Valley, as it is known, in the Hebrew. *(See the following picture).*

(Photograph Courtesy of Shari and JoAnn Vickers)

Even further to the south between the Old City Jerusalem and the Mount of Olives is the Kidron Valley, also mentioned in Joel as the Valley of Jehoshaphat. All of these names relate to where the Battle of Armageddon will take place as mentioned in Rev. 16:16. We will see later that this valley reaches almost 200 miles in length from the valley of Megiddo to the Dead Sea to the Kidron Valley in Jerusalem. *(See following picture).*

(Photograph Courtesy of John and Jana Nowell)

The Kidron Valley is seen behind my friend John with the Old City Jerusalem and the Dome of the Rock in the background. I do not believe John fits the character of a Bedouin nomadic tribesman, do you?

Rev. 11:16
And the four and twenty elders, which sat before God on their seats, fell upon their faces, and worshipped God,
Rev. 11:17
Saying, We give thee thanks, O LORD God Almighty, which art, and wast, and art to come; because thou hast taken to thee thy great power, and hast reigned.
Rev. 11:18
And the nations were angry, and thy wrath is come, and the time of the dead, that they should be judged, and that thou shouldest give reward unto thy servants the prophets, and to the saints, and them that fear thy name, small and great; and shouldest destroy them which destroy the earth.
Rev. 11:19
And the temple of God was opened in heaven, and there was seen in his temple the ark of his testament: and there were lightnings, and

voices, and thunderings, and an earthquake, and great hail.

We see in the verses above another scene in heaven. Once again those in heaven worship God and praise His just judgments that God has pronounced upon the earth and mankind. We see that Jesus is coming again to earth. The nations are still angry at God for what He has done to them. They still will not repent. Verse 18 speaks of the upcoming judgment of nations after the Battle of Armageddon is complete. It foretells of the rewards that will be given to Israel and the saints when they inhabit the land during the millennium period.

We also see the temple in heaven open and the ark of the covenant revealed. We are told that lightning and voices and thunder are seen and heard. Then these are followed by another earthquake and hail. Years ago, a movie, Raiders of the Lost Ark, was made about a fictional fellow called Indiana Jones. His heartfelt mission as an archeologist was to find the lost ark of the covenant on earth. However, after he found it, a Nazi stole it from him and took it to a place to open it and supposedly gain the powers that the ark would bestow upon him. When he opened the ark, lightning, thunder, voices and strange ghost-like beings proceeded out of the ark and these were followed by an earthquake. The scene went on to depict every one of the Nazis being destroyed by the effects of the ark. This was Hollywood's version of this same verse in Revelation. Hollywood had some of it correct, but this ark is in heaven in the heavenly temple.

We will see later during the Battle of Armageddon, that many on earth will die from similar events as a result of Jesus' Second Coming to earth. They will be destroyed by fire. It will not be because of the ark of the covenant, but because of their continued rejection of Jesus as Lord and Savior, the true Ark of the Covenant. Fire will proceed from Jesus in judgment on the unsaved at the Battle of Armageddon.

Jesus' Second Coming to Earth with His Host from Heaven Consisting of His Mighty Angels and Saints

---

As we will see in the scriptures to follow, there is a tremendous amount of supporting scripture relating to the Second Coming and the Battle of Armageddon. I will try my best to place the supporting scripture in as close chronological order as possible. However, please notice that many of the references support several verses in Revelation at this point.

The heavens will open and Jesus and His host from heaven are about to arrive on the scene of what is known as the Second Coming to earth and the Battle of Armageddon. Remember in the introduction I introduced several questions? One of those was, "Will there be a Battle of Armageddon?" The answer is, yes, and it is about to occur.

Rev. 19:11
And I saw heaven opened, and behold a white horse; and he that sat upon him *was* called Faithful and True, and in righteousness he doth judge and make war.

Matt. 24:27,29-30
[27]For as the lightning cometh out of the east, and shineth even unto the west; so shall also the coming of the Son of man be.
[29]Immediately after the tribulation of those days shall the sun be darkened, and the moon shall not give her light, and the stars shall fall from heaven, and the powers of the heavens shall be shaken:
[30]And then shall appear the sign of the Son of man in heaven: and then shall all the tribes of the earth mourn, and they shall see the Son of man coming in the clouds of heaven with power and great glory.

Dan. 7:13
[13]I saw in the night visions, and, behold, *one* like the Son of man came with the clouds of heaven, and came to the Ancient of days, and they brought him near before him.

Acts 1:10-11
[10]And while they looked stedfastly toward heaven as he went up, behold, two men stood by them in white apparel;
[11]Which also said, Ye men of Galilee, why stand ye gazing up into heaven? this same Jesus, which is taken up from you into heaven, shall so come in like manner as ye have seen him go into heaven.

Acts 2:19-20

[19]And I will show wonders in heaven above, and signs in the earth beneath; blood, and fire, and vapour of smoke:

[20]The sun shall be turned into darkness, and the moon into blood, before that great and notable day of the Lord come:

Lk. 21:25-28

[25]And there shall be signs in the sun, and in the moon, and in the stars; and upon the earth distress of nations, with perplexity; the sea and the waves roaring;

[26]Men's hearts failing them for fear, and for looking after those things which are coming on the earth: for the powers of heaven shall be shaken.

[27]And then shall they see the Son of man coming in a cloud with power and great glory.

[28]And when these things begin to come to pass, then look up, and lift up your heads; for your redemption draweth nigh.

Tit. 2:13

[13]Looking for that blessed hope, and the glorious appearing of the great God and our Saviour Jesus Christ;

Zep. 1:14-16

[14]The great day of the LORD is near, it is near, and hasteth greatly, even the voice of the day of the LORD: the mighty man shall cry there bitterly.

[15]That day is a day of wrath, a day of trouble and distress, a day of wasteness and desolation, a day of darkness and gloominess, a day of clouds and thick darkness,

[16]A day of the trumpet and alarm against the fenced cities, and against the high towers.

Is. 24:23

[23]Then the moon shall be confounded, and the sun ashamed, when the LORD of hosts shall reign in mount Zion, and in Jerusalem, and before his ancients gloriously.

Ps. 102:13-23

[13]Thou shalt arise, and have mercy upon Zion: for the time to favour her, yea, the set time, is come.

[14]For thy servants take pleasure in her stones, and favour the dust thereof.

[15]So the heathen shall fear the name of the LORD, and all the kings of the earth thy glory.

[16]When the LORD shall build up Zion, he shall appear in his glory.

[17]He will regard the prayer of the destitute, and not despise their prayer.

[18]This shall be written for the generation to come: and the people which shall be created shall praise the LORD.

[19]For he hath looked down from the height of his sanctuary; from heaven did the LORD behold the earth;
[20]To hear the groaning of the prisoner; to loose those that are appointed to death;
[21]To declare the name of the LORD in Zion, and his praise in Jerusalem;
[22]When the people are gathered together, and the kingdoms, to serve the LORD.
[23]He weakened my strength in the way; he shortened my days.

This type of supporting scripture is what makes Bible study interesting and exciting. It all comes together to tell the story without a lot of commentary being necessary. When we allow the Bible to interpret itself, we can rest assured that man could never produce such a document without the guidance of the Holy Spirit.

We see in the verses above that Jesus will come in the clouds. The sun, moon and stars will be darkened because of His appearing. This is probably because of the magnitude of the host of heaven that will be coming with Him. Shock and horror will grip the unsaved, while I am sure the saved will be jumping for joy. Jesus does not stop in the clouds this time as He did at the Rapture, but will be coming all the way to earth to fulfill the prophecies of His Second Coming to earth.

He has heard the cry of the saved that are on earth. As mentioned earlier in our book, thank God that He shortened the days or else no flesh would have survived. Once again, He is praised for shortening those days.

Rev. 14:14
And I looked, and behold a white cloud, and upon the cloud *one* sat like unto the Son of man, having on his head a golden crown, and in his hand a sharp sickle.
Rev. 19:12
His eyes *were* as a flame of fire, and on his head *were* many crowns; and he had a name written, that no man knew, but he himself.
Rev. 19:13
And he *was* clothed with a vesture dipped in blood: and his name is called The Word of God.

This, of course, is Jesus Christ. He is not coming as a Lamb to be slain for the sins of the world. He is coming in vengeance to execute judgment upon an ungodly mankind. Jesus is love, but He is also the judge of those who reject Him. His judgments will be swift and complete. The sharp sickle is a tool used to harvest grain. This sickle in the hand of the Lord is a sign of judgment. Mankind will reap the results of their evil deeds on earth. Verse 12 describes Jesus whose eyes are "as a flame of fire," which also denotes judgment. John 1:1 says, "In the beginning was the Word, and the Word was with God, and the Word was God." Jesus is the Word!

Is. 63:1-2
[1]Who *is* this that cometh from Edom, with dyed garments from Bozrah? this *that is* glorious in his apparel, travelling in the greatness of his strength? I that speak in righteousness, mighty to save.
[2]Wherefore *art thou* red in thine apparel, and thy garments like him that treadeth in the winefat?

Edom is the southern portion of Jordan where the city Petra is located. Bozrah means "sheep of the fold" or "sheepfold" and is probably the city we call Petra today. The "red... apparel" and "vesture dipped in blood" speak of the death and destruction that Jesus will cause on earth at His Second Coming and specifically around the area of Petra. The Antichrist will try to destroy the remnant Jews at Petra, but Jesus will come to their rescue and the blood of the Antichrist's armies will flow deep.

Rev. 19:14
And the armies *which were* in heaven followed him upon white horses, clothed in fine linen, white and clean.

We now see that Jesus is returning with His armies from heaven, which are the saints who were Raptured just before the beginning of the Tribulation Period. They have already been awarded their fine linen and are arrayed for battle. These white linens represent the righteousness and purity of the saints. In other words, they have already appeared before the Judgment Seat of Christ and have been awarded their rewards for the deeds they performed on earth after they trusted Christ and became a child of God. In addition, He will come with His mighty angels.

Jude 14-15

[14]And Enoch also, the seventh from Adam, prophesied of these, saying, Behold, the Lord cometh with ten thousands of his saints, [15]To execute judgment upon all, and to convince all that are ungodly among them of all their ungodly deeds which they have ungodly committed, and of all their hard *speeches* which ungodly sinners have spoken against him.

Enoch, back in the days before the worldwide flood, preached about the Second Coming of Christ. He preached that the reason for His Second Coming was to "execute judgment." Notice also that he preached that Jesus would come with "ten thousands of his saints," meaning an innumerable amount. For Jesus to come with His saints, means they had to have Raptured sometime before this as I mentioned in the beginning of this book. The Second Coming has been preached since the beginning of time.

Jer. 50:41-42

[41]Behold, a people shall come from the north, and a great nation, and many kings shall be raised up from the coasts of the earth. [42]They shall hold the bow and the lance: they *are* cruel, and will not show mercy: their voice shall roar like the sea, and they shall ride upon horses, *every one* put in array, like a man to the battle, against thee, O daughter of Babylon.

This Godly army is coming to fight the ungodly who are still left on earth and especially the "daughter of Babylon," the Antichrist.

Joel 2:1-11

[1]Blow ye the trumpet in Zion, and sound an alarm in my holy mountain: let all the inhabitants of the land tremble: for the day of the LORD cometh, for *it is* nigh at hand; [2]A day of darkness and of gloominess, a day of clouds and of thick darkness, as the morning spread upon the mountains: a great people and a strong; there hath not been ever the like, neither shall

be any more after it, *even* to the years of many generations.
[3]A fire devoureth before them; and behind them a flame burneth: the land *is* as the garden of Eden before them, and behind them a desolate wilderness; yea, and nothing shall escape them.
[4]The appearance of them *is* as the appearance of horses; and as horsemen, so shall they run.
[5]Like the noise of chariots on the tops of mountains shall they leap, like the noise of a flame of fire that devoureth the stubble, as a strong people set in battle array.
[6]Before their face the people shall be much pained: all faces shall gather blackness.
[7]They shall run like mighty men; they shall climb the wall like men of war; and they shall march every one on his ways, and they shall not break their ranks:
[8]Neither shall one thrust another; they shall walk every one in his path: and *when* they fall upon the sword, they shall not be wounded.
[9]They shall run to and fro in the city; they shall run upon the wall, they shall climb up upon the houses; they shall enter in at the windows like a thief.
[10]The earth shall quake before them; the heavens shall tremble: the sun and the moon shall be dark, and the stars shall withdraw their shining:
[11]And the LORD shall utter his voice before his army: for his camp *is* very great: for *he is* strong that executeth his word: for the day of the LORD *is* great and very terrible; and who can abide it?

These verses in Joel speak of the army from heaven on horses who accompany Jesus at His Second Coming to earth. These are none other than the saints who were Raptured before the Tribulation began. They use fire to devour those before them and they are immortal. Verse 8 states if they should be stuck with a sword, "they shall not be wounded." Therefore, these are saints from heaven who have been given their immortal heavenly glorified bodies which cannot die or feel pain. They will have supernatural abilities and fear will grip everyone in their path. Many movies today depict "super-heroes." Would you like to be a super hero? Place your faith and trust in Jesus Christ today and you will have the opportunity to be one in the future. Not like Hollywood would have you to believe, but in the way that God will allow you to be, after you receive your "glorified" body.

Rev. 19:15
And out of his mouth goeth a sharp sword, that with it he should smite the nations: and he shall rule them with a rod of iron: and he treadeth the winepress of the fierceness and wrath of Almighty God.

Heb. 4:12
[12]For the word of God *is* living and powerful, and sharper than any two-edged sword, piercing even to the division of soul and spirit, and of joints and marrow, and is a discerner of the thoughts and intents of the heart.

We have already discussed that the sharp "twoedged" sword is the Word of God. In Verse 15 the "sharp sword" is the same. Jesus through His Word will smite the nations and rule them. It is the Word of God that convicts the soul of sin and unrighteousness and it is by this Word that all the nations will be judged. The Word of God is pure and can be trusted in its entirety. Many millions of souls have felt the convicting power of the Word of God and have been changed by it. The Word of God will not be used for convicting at this battle, but for judgment.

Ps. 2:9
[9]Thou shalt break them with a rod of iron; thou shalt dash them in pieces like a potter's vessel.

Is. 63:3-6
[3]I have trodden the winepress alone; and of the people *there was* none with me: for I will tread them in mine anger, and trample them in my fury; and their blood shall be sprinkled upon my garments, and I will stain all my raiment.
[4]For the day of vengeance *is* in mine heart, and the year of my redeemed is come.
[5]And I looked, and *there was* none to help; and I wondered that *there was* none to uphold: therefore mine own arm brought salvation unto me; and my fury, it upheld me.
[6]And I will tread down the people in mine anger, and make them drunk in my fury, and I will bring down their strength to the earth.

Zec. 12:2-4,9
[2]Behold, I will make Jerusalem a cup of trembling unto all the people round about, when they shall be in the siege both against Judah *and* against Jerusalem.

³And in that day will I make Jerusalem a burdensome stone for all people: all that burden themselves with it shall be cut in pieces, though all the people of the earth be gathered together against it. ⁴In that day, saith the LORD, I will smite every horse with astonishment, and his rider with madness: and I will open mine eyes upon the house of Judah, and will smite every horse of the people with blindness.
⁹And it shall come to pass in that day, *that* I will seek to destroy all the nations that come against Jerusalem.

Rev. 19:16
And he hath on *his* vesture and on his thigh a name written, KING OF KINGS, AND LORD OF LORDS.

Even though mankind has ridiculed Jesus, cursed His name, tried to eradicate His people, laughed at His witnesses, mocked Him and spat upon Him, He will be seen as the "KING OF KINGS, AND LORD OF LORDS" at His Second-Coming by everyone.

Rev. 19:17
And I saw an angel standing in the sun; and he cried with a loud voice, saying to all the fowls that fly in the midst of heaven, Come and gather yourselves together unto the supper of the great God;

This is not a supper anyone would choose to attend. This supper is for the fowls of the earth to feed on the dead bodies of the unsaved who will be killed as a result of this terrible battle.

Rev. 19:18
That ye may eat the flesh of kings, and the flesh of captains, and the flesh of mighty men, and the flesh of horses, and of them that sit on them, and the flesh of all *men, both* free and bond, both small and great.

God has called the fowls of the air and the beasts to gather together after this battle to feast on the flesh of mankind and horses. It is estimated that there will be millions of people in this battle that will die in a very short period. The birds and beasts will eat the flesh of these high ranking officers and others.

Mt. 24:28

[28]For whersoever the carcase is, there will the eagles be gathered together.

Ez. 39:17-22

[17]And, thou son of man, thus saith the Lord GOD; Speak unto every feathered fowl, and to every beast of the field, Assemble yourselves, and come; gather yourselves on every side to my sacrifice that I do sacrifice for you, *even* a great sacrifice upon the mountains of Israel, that ye may eat flesh, and drink blood.

[18]Ye shall eat the flesh of the mighty, and drink the blood of the princes of the earth, of rams, of lambs, and of goats, of bullocks, all of them fatlings of Bashan.

[19]And ye shall eat fat till ye be full, and drink blood till ye be drunken, of my sacrifice which I have sacrificed for you.

[20]Thus ye shall be filled at my table with horses and chariots, with mighty men, and with all men of war, saith the Lord GOD.

[21]And I will set my glory among the heathen, and all the heathen shall see my judgment that I have executed, and my hand that I have laid upon them.

[22]So the house of Israel shall know that I *am* the LORD their God from that day and forward.

Jer. 30:16

[16]Therefore all they that devour thee shall be devoured; and all thine adversaries, every one of them, shall go into captivity; and they that spoil thee shall be a spoil, and all that prey upon thee will I give for a prey.

Now Begins the Battle of Armageddon and the Bloodbath of the Ages

---

Rev. 19:19
And I saw the beast, and the kings of the earth, and their armies, gathered together to make war against him that sat on the horse, and against his army.

Some have questioned whether this is a real horse or a figurative horse. I believe it is a real horse. When Jesus was about to make His triumphant entry into Jerusalem just before His crucifixion, He rode in on a real horse.

Mt. 21:4-5, 9

⁴All this was done, that it might be fulfilled which was spoken by the prophet, saying,

⁵Tell ye the daughter of Sion, Behold, thy King cometh unto thee, meek, and sitting upon an ass, and a colt the foal of an ass.

⁹And the multitudes that went before, and that followed, cried, saying, Hosanna to the Son of David: Blessed *is* he that cometh in the name of the Lord; Hosanna in the highest.

Zech. 9:9-11

⁹Rejoice greatly, O daughter of Zion; shout, O daughter of Jerusalem: behold, thy King cometh unto thee: he *is* just, and having salvation; lowly, and riding upon an ass, and upon a colt the foal of an ass.

¹⁰And I will cut off the chariot from Ephraim, and the horse from Jerusalem, and the battle bow shall be cut off: and he shall speak peace unto the heathen: and his dominion *shall be* from sea *even* to sea, and from the river *even* to the ends of the earth.

¹¹As for thee also, by the blood of thy covenant I have sent forth thy prisoners out of the pit wherein *is* no water.

Matthew 21:4-5 refer to the partial fulfillment of Zechariah 9:9-11, but it has a twofold prophecy. It was partially fulfilled the first time because He did make a way of salvation and He was "meek" or lowly," but it will be completely fulfilled at the Second Coming as seen in Zechariah 9:10-11. The people of Jesus' day thought Jesus was going to set up His kingdom, therefore they shouted "Hosanna in the Highest," thinking He had "come to save" and become their earthly king. He did come to save the first time, but He will come to rescue the second time and truly be Hosanna on earth. Notice in Matthew that the words "he *is* just, and having salvation" are not mentioned, as seen in Zechariah. That is because the complete fulfillment of Him being "just and having salvation" or His judgments being justified, will not happen until His Second Coming to earth. It has to be a real horse the second time to completely fulfill Zechariah 9:9-11. The same people who do not believe that it is a real horse the second time, do believe that it was a real horse the first time. So why is it so hard for people to believe that it is a real horse the second time?

Rev. 17:14
These shall make war with the Lamb, and the Lamb shall overcome them: for he is Lord of lords, and King of kings: and they that are with him *are* called, and chosen, and faithful.

Notice that the Antichrist and his armies have been gathered together to fight against the "Lamb." As I stated earlier, this is not the same war as with "Gog and Magog" or Russia. At the battle of Gog and Magog, found in Exekiel 38-39, the armies of the north and south are fighting the Antichrist and his armies. Here, all the armies of the world are gathered to fight the coming of Jesus and His host of heaven. The outcome of this war is victory for Jesus.

Rev. 14:15
And another angel came out of the temple, crying with a loud voice to him that sat on the cloud, Thrust in thy sickle, and reap: for the time is come for thee to reap; for the harvest of the earth is ripe.
Rev. 14:16
And he that sat on the cloud thrust in his sickle on the earth; and the earth was reaped.

The one sitting on the cloud is Jesus and the times of the Gentiles is now complete. Their abominations will   be tolerated no longer. This reaping with the sickle will be judgment of these unsaved Gentile nations through war.

Rev. 14:17
And another angel came out of the temple which is in heaven, he also having a sharp sickle.
Rev. 14:18
And another angel came out from the altar, which had power over fire; and cried with a loud cry to him that had the sharp sickle, saying, Thrust in thy sharp sickle, and gather the clusters of the vine of the earth; for her grapes are fully ripe.

"Fully ripe" grapes usually meant they have reached their maturity and are ready to be plucked from the vine and crushed in the wine press. This verse could mean that the evil on earth has been given time to reach the height of its debauchery and it is now time to stop its continued evil growth on mankind. It has been allowed to suck the goodness from the earth and fill its belly with the juice of corruption. It is now time to reap what it has sown.

Rev. 14:19
And the angel thrust in his sickle into the earth, and gathered the vine of the earth, and cast *it* into the great winepress of the wrath of God.

Jer. 25:15-17, 33

[15]For thus saith the LORD God of Israel unto me; Take the wine cup of this fury at my hand, and cause all the nations, to whom I send thee, to drink it.
[16]And they shall drink, and be moved, and be mad, because of the sword that I will send among them.
[17]Then took I the cup at the LORD'S hand, and made all the nations to drink, unto whom the LORD had sent me:

We see that God will cause all nations to reap the results of His fury and suffer death. In this same chapter, Jeremiah begins to name many of the nations that will reap this judgment.

[33]And the slain of the LORD shall be at that day from *one* end of the earth even unto the *other* end of the earth: they shall not be lamented, neither gathered, nor buried; they shall be dung upon the ground.

As seen in verse 33, this destruction will take place throughout the earth and the dead bodies will not be buried. The main battle will take place in the mountains and valleys of Israel, but death will occur throughout the earth for the unsaved. The reader is encouraged to read all of Jeremiah 25 to see how this whole chapter fits perfectly at this stage of prophecy.

Verse 33 proves even further that the Battle of Gog and Magog is not the same as the Battle of Armageddon. The dead will not be buried after Armageddon as seen in verse 33, but the dead will be buried after the battle with Russia and her allies, mentioned in Ezekiel earlier.

Rev. 14:20
And the winepress was trodden without the city, and blood came out of the winepress, even unto the horse bridles, by the space of a thousand *and* six hundred furlongs.

Joel 3:2,12-14
[2]I will also gather all nations, and will bring them down into the valley of Jehoshaphat, and will plead with them there for my people and *for* my heritage Israel, whom they have scattered among the nations, and parted my land.
[12]Let the heathen be wakened, and come up to the valley of Jehoshaphat: for there will I sit to judge all the heathen round about.
[13]Put ye in the sickle, for the harvest is ripe: come, get you down; for the press is full, the vats overflow; for their wickedness *is* great.
[14]Multitudes, multitudes in the valley of decision: for the day of the LORD *is* near in the valley of decision.

Is. 34:5-6
[5]For my sword shall be bathed in heaven: behold, it shall come down upon Idumea, and upon the people of my curse, to judgment.
[6]The sword of the LORD is filled with blood, it is made fat with fatness, *and* with the blood of lambs and goats, with the fat of the kidneys of rams: for the LORD hath a sacrifice in Bozrah, and a great slaughter in the land of Idumea.

This will be the battle of all battles. Good against evil. No war in history has ever seen such carnage. One could combine all the battles ever fought in history and they would still not equal the death and destruction that this war will cause. Eight furlongs are equal to about one mile. One thousand six hundred furlongs equates to about 200 miles in distance. The average height of a full size horse from the ground to its bridle ranges from 38 to 48 inches. If we take a medium-low height to be 42 inches, then we have a scene of blood that would be 3½ feet deep, covering a distance of about 200 miles. This area could probably cover a distance from the Valley of Megiddo and Jezreel Valley on the north, down through the

Jordan River Valley to the Dead Sea on the South, to the Kidron Valley on the west of the Dead Sea. The Kidron Valley flows through Jerusalem southeast to the Dead Sea.

The Kidron Valley is located between the Old City Jerusalem and the Mount of Olives and extends to the Dead Sea. It is almost beyond human comprehension that there could be such a blood bath of this size. This would mean that millions, even hundreds of millions of people, will die in this area to create such a volume of blood. Certainly this will be the most gruesome war of all the ages. Below is a picture of a portion of the Kidron Valley as seen from the Mount of Olives.

(Photograph Courtesy of Shari and JoAnn Vickers)

As I mentioned before, there is a tremendous amount of supporting scripture that refer to the gathering of the armies of the Antichrist, the Second Coming of Jesus and His armies from heaven, the destruction and death of these earthly armies, etc. I will now place much of this supporting scripture in this area of our study.

Joel 3:3, 7, 15-16

[3]And they have cast lots for my people; and have given a boy for an harlot, and sold a girl for wine, that they might drink.

[5]Because ye have taken my silver and my gold, and have carried into your temples my goodly pleasant things:

[6]The children also of Judah and the children of Jerusalem have ye sold unto the Grecians, that ye might remove them far from their border.

[7]Behold, I will raise them out of the place whither ye have sold them, and will return your recompense upon your own head:

[15]The sun and the moon shall be darkened, and the stars shall withdraw their shining.

[16]The LORD also shall roar out of Zion, and utter his voice from Jerusalem; and the heavens and the earth shall shake: but the LORD *will be* the hope of his people, and the strength of the children of Israel.

These verses in Joel speak of how the Antichrist and his demonic armies have treated the Jewish people. They enslaved them, sold them to others for prostitutes and given young girls in exchange for wine. They have stolen virtually everything they could from Israel and Jerusalem. The Antichrist's plan was to annihilate the Jewish race from the earth. However, Jesus appears in His Second Coming and destroys the Antichrist and his perverted God-hating people before they could destroy the Jews.

Zech. 14:1-3

[1]Behold, the day of the LORD cometh, and thy spoil shall be divided in the midst of thee.

[2]For I will gather all nations against Jerusalem to battle; and the city shall be taken, and the houses rifled, and the women ravished; and half of the city shall go forth into captivity, and the residue of the people shall not be cut off from the city.

[3]Then shall the LORD go forth, and fight against those nations, as when he fought in the day of battle.

Once again we see the nations gather against Jerusalem and the perversion that is wrought upon the Jewish people.

Zech. 14:12-13

[12]And this shall be the plague wherewith the LORD will smite all the people that have fought against Jerusalem; Their flesh shall consume away while they stand upon their feet, and their eyes shall consume away in their holes, and their tongue shall consume away in their mouth.
[13]And it shall come to pass in that day, *that* a great tumult from the LORD shall be among them; and they shall lay hold every one on the hand of his neighbour, and his hand shall rise up against the hand of his neighbour.

These verses seem to describe a nuclear explosion. The death of these individuals is the exact description of what happens as a result of a nuclear explosion. Jesus does not have to use nuclear energy to destroy them, because He is the creator of the universe and has more power than nuclear energy. Regardless, these people are consumed in a split second while standing on their feet.

When the remnant Jews who have fled to Petra see the armies of the Antichrist surround them, numbering in the hundreds of millions, they are probably thinking they have no chance. However, Jesus splits the Eastern sky and comes to the rescue. Notice also in verse 13, that the Lord causes all the armies of the Antichrist to be confused to the point that they turn on themselves and kill each other. God, in the past, has caused many armies that opposed Israel to become confused and turn and run when they out numbered the Israelites 1000 to 1 or more. At the Battle of Armageddon, they will turn on each other.

Mal. 4:1-3

[1]For, behold, the day cometh, that shall burn as an oven; and all the proud, yea, and all that do wickedly, shall be stubble: and the day that cometh shall burn them up, saith the LORD of hosts, that it shall leave them neither root nor branch.

[2]But unto you that fear my name shall the Sun of righteousness arise with healing in his wings; and ye shall go forth, and grow up as calves of the stall.
[3]And ye shall tread down the wicked; for they shall be ashes under the soles of your feet in the day that I shall do *this*, saith the LORD of hosts.

Here is another description of how the Antichrist's army will be destroyed and it will be by fire. Is it somewhat ironic that pagan worship has always used some form of fire in their worship? Fire was usually an essential part of their worship. As I stated earlier, God mocks the idol worship of paganism by plaguing the people with the item that is worshipped or by destroying their idols. Here God destroys the same group who worship fire with fire.

Zeph. 1:17-18

[17]And I will bring distress upon men, that they shall walk like blind men, because they have sinned against the LORD: and their blood shall be poured out as dust, and their flesh as the dung.
[18]Neither their silver nor their gold shall be able to deliver them in the day of the LORD'S wrath; but the whole land shall be devoured by the fire of his jealousy: for he shall make even a speedy riddance of all them that dwell in the land.

Mic. 4:11-13

[11]Now also many nations are gathered against thee, that say, Let her be defiled, and let our eye look upon Zion.
[12]But they know not the thoughts of the LORD, neither understand they his counsel: for he shall gather them as the sheaves into the floor.
[13]Arise and thresh, O daughter of Zion: for I will make thine horn iron, and I will make thy hoofs brass: and thou shalt beat in pieces many people: and I will consecrate their gain unto the LORD, and their substance unto the Lord of the whole earth.

Is. 13:3-11

[3]I have commanded my sanctified ones, I have also called my mighty ones for mine anger, *even* them that rejoice in my highness.
[4]The noise of a multitude in the mountains, like as of a great people; a tumultuous noise of the kingdoms of nations gathered together: the LORD of hosts mustereth the host of the battle.
[5]They come from a far country, from the end of heaven, *even* the

LORD, and the weapons of his indignation, to destroy the whole land.

The host of heaven is made up of the Raptured Christians and the Holy Angels.

[6]Howl ye; for the day of the LORD *is* at hand; it shall come as a destruction from the Almighty.
[7]Therefore shall all hands be faint, and every man's heart shall melt:
[8]And they shall be afraid: pangs and sorrows shall take hold of them; they shall be in pain as a woman that travaileth: they shall be amazed one at another; their faces *shall be as* flames.
[9]Behold, the day of the LORD cometh, cruel both with wrath and fierce anger, to lay the land desolate: and he shall destroy the sinners thereof out of it.
[10]For the stars of heaven and the constellations thereof shall not give their light: the sun shall be darkened in his going forth, and the moon shall not cause her light to shine.
[11]And I will punish the world for *their* evil, and the wicked for their iniquity; and I will cause the arrogancy of the proud to cease, and will lay low the haughtiness of the terrible.

In these verses we see that the Lord has brought all these people together for battle from all the nations, not just a few. This is another verse that supports the fact that the war with Gog and Magog is not the same war as this battle at Armageddon. We see that every man's heart will be in absolute fear and their hands will become virtually useless due to fright. Only women can relate to the phrase "as a woman that travaileth," as this refers to the pain of giving birth naturally. I am told that a man can equate to this pain if he has ever had kidney stones. I, for one, can relate for I have had kidney stones. These people will experience similar pain at the coming of the Lord and then death will occur. All sinners will be purged out of the land. We will see the complete fulfillment of this at the Judgment of Nations.

Jer. 50:43

[43]The king of Babylon hath heard the report of them, and his hands waxed feeble: anguish took hold of him, *and* pangs as of a woman in travail.

Some may have thought that the Antichrist has no fear in him. According to Jeremiah, he experiences the same fear that was mentioned in Isaiah above. For seven years this high-minded, haughty, cocky, selfish person has tormented the people on earth. People were so fearful of him and many bowed down to his every whim. Now he experiences the fear of God. Soon he will bow to his knees and receive his just reward. Remember, the Antichrist is still a human, possessed by Satan himself. Satan knows who created him and His name is Jesus. Satan is also afraid of Jesus, for he knows that Jesus is God and will win and judge him.

Dan. 8:25

[25]And through his policy also he shall cause craft to prosper in his hand; and he shall magnify *himself* in his heart, and by peace shall destroy many: he shall also stand up against the Prince of princes; but he shall be broken without hand.

This verse is speaking of the Antichrist. The last part of the verse talks about him fighting against the "Prince of princes" who is Jesus Christ. The outcome will be that the Antichrist will lose.

Is. 34:1-3

[1]Come near, ye nations, to hear; and hearken, ye people: let the earth hear, and all that is therein; the world, and all things that come forth of it.
[2]For the indignation of the LORD *is* upon all nations, and *his* fury upon all their armies: he hath utterly destroyed them, he hath delivered them to the slaughter.
[3]Their slain also shall be cast out, and their stink shall come up out of their carcases, and the mountains shall be melted with their blood.

Ps. 2:1-3

¹Why do the heathen rage, and the people imagine a vain thing?
²The kings of the earth set themselves, and the rulers take counsel together, against the LORD, and against his anointed, *saying*,
³Let us break their bands asunder, and cast away their cords from us.
⁴He that sitteth in the heavens shall laugh: the Lord shall have them in derision.
⁵Then shall he speak unto them in his wrath, and vex them in his sore displeasure.

Ps. 97:3-7, 10

³A fire goeth before him, and burneth up his enemies round about.
⁴His lightnings enlightened the world: the earth saw, and trembled.
⁵The hills melted like wax at the presence of the LORD, at the presence of the Lord of the whole earth.
⁶The heavens declare his righteousness, and all the people see his glory.
⁷Confounded be all they that serve graven images, that boast themselves of idols: worship him, all *ye* gods.
¹⁰Ye that love the LORD, hate evil: he preserveth the souls of his saints; he delivereth them out of the hand of the wicked.

We see that God destroys all the heathen armies, but we also see that He preserves His saints who are still left on earth during this war. The battles will be bloody. All the heathen armies' planning and attempts to conquer Jesus and His army will be like a joke. Jesus will laugh at their attempts and completely overwhelm them.

Mic. 5:9-15

⁹Thine hand shall be lifted up upon thine adversaries, and all thine enemies shall be cut off.
¹⁰And it shall come to pass in that day, saith the LORD, that I will cut off thy horses out of the midst of thee, and I will destroy thy chariots:
¹¹And I will cut off the cities of thy land, and throw down all thy strong holds:
¹²And I will cut off witchcrafts out of thine hand; and thou shalt have no *more* soothsayers:
¹³Thy graven images also will I cut off, and thy standing images out of the midst of thee; and thou shalt no more worship the work

of thine hands.

[14]And I will pluck up thy groves out of the midst of thee: so will I destroy thy cities.

[15]And I will execute vengeance in anger and fury upon the heathen, such as they have not heard.

We see in these verses that God performs a very thorough job of destroying these armies that have come against Him. Not only are the unsaved armies destroyed in the valleys and mountains of Israel, but even their cities from which they came are destroyed.

Today many people throughout the world seek the advice of psychics, palm readers, witches and astrological charts to determine their future or solve problems. Hollywood glorifies these groups of people as being "good." What a spin on evil! As the Bible states in Isaiah, there is a "Woe" pronounced upon such people.

Is. 5:20

[20]Woe unto them that call evil good, and good evil; that put darkness for light, and light for darkness; that put bitter for sweet, and sweet for bitter!

Seeking witchcraft, soothsayers, psychics and worshipping idols has and will always be an abomination to God. These "mediums" are nothing but an attempt to bypass the God of the universe and seek Satan and his demons for advice. God has stated that no one is to seek these types of individuals, because it is nothing but a form of Satan worship. We see that God destroys all these "mediums." Based on this, who would you rather seek, God or these mediums?

Is. 29:6-7

[6]Thou shalt be visited of the LORD of hosts with thunder, and with earthquake, and great noise, with storm and tempest, and the flame of devouring fire.

[7]And the multitude of all the nations that fight against Ariel, even all that fight against her and her munition, and that distress her, shall be as a dream of a night vision.

Ariel is Jerusalem and specifically the Temple Mount area of Jerusalem. We see that when the Lord comes back, He will be preceded by thunder, earthquakes, storms and with a great noise. He will destroy with the flame of fire, those who have come to fight against Him.

Is. 66:15-17

[15]For, behold, the LORD will come with fire, and with his chariots like a whirlwind, to render his anger with fury, and his rebuke with flames of fire.
[16]For by fire and by his sword will the LORD plead with all flesh: and the slain of the LORD shall be many.
[17]They that sanctify themselves, and purify themselves in the gardens behind one *tree* in the midst, eating swine's flesh, and the abomination, and the mouse, shall be consumed together, saith the LORD.

There will be no place to hide from the Lord at His coming. His judgment will find and destroy all the unsaved.

Ps. 110:2, 5-6

[2]The LORD shall send the rod of thy strength out of Zion: rule thou in the midst of thine enemies.
[5]The Lord at thy right hand shall strike through kings in the day of his wrath.
[6]He shall judge among the heathen, he shall fill *the places* with the dead bodies; he shall wound the heads over many countries.

These scriptures speak of "The LORD," Jehovah, will send "the rod of thy strength out of Zion," who is Jesus Christ to "rule." Some would take this to mean that Jesus will not destroy His enemies, but will rule over them. The word "rule" is taken from the original Hebrew word "radah," which means to "tread down." Therefore, He will destroy His enemies just as we have seen in the other texts. The Bible never contradicts itself, as some would presume. The reason I supply so much scripture references is so the reader can see that the Bible truly does interpret itself and there are no contradictions whatsoever.

II Thess. 1:7-10

[7]And to you who are troubled rest with us, when the Lord Jesus shall be revealed from heaven with his mighty angels,
[8]In flaming fire taking vengeance on them that know not God, and that obey not the gospel of our Lord Jesus Christ:
[9]Who shall be punished with everlasting destruction from the presence of the Lord, and from the glory of his power;
[10]When he shall come to be glorified in his saints, and to be admired in all them that believe (because our testimony among you was believed) in that day.

The fact that Jesus is coming again is stated in verse 7. We know from this verse that He will come with His mighty angels and as we have seen from other verses, He will come with His saints, who were Raptured at least seven years prior. This is the day of vengeance of the Lord and it will come upon all those who are unsaved, "that obey not the gospel of our Lord Jesus Christ." The gospel is the good news that Jesus died for our sin, was buried and rose again on the third day. He is God and Savior! Verse 10 speaks about His rule on earth that will begin very soon and He will be joined with His saints from all the ages.

Zech. 12:10

[10]And I will pour upon the house of David, and upon the inhabitants of Jerusalem, the spirit of grace and of supplications: and they shall look upon me whom they have pierced, and they shall mourn for him, as one mourneth for *his* only *son*, and shall be in bitterness for him, as one that is in bitterness for *his* firstborn.

Zechariah tells us that the Jews in Jerusalem shall see that Jesus "whom they have pierced" is really the Messiah. This verse is also a prophetic verse telling the world that Jesus will be pierced and He fulfilled this on the cross of Calvary.

The Battle of Armageddon is Over - Jesus Physically Returns to Earth to Judge the Inhabitants - The Beast and the False Prophet Are Cast Into the Lake of Fire

Zech. 14:4

[4]And his feet shall stand in that day upon the mount of Olives, which *is* before Jerusalem on the east, and the mount of Olives shall cleave in the midst thereof toward the east and toward the west, *and there shall be* a very great valley; and half of the mountain shall remove toward the north, and half of it toward the south.

Job 19:25

[25]For I know *that* my redeemer liveth, and *that* he shall stand at the latter *day* upon the earth:

As we see above, Jesus will physically come back to earth and literally stand on earth in Jerusalem on the Mount of Olives. The Mount of Olives is on one side of the Kidron Valley and the old city of Jerusalem is on the other. According to verse 4 above, there will be a new valley created as the Mount of Olives will split or "rip open." One part of the mountain will move toward the north and the other toward the south creating a valley that flows east to west. This is probably the same valley that creates a river that runs from the Mediterranean Sea to the Dead Sea. This river will bring the Dead Sea to life.

I think it is so awesome that Jesus returns to the Mount of Olives, because when he ascended into heaven after He rose from the grave, it was from this same Mount of Olives.

Acts 1:9-12a

[9]And when he had spoken these things, while they beheld, he was taken up; and a cloud received him out of their sight.

[10]And while they looked stedfastly toward heaven as he went up, behold, two men stood by them in white apparel;

[11]Which also said, Ye men of Galilee, why stand ye gazing up into heaven? this same Jesus, which is taken up from you into heaven, shall so come in like manner as ye have seen him go into

heaven.
[12a]Then returned they unto Jerusalem from the mount called Olivet...

In verse 11, the angels foretell of His Second Coming to earth again to this very same Mount of Olives. He left this earth in power and majesty after conquering death and sin and the grave. He returns in power and majesty to destroy the man of sin, the Antichrist and bind and chain the Devil. As the disciples' hearts were filled with joy, excitement and awe of Jesus as He ascended into heaven, so will those who are saved that are still on earth at His Second Coming. Like the old country preacher said "if that don't set you on fire for God, your wood is wet." In other words, that ought to make you shout, Glory to God!

At this point, the battle of Armageddon is now over and the armies of Jesus have won. The Antichrist and Satan have had their short reign over earth, but it is now time for Jesus to rule and reign and the saved are excited. See the rejoicing in the verses below.

Ps. 98:1-9

[1]O sing unto the LORD a new song; for he hath done marvellous things: his right hand, and his holy arm, hath gotten him the victory.
[2]The LORD hath made known his salvation: his righteousness hath he openly showed in the sight of the heathen.
[3]He hath remembered his mercy and his truth toward the house of Israel: all the ends of the earth have seen the salvation of our God.
[4]Make a joyful noise unto the LORD, all the earth: make a loud noise, and rejoice, and sing praise.
[5]Sing unto the LORD with the harp; with the harp, and the voice of a psalm.
[6]With trumpets and sound of cornet make a joyful noise before the LORD, the King.
[7]Let the sea roar, and the fulness thereof; the world, and they that dwell therein.
[8]Let the floods clap *their* hands: let the hills be joyful together
[9]Before the LORD; for he cometh to judge the earth: with

righteousness shall he judge the world, and the people with equity.

Rev. 19:20
And the beast was taken, and with him the false prophet that wrought miracles before him, with which he deceived them that had received the mark of the beast, and them that worshipped his image. These both were cast alive into a lake of fire burning with brimstone.

Dan. 7:10-11
[10] A fiery stream issued and came forth from before him: thousand thousands ministered unto him, and ten thousand times ten thousand stood before him: the judgment was set, and the books were opened.
[11] I beheld then because of the voice of the great words which the horn spake: I beheld *even* till the beast was slain, and his body destroyed, and given to the burning flame.

Dan. 7:26
[26] But the judgment shall sit, and they shall take away his dominion, to consume and to destroy *it* unto the end.

Notice that the Antichrist, "the horn" in verse 11, is still speaking "great" or arrogant "words" towards Jesus, even in his defeat. The Antichrist and the False Prophet are now taken and cast alive into the "lake of fire." The soul is the real being of a person such as the emotions, the feelings, the senses, etc. The soul of these two will suffer in the flames of fire forever.

They were the ones who deceived the nations and caused them to take the mark of the beast. Notice in Daniel that an unnumbered amount of witnesses watched this scene unfold. These are the holy angels and saints that witness this event. As far as I can determine, these are the first humans to be cast into the "lake of fire." Later in our study we will see all the unsaved will eventually be cast into the lake of fire at the Great White Throne of Judgment.

The Judgment of the Sheep and Goat Nations

Rev. 19:21
And the remnant were slain with the sword of him that sat upon the horse, which *sword* proceeded out of his mouth: and all the fowls were filled with their flesh.

Jesus destroys the rest of the armies of the Antichrist and the birds feast on their remaining flesh. We have already seen in Daniel 7:10 above that the books are opened for judgment. This judgment is not the final judgment, but to determine how the nations and people who are still alive on earth are to be judged according to their treatment of God's saints during the Tribulation Period. This is commonly referred to in Bible terms as "The Judgment of the Nations." It is also commonly referred to as the "judgment of the sheep and goat nations." Sheep are the believers who are still alive on earth and goats are the unbelievers who are still alive on earth. The rest of the unsaved who are left on earth are about to be judged and cast into hell to await the final judgment, which is known as the Great White Throne Judgment. The Judgment of Nations is not the same as the Great White Throne Judgment. The Great White Throne Judgment will happen at least one thousand years in the future, whereas the Judgment of Nations happen immediately after the end of the Battle of Armageddon.

Following are supporting scripture dealing with the judgment of the nations and people who are still alive on earth after the Battle of Armageddon is complete. Those who are unsaved will be cast into hell to await final judgment. The earth will have been purged of all unsaved human beings, leaving only the saved to replenish the earth.

Mt.24:40-42
[40]Then shall two be in the field; the one shall be taken, and the other left.
[41]Two *women shall be* grinding at the mill; the one shall be taken, and the other left.
[42]Watch therefore: for ye know not what hour your Lord doth come.

Mt. 25:31-34

[31]When the Son of man shall come in his glory, and all the holy angels with him, then shall he sit upon the throne of his glory:

[32]And before him shall be gathered all nations: and he shall separate them one from another, as a shepherd divideth *his* sheep from the goats:

[33]And he shall set the sheep on his right hand, but the goats on the left.

[34]Then shall the King say unto them on his right hand, Come, ye blessed of my Father, inherit the kingdom prepared for you from the foundation of the world:

Mt. 25:41,46

[41]Then shall he say also unto them on the left hand, Depart from me, ye cursed, into everlasting fire, prepared for the devil and his angels:

[46]And these shall go away into everlasting punishment: but the righteous into life eternal.

Mt. 13:41-43

[41]The Son of man shall send forth his angels, and they shall gather out of his kingdom all things that offend, and them which do iniquity;

[42]And shall cast them into a furnace of fire: there shall be wailing and gnashing of teeth.

[43]Then shall the righteous shine forth as the sun in the kingdom of their Father. Who hath ears to hear, let him hear.

These verses in Matthew speak of the time after Jesus returns to earth in His Second Coming when He will judge those who are still alive on earth to determine if they are believers or unbelievers. All unbelievers will be cast into Hell and all believers will inherit and replenish the earth.

Is. 11:1-4

[1]And there shall come forth a rod out of the stem of Jesse, and a Branch shall grow out of his roots:

[2]And the spirit of the LORD shall rest upon him, the spirit of wisdom and understanding, the spirit of counsel and might, the spirit of knowledge and of the fear of the LORD;

[3]And shall make him of quick understanding in the fear of the LORD: and he shall not judge after the sight of his eyes, neither reprove after the hearing of his ears:

[4]But with righteousness shall he judge the poor, and reprove with equity for the meek of the earth: and he shall smite the earth with the rod of his mouth, and with the breath of his lips shall he slay the wicked.

The "rod out of the stem of Jesse and a Branch" is Jesus Christ. He will be the judge of these nations and He will destroy those unbelievers who are still left on the earth after His Second Coming.

Ez. 34:11-13

[11]For thus saith the Lord GOD; Behold, I, *even* I, will both search my sheep, and seek them out.

[12]As a shepherd seeketh out his flock in the day that he is among his sheep *that are* scattered; so will I seek out my sheep, and will deliver them out of all places where they have been scattered in the cloudy and dark day.

[13]And I will bring them out from the people, and gather them from the countries, and will bring them to their own land, and feed them upon the mountains of Israel by the rivers, and in all the inhabited places of the country.

Ezekiel talks about the gathering of all the saved "sheep" that are scattered throughout the world. Jesus will gather them to Israel to inhabit the land.

Zep. 3:8

[8]Therefore wait ye upon me, saith the LORD, until the day that I rise up to the prey: for my determination *is* to gather the nations, that I may assemble the kingdoms, to pour upon them mine indignation, *even* all my fierce anger: for all the earth shall be devoured with the fire of my jealousy.

Once again, Jesus will gather all the unbelieving people to the judgment of nations and their bodies will be destroyed and their souls will go into Hell.

Ob. 1:15

[15]For the day of the LORD *is* near upon all the heathen: as thou hast done, it shall be done unto thee: thy reward shall return upon thine own head.

Obadiah prefaces this verse with a discussion of how the unsaved, whom are still alive at Jesus' Second Coming, should not have treated His people the way they did. As a result, they will reap death and Hell. Obadiah goes on to say that the saved will inherit the earth.

Jer. 46:28

[28]Fear thou not, O Jacob my servant, saith the LORD: for I *am* with thee; for I will make a full end of all the nations whither I have driven thee: but I will not make a full end of thee, but correct thee in measure; yet will I not leave thee wholly unpunished.

Jer. 30:11, 23-24

[11]For I *am* with thee, saith the LORD, to save thee: though I make a full end of all nations whither I have scattered thee, yet will I not make a full end of thee: but I will correct thee in measure, and will not leave thee altogether unpunished.
[23]Behold, the whirlwind of the LORD goeth forth with fury, a continuing whirlwind: it shall fall with pain upon the head of the wicked.
[24]The fierce anger of the LORD shall not return, until he have done *it*, and until he have performed the intents of his heart: in the latter days ye shall consider it.

Is. 24:21-22

[21]And it shall come to pass in that day, *that* the LORD shall punish the host of the high ones *that are* on high, and the kings of the earth upon the earth.
[22]And they shall be gathered together, *as* prisoners are gathered in the pit, and shall be shut up in the prison, and after many days shall they be visited.

Jeremiah talks about the judgment of these nations as it relates to how they have treated Israel during the Tribulation Period. Isaiah talks about two groups that will be cast into the "pit." The group, "host of high ones *that are* on high," refer to the fallen angels or demons. The other group refers to the "kings of the earth" that fought against Jesus and His host from heaven. Isaiah states their punishment will be to cast them into the "pit." The pit is Hell. The phrase "after many days shall they be visited" refers to the last judgment called the Great White Throne of Judgment, which will happen one thousand years in the future. The souls of the humans will be reunited with their earthly body and will be brought out of Hell and judged and cast into the Lake of Fire. The demonic angels will not be judged again, since their judgment was sealed when they rebelled with Satan against God in the beginning of time. At that time, they will be cast into the Lake of Fire.

Ps. 82:8

[8]Arise, O God, judge the earth: for thou shalt inherit all nations.

Ps. 96:10,13

[10]Say among the heathen *that* the LORD reigneth: the world also shall be established that it shall not be moved: he shall judge the people righteously.

[13]Before the LORD: for he cometh, for he cometh to judge the earth: he shall judge the world with righteousness, and the people with his truth.

God will judge the nations and will then set up His kingdom on earth.

Mk. 13:26-27

[26]And then shall they see the Son of man coming in the clouds with great power and glory.

[27]And then shall he send his angels, and shall gather together his elect from the four winds, from the uttermost part of the earth to the uttermost part of heaven.

As we see in Mark, Jesus will send His angels to gather the "elect" or the saved who are still alive after the Tribulation. This is part of the gathering to the judgment of nations. These will be the sheep or the believers.

14

Satan Bound and Chained
The Resurrection of Dead Believers

**Satan Bound and Chained and Cast Into the Bottomless
Pit for One Thousand Years**

Rev. 20:1
And I saw an angel come down from heaven, having the key of the
bottomless pit and a great chain in his hand.
Rev. 20:2
And he laid hold on the dragon, that old serpent, which is the Devil,
and Satan, and bound him a thousand years,
Rev. 20:3
And cast him into the bottomless pit, and shut him up, and set a seal
upon him, that he should deceive the nations no more, till the
thousand years should be fulfilled: and after that he must be loosed
a little season.

We see now that Satan is bound and chained and cast into
the "bottomless pit" for one thousand years. This bottomless
pit is Hell or the "abyss." The seal that is "set upon him" is a
seal that no one can break except Jesus Christ himself. This
seal is not placed on anyone else that has been cast into Hell.
There have been demonic angels who have been chained, but
this "seal" was not mentioned about them. It could mean that
this seal is set on Satan so Jesus can loose him one thousand
years later.

Many Amillennial theologians (those who do not believe in
a Millennial reign of Christ on earth) believe that Satan was
bound at the cross and at the ascension of Christ. This theory

has no foundation in the literal interpretation of scripture. The Amillennial theory was proposed by Augustine, back in the 4th Century A.D., to the Church at Rome. Augustine interpreted scripture by spiritualizing it as opposed to taking scripture literally. By spiritualizing scripture, the personal meaning of scripture is removed and it makes God an impersonal God. Literal interpretation of scripture does not mean that symbolism and spiritual applications cannot be interpreted as such. It means, as I stated before, "when the plain sense of scripture makes common sense, seek no other sense, lest it become nonsense." Jesus did take the keys to Death and Hell with Him to His throne, but this did not signify that Satan was bound in the bottomless pit at that time.

I Pet. 5:8-9

[8]Be sober, be vigilant; because your adversary the devil, as a roaring lion, walketh about, seeking whom he may devour:
[9]Whom resist stedfast in the faith, knowing that the same afflictions are accomplished in your brethren that are in the world.

As seen in First Peter, Satan was still loose after the ascension and is the adversary to all and especially the saints of God. Some would say, "this means his influence is affecting people, not him personally!" Everything about these two verses speak of a literal being, "the devil," Satan, and the fact that he is mobile and not bound. Notice that he "walketh about" throughout "the world" as verse 9 explains. The word "devil" is used fifty times in the New Testament. Twenty-five times it is taken from the Greek word "diabolos" which means Satan and the other twenty-five times it is taken from two other Greek words "daimonizomai" and "daimonion" which means demons. The Greek word used in verse 8 above for "devil' is "diabolos" meaning Satan. The same "diabolos" is used in Matthew 4:1, "Then was Jesus led up of the Spirit into the wilderness to be tempted of the devil." Was this not the literal "Devil/Satan" in this verse? Yes, this is the same Devil and no, my friend, the Devil has not been and will not be bound and chained until the point of time just after the Second Coming of Christ to earth.

Satan is bound after the Tribulation and the Second Coming and he will be loosed again one thousand years later. We will discuss the loosening of Satan later in our study.

Is. 14:7-12, 15-19

[7] The whole earth is at rest, *and* is quiet: they break forth into singing.

[8] Yea, the fir trees rejoice at thee, *and* the cedars of Lebanon, *saying,* Since thou art laid down, no feller is come up against us.

[9] Hell from beneath is moved for thee to meet *thee* at thy coming: it stirreth up the dead for thee, *even* all the chief ones of the earth; it hath raised up from their thrones all the kings of the nations.

[10] All they shall speak and say unto thee, Art thou also become weak as we? art thou become like unto us?

[11] Thy pomp is brought down to the grave, *and* the noise of thy viols: the worm is spread under thee, and the worms cover thee.

[12] How art thou fallen from heaven, O Lucifer, son of the morning! *how* art thou cut down to the ground, which didst weaken the nations!

[15] Yet thou shalt be brought down to hell, to the sides of the pit.

[16] They that see thee shall narrowly look upon thee, *and* consider thee, *saying, Is* this the man that made the earth to tremble, that did shake kingdoms;

[17] *That* made the world as a wilderness, and destroyed the cities thereof; *that* opened not the house of his prisoners?

[18] All the kings of the nations, *even* all of them, lie in glory, every one in his own house.

[19] But thou art cast out of thy grave like an abominable branch, *and as* the raiment of those that are slain, thrust through with a sword, that go down to the stones of the pit; as a carcase trodden under feet.

Is. 29:20

[20] For the terrible one is brought to nought, and the scorner is consumed, and all that watch for iniquity are cut off:

As we see in Isaiah, there will be rejoicing by all of creation at the binding of Satan to the "pit" or "Sheol." Sheol is the Hebrew name used for the English word "hell" or Greek word "Hades." It is a place where the unbeliever's departed soul will await final judgment at the Great White Throne of Judgment and then cast into the Lake of Fire. This is not "purgatory" as no such place exists. Catholics and some other religious groups teach that you can buy or have your living relatives pray you out of "purgatory." Never! When you die, if you are a born-again Christian, you will immediately go to be with Christ in Heaven. Paul told us in II Corinthians 5:8, "We are confident, *I say*, and willing rather to be absent from the body, and to be present with the Lord." If you are not a born-again Christian, your soul will go to Hell and there will be no chance to get out.

Jesus told a story of a rich man and a poor beggar named Lazarus. The rich man, who was not saved, died and went to Hell, and Lazarus, who put his trust in the Lord, died and went to be with the Lord. Jesus told the rich man that he could never get out of Hell. Luke 16:26 states, "And beside all this, between us and you there is a great gulf fixed: so that they which would pass from hence to you cannot; neither can they pass to us, that *would come* from thence." The only chance a person has to assure ones self of heaven, is to accept Jesus Christ as Lord and Savior on earth with a true sincere heart.

Satan is bound with a special seal so he can be loosed toward the end of the Millennial Reign of Christ to expose those who were born during the Millennium who never put their trust in Jesus as Lord and Savior.

The Marriage Supper of the Lamb - The Resurrection of the Martyred Tribulation Saints and the Old Testament Saints

---

Rev. 19:9
And he saith unto me, Write, Blessed *are* they which are called unto the marriage supper of the Lamb. And he saith unto me, These are the true sayings of God.

This verse announces the Marriage Supper of the Lamb

that will take place on earth during the millennium period. It tells of the "marriage supper of the Lamb" or feast. Many believe this feast will take place on earth shortly after the Battle of Armageddon is complete and all the earth is rid of Satan, his demons and the unsaved who are still alive at Jesus' Second Coming. I also believe this feast will take place on earth after these events and will very possibly continue throughout the millennium period. "Blessed are they which are called" refers to the guests of the bridegroom.

Let's briefly review the typical marriage process during Biblical times. As you study this process, Jesus Christ is the bridegroom and those saved after His ascension to heaven are His bride or what is called the Church.

The bridegroom chose a bride and would go to the family of the bride and propose his covenant. Jesus did this for us during His earthly ministry. His covenant to us was to save all who came to Him and that they will rule and reign with Him in His kingdom. The Jewish grooms always paid a costly "dowry" to the family for raising a godly woman. Jesus paid this costly price when He was beaten, bruised and died on the cross for our sins. Once the terms were established with the family, the agreement was sealed by drinking a cup of wine or grape juice. Jesus fulfilled this promise by drinking of the "cup" of crucifixion. The agreement was sealed at the day of Pentecost, when the Holy Spirit came to live inside every believer at salvation. The Holy Spirit was the seal of His covenant for His bride.

In the Betrothal Period, the groom would leave his betrothed bride with her family and go back to his father's house to rebuild or add a new section onto the house for his bride. Jesus did this when He ascended to heaven to prepare a mansion for His bride in heaven. He would also make ready a seven-day preparation for the wedding party. The groom would then come back for his bride and "steal her away" for the wedding celebration that would last for seven days. The only warning given to the bride was a shout or blow from a "shofar," a ram's horn. I believe this could very well relate to the Rapture of the Bride of Christ, the Church. Then the seven-day wedding ceremony would begin and the groom and his bride would stay in the wedding chamber for these seven days. I believe this relates to the seven-year Tribulation Period. When the seven days were complete and the marriage consummated, the friend of the groom would announce to everyone that the marriage is complete and that the wedding supper, or "marriage supper," would begin. This relates to the announcement of the Second Coming of Jesus and His Bride to earth. The guests were invited to the supper and joy broke out throughout the area. The guests will be all the Old Testament Saints, the martyred Tribulation Saints and those saints who are still alive at His coming. The whole earth will be elated at this announcement.

As we see with the traditional wedding during Biblical times, the marriage supper will happen during the millennium. I would encourage you to do a more detailed study of the Biblical marriage and betrothal stages to see how neatly it represents the ages of time as I summarized above. Our western marriage ceremonies do not compare to those in Biblical times.

Revelation 19:9 above states, "Blessed are they which are called unto the marriage supper of the Lamb." We are about to see the resurrection of the Tribulation Saints who were martyred for their faith and the Old Testament Saints. Resurrection always refers to the body because the soul never dies.

Rev. 7:9
After this I beheld, and, lo, a great multitude, which no man could number, of all nations, and kindreds, and people, and tongues, stood before the throne, and before the Lamb, clothed with white robes, and palms in their hands;
Rev. 7:10
And cried with a loud voice, saying, Salvation to our God which sitteth upon the throne, and unto the Lamb.
Rev. 7:11
And all the angels stood round about the throne, and *about* the elders and the four beasts, and fell before the throne on their faces,

and worshipped God,
Rev. 7:12
Saying, Amen: Blessing, and glory, and wisdom, and thanksgiving, and honour, and power, and might, *be* unto our God for ever and ever. Amen.
Rev. 7:13
And one of the elders answered, saying unto me, What are these which are arrayed in white robes? and whence came they?
Rev. 7:14
And I said unto him, Sir, thou knowest. And he said to me, These are they which came out of great tribulation, and have washed their robes, and made them white in the blood of the Lamb.
Rev. 7:15
Therefore are they before the throne of God, and serve him day and night in his temple: and he that sitteth on the throne shall dwell among them.

Notice that Verse 15 speaks about the fact that Jesus will dwell among those who are resurrected. This is the Millennial Reign of Christ that is about to begin on earth. In the verses above we see the Tribulation saints that were killed for their faith are now resurrected and will become some of the guests of the Bridegroom at the Marriage Supper of the Lamb. There is a multitude of these saints from every nation of the world. They have also received their white robes.

Rev. 7:16
They shall hunger no more, neither thirst any more; neither shall the sun light on them, nor any heat.
Rev. 7:17
For the Lamb which is in the midst of the throne shall feed them, and shall lead them unto living fountains of waters: and God shall wipe away all tears from their eyes.

Verses 16-17 refer to the future, *after* the Millennial Reign. These do not refer to the Millennial Reign because of several phrases used in these verses. Verse 15 refers to the Millennium Period because "day and night in his temple" is used. During the New Heavens and New Earth, which is the end of the ages, there will only be daytime and there will be no temple. Verses 16-17 refer to the New Heavens and New Earth when there will be no more sun, no temple and God will wipe away all tears. The sun will still shine during the Millennium.

See Chapter 17 of this book for more detail information on the New Heavens and New Earth. Revelation 7:16-17 will be used again in Chapter 17 where they actually fall in the chronology of events.

Rev. 20:4
And I saw thrones, and they sat upon them, and judgment was given unto them: and *I saw* the souls of them that were beheaded for the witness of Jesus, and for the word of God, and which had not worshipped the beast, neither his image, neither had received *his* mark upon their foreheads, or in their hands; and they lived and reigned with Christ a thousand years.

We are told that the reign of Christ on earth will be one thousand years. Is this literal? It certainly is and these martyred saints will reign with Christ, along with the Bride of Christ (the Church) and the Old Testament Saints for this one thousand year period. Over whom will these reign? They will reign over all those who were saved during the Tribulation that did not die. Everyone left on earth at this time are believers and they will inhabit the Millennial Kingdom.

I Cor. 15:23
²³But every man in his own order: Christ the firstfruits; afterward they that are Christ's at his coming.

There will be a resurrection at Christ's second coming.

Lk. 22:29-30
²⁹And I appoint unto you a kingdom, as my Father hath appointed unto me;
³⁰That ye may eat and drink at my table in my kingdom, and sit on thrones judging the twelve tribes of Israel.

Mt. 19:28
²⁸And Jesus said unto them, Verily I say unto you, That ye which have followed me, in the regeneration when the Son of man shall

sit in the throne of his glory, ye also shall sit upon twelve thrones, judging the twelve tribes of Israel.

Corinthians tells us there will be a resurrection at His Second Coming. The verses in Luke and Matthew above were spoken by Jesus to His twelve disciples, telling them that they would sit on twelve thrones and judge the twelve tribes of Israel. Notice in Matthew He qualifies His disciples with the phrase "followed me, in the regeneration," meaning that Judas Iscariot would not sit on one of these thrones because he did not become regenerated or saved. I believe Paul is the twelfth disciple. Notice also that we are told here that there will be representatives of all the twelve tribes of Israel occupying the Millennial Kingdom.

Rev. 20:5
But the rest of the dead lived not again until the thousand years were finished. This *is* the first resurrection.

This verse clearly shows that there will be a resurrection of the just and then one thousand years later a resurrection of the unjust or unsaved. The resurrection of the unjust is also called the "second death."

Lk. 14:14
[14]And thou shalt be blessed; for they cannot recompense thee: for thou shalt be recompensed at the resurrection of the just.

In Luke Jesus mentions the resurrection of the just, which is the first resurrection.

Is. 24:22
[22]And they shall be gathered together, *as* prisoners are gathered in the pit, and shall be shut up in the prison, and after many days shall they be visited.

In Isaiah, we see every unsaved individual who is left on earth after the Battle of Armageddon is cast into the pit, as I mentioned earlier. The phrase "after many days shall they be visited" refers to the Great White Throne of Judgment that will occur after the one thousand-year reign of Christ on earth. This verse also denotes that the two resurrections are separated and not combined.

Rev. 20:6
Blessed and holy *is* he that hath part in the first resurrection: on such the second death hath no power, but they shall be priests of God and of Christ, and shall reign with him a thousand years.

The resurrection of the Old Testament Saints will happen at this time also. These Old Testament Saints include both Gentiles and Jews from Adam to the last saint to die before the Church began in the New Testament. All the bodies of all believers of all the ages past will have resurrected by this time because they are a part of the "first resurrection." The last resurrection is called the "second death." Those in the first resurrection will never be affected by this "second death." The Second Death, as we will see later, is the Lake of Fire.

The First Resurrection Participants

Let us review all those who will have a part of this "first resurrection."

First Resurrection
1. Jesus Christ on the Third Day
2. Rapture of the Church, just before the Tribulation
3. The Two Special Witnesses of the Tribulation Period, at the middle of the Tribulation
4. The 144,000 Witnesses of the Tribulation Period, at the middle of the Tribulation
5. The Martyred Tribulation Saints, at the beginning of the Millennium
6. The Old Testament Saints, at the beginning of the Millennium
7. Millennial Saints both dead and alive at the end of the Millennial Period

Dan. 12:2

²And many of them that sleep in the dust of the earth shall awake, some to everlasting life, and some to shame *and* everlasting contempt.

Daniel talks about the resurrection to "everlasting life" and another resurrection of "everlasting contempt." Old Testament saints are to be resurrected at the beginning of the Millennium. As we saw in Revelation 20:5, there will be a resurrection of the unsaved dead after the thousand years.

Job 19:25-27

²⁵For I know *that* my redeemer liveth, and *that* he shall stand at the latter *day* upon the earth:
²⁶And *though* after my skin *worms* destroy this *body*, yet in my flesh shall I see God:
²⁷Whom I shall see for myself, and mine eyes shall behold, and not another; *though* my reins be consumed within me.

Job believes in the resurrection of his body and tells us that it will be in the "latter day upon the earth." He also states that in "my flesh shall I see God" and that his own eyes will see Him. Job clearly tells us there will be a resurrection of his body and he will be back on this earth and will see God on this earth in the latter days. These three verses alone give us much knowledge of the end times.

Is. 26:19-20

¹⁹Thy dead *men* shall live, *together with* my dead body shall they arise. Awake and sing, ye that dwell in dust: for thy dew *is as* the dew of herbs, and the earth shall cast out the dead.
²⁰Come, my people, enter thou into thy chambers, and shut thy doors about thee: hide thyself as it were for a little moment, until the indignation be overpast.

Isaiah speaks of the resurrection and he tells us that it will be after the "indignation be overpast." In other words, the resurrection of these Old Testament Saints

will be after Satan, the Antichrist, the False Prophet
and all the unsaved are purged from the earth. He
includes his body in this resurrection also.

Hos. 13:14

[14]I will ransom them from the power of the grave; I will redeem
them from death: O death, I will be thy plagues; O grave, I will be
thy destruction: repentance shall be hid from mine eyes.

John 6:39-40, 44

[39]And this is the Father's will which hath sent me, that of all
which he hath given me I should lose nothing, but should raise it
up again at the last day.
[40]And this is the will of him that sent me, that every one which
seeth the Son, and believeth on him, may have everlasting life:
and I will raise him up at the last day.
[44]No man can come to me, except the Father which hath sent me
draw him: and I will raise him up at the last day.

John 11:23-24

[23]Jesus saith unto her, Thy brother shall rise again.
[24]Martha saith unto him, I know that he shall rise again in the
resurrection at the last day.

All of these references above speak of the
resurrection of Old Testament Saints. In John 11, Jesus
is speaking about Lazarus, and Martha agrees that
there will be a resurrection. Jesus went on to say to
Martha, not only will there be a resurrection, but that
He Himself is the resurrection and without Him there
would be no resurrection.

Now that the resurrection of all believers has
occurred, it is now time for them to enjoy a time of
bliss that has never existed on earth. This time of bliss
is called the Millennial Reign of Christ on earth.

15

The Thousand-Year Reign of Christ
The Millennium

We have seen in several of the previous verses, that there will be a one thousand-year period where Jesus will rule and reign on earth with His saints from all the ages. We will discuss the fact of the Millennial Reign, the inhabitants, the living conditions, who will reign, the temple, the teachings and a host of other conditions that will pervade this time period. There seems to be more scripture referring to this period of time than virtually any other subject found in the Bible. Many scripture references in the Bible that refer to the Kingdom of Heaven refers to the Millennium Period also. There will be a tremendous amount of references for your study, but this certainly will not be an exhaustive study. For those who think that the Old Testament is not to be used anymore since the New Testament has been written, you will be surprised to see that the Old Testament has more to say about end time prophecy than does the New Testament. As relates to the Millennium, the Old Testament gives more detail descriptions of this period than one could ever imagine. All scripture, both Old and New, is given to us to use in equipping the believer and convicting the unbeliever. It is all inspired and not "one jot or one tittle" will pass from this Word until everything is fulfilled.

The Fact of the Millennial Reign of Christ

We have already reviewed scripture that presents the fact

of the reign of Christ on earth with His saints for one thousand years. Let us consider some additional references to prove even further this fact.

Mt. 6:10

[10]Thy kingdom come. Thy will be done in earth, as *it is* in heaven.

This is what some would call "The Lord's Prayer." It would be okay to classify it in that manner, but it could be more appropriately called "The Disciple's Prayer," since Jesus is telling His disciples how to pray. We are all to pray for His kingdom to come.

Dan. 7:14, 18, 22, 27

[14]And there was given him dominion, and glory, and a kingdom, that all people, nations, and languages, should serve him: his dominion *is* an everlasting dominion, which shall not pass away, and his kingdom *that* which shall not be destroyed.
[18]But the saints of the most High shall take the kingdom, and possess the kingdom for ever, even for ever and ever.
[22]Until the Ancient of days came, and judgment was given to the saints of the most High; and the time came that the saints possessed the kingdom.
[27]And the kingdom and dominion, and the greatness of the kingdom under the whole heaven, shall be given to the people of the saints of the most High, whose kingdom *is* an everlasting kingdom, and all dominions shall serve and obey him.

Dan. 9:24

[24]Seventy weeks are determined upon thy people and upon thy holy city, to finish the transgression, and to make an end of sins, and to make reconciliation for iniquity, and to bring in everlasting righteousness, and to seal up the vision and prophecy, and to anoint the most Holy.

In these scriptures found in Daniel, it is clearly seen that there will be a kingdom set up on earth in the last days. It will be an everlasting kingdom that will never be destroyed. We are also told that the saints will inhabit this kingdom. Some might say that this is speaking of a heavenly kingdom and not a kingdom on earth. Verse 27 states "the kingdom under the whole heaven," which specifically refers to it being set up on earth. The Bible has been very clear to state when events take place in "heaven" and in this verse it clearly states that it will take place on earth. We also see in Daniel 9:24 that the "Seventy weeks" of Daniel's prophecy will have been fulfilled before this kingdom is set up. We also see that the Most Holy will be anointed at this time.

Is. 2:2-4

[2]And it shall come to pass in the last days, *that* the mountain of the LORD'S house shall be established in the top of the mountains, and shall be exalted above the hills; and all nations shall flow unto it.
[3]And many people shall go and say, Come ye, and let us go up to the mountain of the LORD, to the house of the God of Jacob; and he will teach us of his ways, and we will walk in his paths: for out of Zion shall go forth the law, and the word of the LORD from Jerusalem.
[4]And he shall judge among the nations, and shall rebuke many people: and they shall beat their swords into plowshares, and their spears into pruninghooks: nation shall not lift up sword against nation, neither shall they learn war any more.

Is. 61:11

[11]For as the earth bringeth forth her bud, and as the garden causeth the things that are sown in it to spring forth; so the Lord GOD will cause righteousness and praise to spring forth before all the nations.

Isaiah tells us that in the last days God will establish His house in the top of the mountains and that every nation will come to it to worship. This will be in Jerusalem.

Notice in verse 4 a phrase that should be familiar to all Americans, "they shall beat their swords into plowshares, and their spears into pruninghooks." In the United Nations' garden stands a statue. In 1959 the Soviet Union donated this statue of a nude man with a hammer raised high in the sky, beating his sword into a plowshare. The statue was inscribed with the phrase "We Shall Beat Our Swords Into Plowshares." Does it not seem hypocritical to you that this statue is donated by the one country of that era which created more havoc, death and destruction across the world than even Hitler did during his reign? Is it not also hypocritical that this godless country is quoting God's scripture? Satan can and has confused the masses. I am sure the United States, who was considered a "Christian Nation" at that time, was impressed and certainly the United Nations were impressed. Even though the United Nations may have been created with good intentions, it has become the laughing stock of the world because they seem powerless to help the world and seem to only suck countries dry of their financial support, such as the United States.

In Isaiah 61:11 there will be a time on earth where righteousness and praise will be the center of all the nations of the earth. There has never been a time like this and this verse is foretelling the time of the Millennium.

II Sam. 7:10,12,13,16

[10]Moreover I will appoint a place for my people Israel, and will plant them, that they may dwell in a place of their own, and move no more; neither shall the children of wickedness afflict them any more, as beforetime,

[12]And when thy days be fulfilled, and thou shalt sleep with thy fathers, I will set up thy seed after thee, which shall proceed out of thy bowels, and I will establish his kingdom.

[13]He shall build an house for my name, and I will stablish the throne of his kingdom for ever.

[16]And thine house and thy kingdom shall be established for ever before thee: thy throne shall be established for ever.

The Lord is telling the prophet Nathan to tell David about what He is going to establish in the last days for Israel. He will establish His kingdom and a place for Israel to dwell where there will be no more wickedness. This is speaking of the earthly kingdom and David will be there also to rule in the kingdom.

Dan. 2:44

[44]And in the days of these kings shall the God of heaven set up a kingdom, which shall never be destroyed: and the kingdom shall not be left to other people, *but* it shall break in pieces and consume all these kingdoms, and it shall stand for ever.

Daniel was interpreting Nebuchadnezzar's dream of the statues or images, the foretelling of future rulers of the world from Nebuchadnezzar to the Antichrist. He then tells of God's kingdom that will stand forever and not be destroyed after all of these others are destroyed.

The Inhabitants of the Millennium

Now that I have proven the fact that the Millennium will exist on earth after the Tribulation Period, let us see who will inhabit this earthly kingdom. I have already presented many references in our previous chapter that identify some of these inhabitants. As we saw in the "first resurrection," the immortal inhabitants will be Christ; those believers from the Church Age that were Raptured; those from the Tribulation such as the Two Witnesses, the 144,000 witnesses and those believers who were martyred during the Tribulation for their faith; and those believers from the Old Testament era. As a result of the first resurrection, all of the bodies of these believers have taken on immortal characteristics in the same fashion as Jesus, yet not in the form of deity. In addition to the immortal inhabitants, there will be mortal believers who were alive and survived the Tribulation Period, such as the remnant believing Jews who fled to Petra and the believing Gentiles throughout the world. These mortals will also replenish the earth with their future offspring who will also inhabit the earth during the Millennium.

Ez. 48:35

[35]*It was* round about eighteen thousand *measures*: and the name of the city from *that* day *shall be*, The LORD *is* there.

The Lord Jesus Christ will be there and the name of

the city of Jerusalem will be "The LORD is there."

Zech. 8:4-8, 12, 20-22

[4]Thus saith the LORD of hosts; There shall yet old men and old women dwell in the streets of Jerusalem, and every man with his staff in his hand for very age.

[5]And the streets of the city shall be full of boys and girls playing in the streets thereof.

[6]Thus saith the LORD of hosts; If it be marvellous in the eyes of the remnant of this people in these days, should it also be marvellous in mine eyes? saith the LORD of hosts.

[7]Thus saith the LORD of hosts; Behold, I will save my people from the east country, and from the west country;

[8]And I will bring them, and they shall dwell in the midst of Jerusalem: and they shall be my people, and I will be their God, in truth and in righteousness.

[12]For the seed *shall be* prosperous; the vine shall give her fruit, and the ground shall give her increase, and the heavens shall give their dew; and I will cause the remnant of this people to possess all these *things*.

[20]Thus saith the LORD of hosts; *It shall* yet *come to pass*, that there shall come people, and the inhabitants of many cities:

[21]And the inhabitants of one *city* shall go to another, saying, Let us go speedily to pray before the LORD, and to seek the LORD of hosts: I will go also.

[22]Yea, many people and strong nations shall come to seek the LORD of hosts in Jerusalem, and to pray before the LORD.

Zechariah tells us who will inhabit the kingdom on earth in a very clear vision. In Jerusalem itself, there will be old men and women, boys and girls playing and the remnant Jews. There will be people from all over the world who will come to Jerusalem to live during the Millennium. People will also come from around the world to worship Jesus in Jerusalem.

Zech. 14:16

[16]And it shall come to pass, *that* every one that is left of all the nations which came against Jerusalem shall even go up from year to year to worship the King, the LORD of hosts, and to keep the feast of tabernacles.

We see in this verse that some of the mortal people who will inhabit the kingdom will be those believers who survived the Tribulation.

Is. 4:2-3

[2]In that day shall the branch of the LORD be beautiful and glorious, and the fruit of the earth *shall be* excellent and comely for them that are escaped of Israel.
[3]And it shall come to pass, *that he that is* left in Zion, and *he that* remaineth in Jerusalem, shall be called holy, *even* every one that is written among the living in Jerusalem:

Isaiah tells us that those Jews who "escaped" or survived the onslaught of Jerusalem at the last battle will live in Jerusalem. He also states that these are believers, "even every one that is written among the living," for they will be called "holy."

Is. 14:1

[1]For the LORD will have mercy on Jacob, and will yet choose Israel, and set them in their own land: and the strangers shall be joined with them, and they shall cleave to the house of Jacob.

Is. 27:12-13

[12]And it shall come to pass in that day, *that* the LORD shall beat off from the channel of the river unto the stream of Egypt, and ye shall be gathered one by one, O ye children of Israel.
[13]And it shall come to pass in that day, *that* the great trumpet shall be blown, and they shall come which were ready to perish in the land of Assyria, and the outcasts in the land of Egypt, and shall worship the LORD in the holy mount at Jerusalem.

Is. 54:3

[3]For thou shalt break forth on the right hand and on the left; and thy seed shall inherit the Gentiles, and make the desolate cities to be inhabited.

Is. 61:4-5, 9

[4]And they shall build the old wastes, they shall raise up the former desolations, and they shall repair the waste cities, the desolations of many generations.
[5]And strangers shall stand and feed your flocks, and the sons of the alien *shall be* your plowmen and your vinedressers.
[9]And their seed shall be known among the Gentiles, and their offspring among the people: all that see them shall acknowledge them, that they *are* the seed *which* the LORD hath blessed.

Is. 66:20

[20]And they shall bring all your brethren *for* an offering unto the LORD out of all nations upon horses, and in chariots, and in litters, and upon mules, and upon swift beasts, to my holy mountain Jerusalem, saith the LORD, as the children of Israel bring an offering in a clean vessel into the house of the LORD.

The saved of Israel will inhabit the land along with non-Jews. They will inhabit cities that have become "desolate" as a result of the previous Tribulation Period and the plagues and wars that ravished them. These living Jews will be known among all nations and they will have children during the Millennium. There will also be children born to Gentiles that are still living.

Hos. 2:16-23

[16]And it shall be at that day, saith the LORD, *that* thou shalt call me Ishi; and shalt call me no more Baali.

[17]For I will take away the names of Baalim out of her mouth, and they shall no more be remembered by their name.

[18]And in that day will I make a covenant for them with the beasts of the field, and with the fowls of heaven, and *with* the creeping things of the ground: and I will break the bow and the sword and the battle out of the earth, and will make them to lie down safely.

[19]And I will betroth thee unto me for ever; yea, I will betroth thee unto me in righteousness, and in judgment, and in lovingkindness, and in mercies.

[20]I will even betroth thee unto me in faithfulness: and thou shalt know the LORD.

[21]And it shall come to pass in that day, I will hear, saith the LORD, I will hear the heavens, and they shall hear the earth;

[22]And the earth shall hear the corn, and the wine, and the oil; and they shall hear Jezreel.

[23]And I will sow her unto me in the earth; and I will have mercy upon her that had not obtained mercy; and I will say to *them which were* not my people, Thou *art* my people; and they shall say, *Thou art* my God.

Hos. 14:4-7

[4]I will heal their backsliding, I will love them freely: for mine anger is turned away from him.

[5]I will be as the dew unto Israel: he shall grow as the lily, and cast forth his roots as Lebanon.

[6]His branches shall spread, and his beauty shall be as the olive tree, and his smell as Lebanon.

[7]They that dwell under his shadow shall return; they shall revive *as* the corn, and grow as the vine: the scent thereof *shall be* as the wine of Lebanon.

These chapters show a beautiful prophecy by the LORD Jehovah to Israel, telling them of their future in the kingdom on earth. The word "Ishi" in the Hebrew means "my husband" and the word "Baali" means "my lord." Israel, as a people, has always been considered the wife of God Jehovah. As the Church is the "Bride of Christ the Son," so Israel is the "wife of God Jehovah" or the mother nation of Jesus Christ. However, Israel throughout centuries rejected God and finally at the cross they rejected God's only Son and His salvation. God decided since Israel became an adulterer by worshipping other gods, He would turn to the Gentiles to save them from their sin and provoke Israel to jealousy. Israel finally realizes their sin during the Tribulation and God restores them and gives them the inheritance He promised them from the beginning. The Millennium was designed for restoration of Israel to God and He will renew them as His wife.

Ob. 1:17

[17]But upon mount Zion shall be deliverance, and there shall be holiness; and the house of Jacob shall possess their possessions.

Ez. 28:25-26

[25]Thus saith the Lord GOD; When I shall have gathered the house of Israel from the people among whom they are scattered, and shall be sanctified in them in the sight of the heathen, then shall they dwell in their land that I have given to my servant Jacob.

[26]And they shall dwell safely therein, and shall build houses, and plant vineyards; yea, they shall dwell with confidence, when I have executed judgments upon all those that despise them round about them; and they shall know that I *am* the LORD their God.

Ez. 36:8-15, 37-38

[8]But ye, O mountains of Israel, ye shall shoot forth your branches, and yield your fruit to my people of Israel; for they are at hand to come.

[9]For, behold, I *am* for you, and I will turn unto you, and ye shall

be tilled and sown:

¹⁰And I will multiply men upon you, all the house of Israel, *even* all of it: and the cities shall be inhabited, and the wastes shall be builded:

¹¹And I will multiply upon you man and beast; and they shall increase and bring fruit: and I will settle you after your old estates, and will do better *unto you* than at your beginnings: and ye shall know that I *am* the LORD.

¹²Yea, I will cause men to walk upon you, *even* my people Israel; and they shall possess thee, and thou shalt be their inheritance, and thou shalt no more henceforth bereave them *of men*.

¹³Thus saith the Lord GOD; Because they say unto you, Thou *land* devourest up men, and hast bereaved thy nations;

¹⁴Therefore thou shalt devour men no more, neither bereave thy nations any more, saith the Lord GOD.

¹⁵Neither will I cause *men* to hear in thee the shame of the heathen any more, neither shalt thou bear the reproach of the people any more, neither shalt thou cause thy nations to fall any more, saith the Lord GOD.

³⁷Thus saith the Lord GOD; I will yet *for* this be inquired of by the house of Israel, to do *it* for them; I will increase them with men like a flock.

³⁸As the holy flock, as the flock of Jerusalem in her solemn feasts; so shall the waste cities be filled with flocks of men: and they shall know that I *am* the LORD.

Ez. 37:21-22

²¹And say unto them, Thus saith the Lord GOD; Behold, I will take the children of Israel from among the heathen, whither they be gone, and will gather them on every side, and bring them into their own land:

²²And I will make them one nation in the land upon the mountains of Israel; and one king shall be king to them all: and they shall be no more two nations, neither shall they be divided into two kingdoms any more at all:

In the references above we see further proof of Israel occupying their nation and that other people will occupy other nations in this time of bliss and righteousness on earth. They will multiply during this thousand years of bliss and have children. Today we have a world birth rate of over 20 births/1000 population and almost 9 deaths/1000 population. During the Millennium the birth rate will increase exponentially and the death rate will decrease exponentially. We do not know how many people will inhabit the Millennium in the beginning, nor do we know what the birth rate will be, but we can be sure that this earth will hold all that God allows.

We also see that there will be one Supreme King and that King will be Jesus Christ.

Ps. 69:34-36

[34]Let the heaven and earth praise him, the seas, and every thing that moveth therein.
[35]For God will save Zion, and will build the cities of Judah: that they may dwell there, and have it in possession.
[36]The seed also of his servants shall inherit it: and they that love his name shall dwell therein.

Ps. 105:6-11

[6]O ye seed of Abraham his servant, ye children of Jacob his chosen.
[7]He *is* the LORD our God: his judgments *are* in all the earth.
[8]He hath remembered his covenant for ever, the word *which* he commanded to a thousand generations.
[9]Which *covenant* he made with Abraham, and his oath unto Isaac;
[10]And confirmed the same unto Jacob for a law, *and* to Israel *for* an everlasting covenant:
[11]Saying, Unto thee will I give the land of Canaan, the lot of your inheritance:

Psalms tells us also that Israel will possess and inherit their land as promised by God.

The Living Conditions During the Millennium

Now let's look at some of the living conditions that will exist throughout this Millennial Period. This will certainly be a time of joy and bliss. Cities will be rebuilt and crops will grow all year round. Many will live for hundreds of years, as was the case before the flood. When a person reaches 100 years of age, they will still be considered a child when compared to those who are in their 900's. Their bodies will not grow old as fast as ours do today. We will see harmony with man and wild beast, children and snakes, wild beast and tame beast and a host of other scenarios will occur during this time. Satan and all his demon angels are not present on the earth to torment mankind, however, people will continue to sin during this period. Some of the children born during this time will not accept Jesus as their personal Savior, as we will see toward the end of the Millennium.

Zep. 3:9

⁹For then will I turn to the people a pure language, that they may all call upon the name of the LORD, to serve him with one consent.

There will be one language spoken on the earth during the Millennium. What a change! Back at the Tower of Babel, the earth was speaking one language. God saw they were using this one language to worship idols and created their own "religion" of cult worship. Therefore, He confused them by causing them to speak all different kinds of languages and caused them to scatter throughout the world. During the Millennium, this curse of languages will be removed and everyone will speak the same language once again. Why would God do this? Because He knows righteousness will rule the world during the Millennium and wants everyone to understand everything that will be taught and be able to converse with whomever they please and learn all they can. No one will have an excuse of saying they did not understand their teacher because they did not understand the language.

Amos 9:13-15

¹³Behold, the days come, saith the LORD, that the plowman shall overtake the reaper, and the treader of grapes him that soweth seed; and the mountains shall drop sweet wine, and all the hills shall melt.

¹⁴And I will bring again the captivity of my people of Israel, and they shall build the waste cities, and inhabit *them*; and they shall plant vineyards, and drink the wine thereof; they shall also make gardens, and eat the fruit of them.

¹⁵And I will plant them upon their land, and they shall no more be

pulled up out of their land which I have given them, saith the
LORD thy God.

In Amos, the Lord tells us that crops will grow
year-round and they will grow as fast as they are
planted and reaped. There probably will be no need for
canning and storage of food because of the tremendous
quantity and availability of food throughout each year.
The cities that were destroyed during the Tribulation
Period will be rebuilt. I imagine there will be many
record-breaking fruits and vegetables that would make
our American State Fair winners look like dwarfs.

Joel 2:22-26

[22]Be not afraid, ye beasts of the field: for the pastures of the
wilderness do spring, for the tree beareth her fruit, the fig tree and
the vine do yield their strength.
[23]Be glad then, ye children of Zion, and rejoice in the LORD your
God: for he hath given you the former rain moderately, and he
will cause to come down for you the rain, the former rain, and the
latter rain in the first *month*.
[24]And the floors shall be full of wheat, and the vats shall overflow
with wine and oil.
[25]And I will restore to you the years that the locust hath eaten, the
cankerworm, and the caterpillar, and the palmerworm, my great
army which I sent among you.
[26]And ye shall eat in plenty, and be satisfied, and praise the name
of the LORD your God, that hath dealt wondrously with you: and
my people shall never be ashamed.

In Joel, we see that the Lord tells the inhabitants of
the Millennium that all of creation will rejoice and not
have fear, even the animals. There will be such an
abundance of food that even the storage houses will
not be able to contain them. We will not see the hungry
children and adults' stomachs bloated because of lack
of food as we see on earth today. Everyone will eat and
never go hungry with all the food they could ever
imagine. Do you remember that all the grass, trees and
vegetation were burned up during the Tribulation

Period? Verse 25 reminds them of the plagues that God sent upon the earth during the Tribulation Period and He states that He will restore all of the land.

Ez. 36:29-30, 33-35

[29]I will also save you from all your uncleannesses: and I will call for the corn, and will increase it, and lay no famine upon you.
[30]And I will multiply the fruit of the tree, and the increase of the field, that ye shall receive no more reproach of famine among the heathen.
[33]Thus saith the Lord GOD; In the day that I shall have cleansed you from all your iniquities I will also cause *you* to dwell in the cities, and the wastes shall be builded.
[34]And the desolate land shall be tilled, whereas it lay desolate in the sight of all that passed by.
[35]And they shall say, This land that was desolate is become like the garden of Eden; and the waste and desolate and ruined cities *are become* fenced, *and* are inhabited.

Is. 51:3

[3]For the LORD shall comfort Zion: he will comfort all her waste places; and he will make her wilderness like Eden, and her desert like the garden of the LORD; joy and gladness shall be found therein, thanksgiving, and the voice of melody.

In Ezekiel and Isaiah, we see more evidence of the bliss during this period. Corn, fruit and anything grown in the fields will flourish. There will be no more famine on earth. The cities will be rebuilt and the land that was destroyed during the Tribulation will blossom and look like the most famous non-cursed garden ever known to man, the Garden of Eden. If we could visualize the destruction that happened throughout the world during the Tribulation, we would think to ourselves that this land would never produce again. However, with God, nothing is impossible. Notice in Isaiah the attitude of those occupying the kingdom. There will be "joy and gladness... thanksgiving, and... melody." There has never been a time on earth filled with such joy as the Millennium. If you are a believer in Christ and have trusted Him as your Lord and Savior, you will have a part in seeing all of this on earth in the future. What a sight to behold! What a joy to know that we will be a part of this wonderful experience! We should tell others so they can have this excitement in their souls as well and become a part of this same experience!

Ez. 34:25-29

^{25}And I will make with them a covenant of peace, and will cause the evil beasts to cease out of the land: and they shall dwell safely in the wilderness, and sleep in the woods.
^{26}And I will make them and the places round about my hill a blessing; and I will cause the shower to come down in his season; there shall be showers of blessing.
^{27}And the tree of the field shall yield her fruit, and the earth shall yield her increase, and they shall be safe in their land, and shall know that I *am* the LORD, when I have broken the bands of their yoke, and delivered them out of the hand of those that served themselves of them.
^{28}And they shall no more be a prey to the heathen, neither shall the beast of the land devour them; but they shall dwell safely, and none shall make *them* afraid.
^{29}And I will raise up for them a plant of renown, and they shall be no more consumed with hunger in the land, neither bear the shame of the heathen any more.

Did anything familiar jump out at you in these verses? It did for me! Notice verse 26, the phrase "there shall be showers of blessing." A great hymn with the same name was taken from this phrase which was written by Daniel W. Whittle. "Major" Whittle, as he was known, was a great evangelist in the late 1800's who penned the words to this song in 1883. It has been sung throughout churches for over a century as he captured the bliss of the Millennium.

There will be no evil beasts, trees will yield fruit abundantly, no one will go hungry and they will not have to fear anyone anymore.

Is. 35:1-2, 5-10

^{1}The wilderness and the solitary place shall be glad for them; and the desert shall rejoice, and blossom as the rose.

²It shall blossom abundantly, and rejoice even with joy and singing: the glory of Lebanon shall be given unto it, the excellency of Carmel and Sharon, they shall see the glory of the LORD, *and* the excellency of our God.

⁵Then the eyes of the blind shall be opened, and the ears of the deaf shall be unstopped.

⁶Then shall the lame *man* leap as an hart, and the tongue of the dumb sing: for in the wilderness shall waters break out, and streams in the desert.

⁷And the parched ground shall become a pool, and the thirsty land springs of water: in the habitation of dragons, where each lay, *shall be* grass with reeds and rushes.

⁸And an highway shall be there, and a way, and it shall be called The way of holiness; the unclean shall not pass over it; but it *shall be* for those: the wayfaring men, though fools, shall not err *therein*.

⁹No lion shall be there, nor *any* ravenous beast shall go up thereon, it shall not be found there; but the redeemed shall walk *there*:

¹⁰And the ransomed of the LORD shall return, and come to Zion with songs and everlasting joy upon their heads: they shall obtain joy and gladness, and sorrow and sighing shall flee away.

Once again, the glory of this period is almost beyond human comprehension. The desert will blossom as a rose and will be filled with drinkable water. Remember during the Tribulation Period, all of the drinkable water was destroyed by turning to blood? Not any more! Even the deserts will be filled with springs and pools of water. Jesus will heal the sick, the blind will see, the deaf will hear, those that cannot speak or talk will talk and sing, and the lame will walk. All the mortal human beings that enter into the Millennium will be healed of all their ailments and diseases. There will be such rejoicing that people will sing with joy and they will have no more sorrow. There will be a special highway called "The way of holiness," or as some scholars call "the Kings Highway."

Is. 43:18-21

¹⁸Remember ye not the former things, neither consider the things of old.
¹⁹Behold, I will do a new thing; now it shall spring forth; shall ye not know it? I will even make a way in the wilderness, *and* rivers in the desert.
²⁰The beast of the field shall honour me, the dragons and the owls: because I give waters in the wilderness, *and* rivers in the desert, to give drink to my people, my chosen.
²¹This people have I formed for myself; they shall show forth my praise.

God tells the Israelites that have lived to this point, to not remember the things of old or things in the past. He will put rivers in the desert and all of creation will honor Him during this period. He chose Israel from the beginning and Israel will finally give Him the praise that is due.

Is. 30:18-19, 23-26

¹⁸And therefore will the LORD wait, that he may be gracious unto you, and therefore will he be exalted, that he may have mercy upon you: for the LORD *is* a God of judgment: blessed *are* all they that wait for him.
¹⁹For the people shall dwell in Zion at Jerusalem: thou shalt weep no more: he will be very gracious unto thee at the voice of thy cry; when he shall hear it, he will answer thee.
²³Then shall he give the rain of thy seed, that thou shalt sow the ground withal; and bread of the increase of the earth, and it shall be fat and plenteous: in that day shall thy cattle feed in large pastures.
²⁴The oxen likewise and the young asses that ear the ground shall eat clean provender, which hath been winnowed with the shovel and with the fan.
²⁵And there shall be upon every high mountain, and upon every high hill, rivers *and* streams of waters in the day of the great slaughter, when the towers fall.
²⁶Moreover the light of the moon shall be as the light of the sun, and the light of the sun shall be sevenfold, as the light of seven days, in the day that the LORD bindeth up the breach of his people, and healeth the stroke of their wound.

Is. 65:19, 24

¹⁹And I will rejoice in Jerusalem, and joy in my people: and the

voice of weeping shall be no more heard in her, nor the voice of crying.
[24]And it shall come to pass, that before they call, I will answer; and while they are yet speaking, I will hear.

Chapter 30:19 and 65:19, 24, specifically state that they will weep no more and God shall hear their prayers before they even pray them and have their answers delivered immediately. Some scholars believe there will be no crying or weeping throughout all the earth throughout the duration of the Millennium. Others state that all the tears will not be wiped away until after the Great White Throne of Judgment. To this I would reply, that tears at the Great White Throne Judgment will probably flow again by most believers as we see loved ones and friends from the past being cast into the Lake of Fire. In addition, these verses relating to crying and weeping could be referring to the area of Jerusalem only, since it specifically states "in Zion at Jerusalem" or "in Jerusalem." Regardless, all tears of all believers will be wiped away by God, whether during the Millennium or after the Millennium.

God knows the thoughts of every individual and hears the prayers of His believers. Sometimes the answers to our prayers are delayed because Satan and his demons try to intervene and stop them from being delivered by God's angels. This happened when Daniel was praying and the holy angel was hindered by Satan from delivering the answer for a while. Since Satan and his demons will not be present during this period, God's answers will be immediate. Notice in verse 18, there is a phrase that all believers should exercise in their daily prayer life and that is "blessed are all they that wait for him." It would do us all good to "wait" on the Lord instead of jumping out prematurely and forcing answers to our prayers. Sometimes we may try to force doors to open in our life that God did not want opened.

Notice that all of the earth will flourish and overflow with plenty. Remember during the Tribulation that the sun, moon and the stars were dimmed by God? In verse 26 we see the moon and the sun will be brighter than ever before. The moon will shine with the brightness that the sun does today and the sun will be seven times brighter than before. Today, some scientists are concerned about the ozone layer of the earth being depleted. I wonder what the scientists would say about this verse. Of course they would state that this would be impossible, because the earth would be burned up and no life could live. This verse shows specifically that God is in complete control of this earth and all the universes He created. He can and will control life and the sun, moon and stars. I would be willing to say that there will be no need of sunscreen during the Millennium. Does this mean that we should act irresponsibly when it comes to taking care of this earth when possible? No! We should act as responsible stewards of God's creation, but understand that God will not allow anything to go beyond the boundaries that He has established. Christians need to be careful not to jump on the "bandwagon" of "doomsday" scientists who claim our earth's atmosphere could become depleted. God will never allow that to happen.

Jer. 46:27

[27]But fear not thou, O my servant Jacob, and be not dismayed, O Israel: for, behold, I will save thee from afar off, and thy seed from the land of their captivity; and Jacob shall return, and be in rest and at ease, and none shall make *him* afraid.

Israel will be at rest during the Millennium Period and will not have any reason to fear anymore. Israel, since their beginning, have had to fear for their safety and existence. Satan has tried to annihilate the Jewish nation from the beginning. They will never have to worry about that again.

Is. 11:6-9

[6]The wolf also shall dwell with the lamb, and the leopard shall lie down with the kid; and the calf and the young lion and the fatling together; and a little child shall lead them.
[7]And the cow and the bear shall feed; their young ones shall lie down together: and the lion shall eat straw like the ox.
[8]And the sucking child shall play on the hole of the asp, and the weaned child shall put his hand on the cockatrice' den.
[9]They shall not hurt nor destroy in all my holy mountain: for the earth shall be full of the knowledge of the LORD, as the waters cover the sea.

When Adam was created and walked upon the earth with all of God's creation, the animals were all in harmony. After Adam sinned in the Garden of Eden, he thrust the whole world into a curse. Many of the animals that we know as wild beasts, began to feed on other animals as prey and the earth brought forth thorns and thistles. During the Millennium, a portion of the curse will be lifted and harmony amongst humans and animals will once again rule the earth as it did originally. Not all of the curse will be lifted, because the curse came about because of sin. Sin will still be present during the Millennium and therefore some of the curse will remain because of sin. Man will continue to till the ground and there will still be death, but sin will not abound as it had in the past.

Notice the relationships in the verses above with animals that are mortal enemies today, yet in the Millennium they are like our home pets, yet living in more harmony than do our home pets. Can you imagine the wolf dwelling with the lamb, the leopard with the goat, the calf and the young lion? And on top of all of that, a young child will be able to lead them like you would walk your dog. Look at some other differences such as the cow and the bear will feed together, their young ones sleep and play together. Notice the change in the lion's habit, the King of the Beasts. He will graze on straw like an ox. There will not be any need for zoos during this time, for the whole earth will be one big zoo without cages. A sucking child, a newborn, will play in the territory of the asp snake. Many believe this snake is the cobra. Also notice that a "weaned" child, or small child, could put his hand in a "cockatrice' den" and not be harmed. Cockatrice could be another snake found in this area, which is called the "yellow viper." It is considered the most venomous snake in the area. However, mothers and fathers will have no concern for the safety of their children, because the Lord said "they shall not hurt nor destroy" during the Millennium. There will be no poisonous or venomous snakes, since their venom was used for protection and capturing other prey.

Is. 14:7-8

[7]The whole earth is at rest, *and* is quiet: they break forth into singing.

[8]Yea, the fir trees rejoice at thee, *and* the cedars of Lebanon, *saying*, Since thou art laid down, no feller is come up against us.

Isaiah is talking about Satan being bound and chained causes the whole earth to be at rest and spring forth with singing. This rest period is the Millennial Reign of Christ. Even the trees rejoice because Satan who was the first to rebel against God is now bound and chained. Because righteousness will be the rule during this time and because God has placed His blessings on this period of time, creation will blossom and bloom as never before.

Is. 65:20, 25

[20]There shall be no more thence an infant of days, nor an old man that hath not filled his days: for the child shall die an hundred years old; but the sinner *being* an hundred years old shall be accursed.

[25]The wolf and the lamb shall feed together, and the lion shall eat straw like the bullock: and dust *shall be* the serpent's meat. They shall not hurt nor destroy in all my holy mountain, saith the LORD.

Isaiah states that during the Millennium, no one will die in their infancy. Everyone will live to a ripe old age. People will still be considered children at the age of 100. I assume that since mankind will live up to 900 years and older, then 100 would seem like a young "whippersnapper." There seems to be death during this time frame, although it must be rare. Verse 20 speaks of death, but not until at least the age of 100. I believe that death will be rare, since it is not mentioned anywhere else but here. This verse also tells us that there will be some that are born during the Millennium who grow up and never trust Jesus as their personal Savior. Verse 20 tells us that sin is a natural thing found within everyone and that it will not be excused during this period also. People must still put their faith and trust in Jesus, as has been the case for the all ages. We will see, towards the end of the Millennium, that these same unbelievers will revolt against Jesus and their revolt will be crushed immediately.

Verse 25 reiterates the role of the animal kingdom during this period and that they shall not hurt or destroy during this time.

Who Will Reign During the Millennium

I have already mentioned some who will reign during this period such as: Jesus Christ, the Church Age believers, the Old Testament saints and the Tribulation saints who were martyred. I will provide more references to support these, along with some references to show that David will once again rule over Israel in his glorified body that was given to him at the resurrection. These groups will rule over those who survive the Tribulation Period and their generations to follow.

Rule is probably not the best English word to describe this Millennial Period. Overseer or teacher or one who is considered a wise counselor may be a better term, because the people during this time period will not have rebellious attitudes that we see today. This does not mean that within the heart of some of the people, rebellion may not exist. It simply means that the people will not "come out of the closet," so to speak, until Satan is loosed again to expose them. It would not be the "politically correct" thing to do until they have a leader who fosters rebellion, such as Satan.

It would be wonderful today if people would not feel boldness to expose their sins in the streets. The reason people feel bold and not sorry for their sin today, is because righteousness does not rule their hearts and the righteous people today do not stand up and condemn their actions as sin. I believe if someone tries to become bold during the Millennium and stand proud of their sin, that they will be silenced immediately. Since righteousness will be the overwhelming rule during this period, people will not be impressed to expose their sins before mankind.

Now let us view some references relating to those who will reign during the Millennium.

1. Jesus Christ will reign on earth from Jerusalem during the Millennium.

> Lk.1:30-33
>
> [30]And the angel said unto her, Fear not, Mary: for thou hast found favour with God.
> [31]And, behold, thou shalt conceive in thy womb, and bring forth a son, and shalt call his name JESUS.
> [32]He shall be great, and shall be called the Son of the Highest: and the Lord God shall give unto him the throne of his father David:
> [33]And he shall reign over the house of Jacob for ever; and of his kingdom there shall be no end.

> Is. 24:23
>
> [23]Then the moon shall be confounded, and the sun ashamed, when the LORD of hosts shall reign in mount Zion, and in Jerusalem, and before his ancients gloriously.

Is. 52:7-8

[7]How beautiful upon the mountains are the feet of him that bringeth good tidings, that publisheth peace; that bringeth good tidings of good, that publisheth salvation; that saith unto Zion, Thy God reigneth!
[8]Thy watchmen shall lift up the voice; with the voice together shall they sing: for they shall see eye to eye, when the LORD shall bring again Zion.

The people will see Jesus "eye to eye." He will be physically ruling on earth during the Millennium.

Is. 59:20

[20]And the Redeemer shall come to Zion, and unto them that turn from transgression in Jacob, saith the LORD.

Is. 11:10

[10]And in that day there shall be a root of Jesse, which shall stand for an ensign of the people; to it shall the Gentiles seek: and his rest shall be glorious.

As I mentioned earlier in this book, the "root of Jesse" refers to the Lord Jesus Christ.

Is. 12:6

[6]Cry out and shout, thou inhabitant of Zion: for great *is* the Holy One of Israel in the midst of thee.

Ez. 43:7, 9

[7]And he said unto me, Son of man, the place of my throne, and the place of the soles of my feet, where I will dwell in the midst of the children of Israel for ever, and my holy name, shall the house of Israel no more defile, *neither* they, nor their kings, by their whoredom, nor by the carcases of their kings in their high places.
[9]Now let them put away their whoredom, and the carcases of their kings, far from me, and I will dwell in the midst of them for ever.

Again, we see that Jesus will physically dwell on earth in Jerusalem on his throne.

Jer. 23:5-6

[5]Behold, the days come, saith the LORD, that I will raise unto David a righteous Branch, and a King shall reign and prosper, and shall execute judgment and justice in the earth.
[6]In his days Judah shall be saved, and Israel shall dwell safely: and this *is* his name whereby he shall be called, THE LORD OUR

RIGHTEOUSNESS.

Ps. 2:6

⁶Yet have I set my king upon my holy hill of Zion.

Ps. 99:1-2

¹The LORD reigneth; let the people tremble: he sitteth *between* the cherubims; let the earth be moved.
²The LORD *is* great in Zion; and he *is* high above all the people.

Zech. 8:3

³Thus saith the LORD; I am returned unto Zion, and will dwell in the midst of Jerusalem: and Jerusalem shall be called a city of truth; and the mountain of the LORD of hosts the holy mountain.

Zech. 14:9

⁹And the LORD shall be king over all the earth: in that day shall there be one LORD, and his name one.

Zech. 2:10-11

¹⁰Sing and rejoice, O daughter of Zion: for, lo, I come, and I will dwell in the midst of thee, saith the LORD.
¹¹And many nations shall be joined to the LORD in that day, and shall be my people: and I will dwell in the midst of thee, and thou shalt know that the LORD of hosts hath sent me unto thee.

Zech. 9:10

¹⁰And I will cut off the chariot from Ephraim, and the horse from Jerusalem, and the battle bow shall be cut off: and he shall speak peace unto the heathen: and his dominion *shall be* from sea *even* to sea, and from the river *even* to the ends of the earth.

Some theologians would state that this period when Jesus rules and reigns is not necessarily during a "millennial" time on earth, but will be after the new heavens and the new earth are created. However, when the new heavens and new earth are created there will be "no more sea" as stated in Revelation 21:1. Therefore, this does specifically refer to the Millennial Reign of Christ.

Zep. 3:15-17

¹⁵The LORD hath taken away thy judgments, he hath cast out thine enemy: the king of Israel, *even* the LORD, *is* in the midst of thee: thou shalt not see evil any more.
¹⁶In that day it shall be said to Jerusalem, Fear thou not: *and to* Zion, Let not thine hands be slack.
¹⁷The LORD thy God in the midst of thee *is* mighty; he will save, he will rejoice over thee with joy; he will rest in his love, he will

joy over thee with singing.

Joel 2:27

^{27}And ye shall know that I *am* in the midst of Israel, and *that* I *am* the LORD your God, and none else: and my people shall never be ashamed.

Joel 3:17, 21

^{17}So shall ye know that I *am* the LORD your God dwelling in Zion, my holy mountain: then shall Jerusalem be holy, and there shall no strangers pass through her any more.

^{21}For I will cleanse their blood *that* I have not cleansed: for the LORD dwelleth in Zion.

All of the scripture above refer to Jesus' rule and reign on earth during the Millennium.

2. David will also reign with Christ over Israel during the Millennium.

Ez. 34:23-24

^{23}And I will set up one shepherd over them, and he shall feed them, *even* my servant David; he shall feed them, and he shall be their shepherd.

^{24}And I the LORD will be their God, and my servant David a prince among them; I the LORD have spoken *it*.

Ez. 37:24-25

^{24}And David my servant *shall be* king over them; and they all shall have one shepherd: they shall also walk in my judgments, and observe my statutes, and do them.

^{25}And they shall dwell in the land that I have given unto Jacob my servant, wherein your fathers have dwelt; and they shall dwell therein, *even* they, and their children, and their children's children for ever: and my servant David *shall be* their prince for ever.

Is. 9:7

^{7}Of the increase of *his* government and peace *there shall be* no end, upon the throne of David, and upon his kingdom, to order it, and to establish it with judgment and with justice from henceforth even for ever. The zeal of the LORD of hosts will perform this.

Hos. 3:5

^{5}Afterward shall the children of Israel return, and seek the LORD their God, and David their king; and shall fear the LORD and his goodness in the latter days.

Jer. 30:9

^{9}But they shall serve the LORD their God, and David their king, whom I will raise up unto them.

In the verses above, we see that David will also be a king and prince amongst his people Israel. Some might say that these verses contradict some of the verses relating to Jesus Christ above. And others might say that these verses, relating to David, are really metaphorically speaking of Jesus and not David himself. First, let us clarify that just because David is said to be a king or prince over Israel, does not take away from the rule of Jesus Christ. Jesus will be the Supreme ruler over all the earth and there will be other kings and princes ruling other specific countries, such as David who will rule Israel again. As relates to David being a "type of Christ" or a metaphor for Christ, I believe these verses are speaking directly about David himself. Isaiah 9:7 is speaking of Jesus, but it mentions the fact that there will be "the throne of David" also. Jeremiah makes it clear that David will be resurrected and reign as Israel's king again.

3. Those from the Church Age, the Tribulation Saints who were martyred and the Old Testament saints will also reign with Christ. We have already seen in Revelation 20:4 the thrones and the people who sat on them and that the martyred Tribulation Saints will reign with Christ for one thousand years.

Jer. 23:4

[4] And I will set up shepherds over them which shall feed them: and they shall fear no more, nor be dismayed, neither shall they be lacking, saith the LORD.

II Tim. 2:12

[12] If we suffer, we shall also reign with *him*: if we deny *him*, he also will deny us:

I Cor. 6:2

[2] Do ye not know that the saints shall judge the world? and if the world shall be judged by you, are ye unworthy to judge the smallest matters?

Rev. 1:6

[6] And hath made us kings and priests unto God and his Father; to him *be* glory and dominion for ever and ever. Amen.

As seen in the verses above, Old Testament and Church Age Saints that have been resurrected will reign with Christ during this time.

Lk. 19:16-19

¹⁶Then came the first, saying, Lord, thy pound hath gained ten pounds.
¹⁷And he said unto him, Well, thou good servant: because thou hast been faithful in a very little, have thou authority over ten cities.
¹⁸And the second came, saying, Lord, thy pound hath gained five pounds.
¹⁹And he said likewise to him, Be thou also over five cities.

This is a parable of the "pounds" or the good stewards and is a story of how a Christian who was given responsibility during their life on earth will rule over areas based on their performance as a Christian. Even though this parable uses money to show how God will assign responsibility during the Millennium, stewardship also relates to your time, your love for others, your eagerness to spread the gospel, etc. The main idea of this parable is that some Christians will rule over more areas than others based on their good works while alive on earth before the Rapture.

The Temple During the Millennium

There will be a temple present during the Millennium Period of Christ's reign on earth. Let us see more about this temple.

Joel 3:18

¹⁸And it shall come to pass in that day, *that* the mountains shall drop down new wine, and the hills shall flow with milk, and all the rivers of Judah shall flow with waters, and a fountain shall come forth of the house of the LORD, and shall water the valley of Shittim.

Hag. 2:7-9

⁷And I will shake all nations, and the desire of all nations shall come: and I will fill this house with glory, saith the LORD of

hosts.

[8]The silver *is* mine, and the gold *is* mine, saith the LORD of hosts. [9]The glory of this latter house shall be greater than of the former, saith the LORD of hosts: and in this place will I give peace, saith the LORD of hosts.

Mic. 4:1-2

[1]But in the last days it shall come to pass, *that* the mountain of the house of the LORD shall be established in the top of the mountains, and it shall be exalted above the hills; and people shall flow unto it.

[2]And many nations shall come, and say, Come, and let us go up to the mountain of the LORD, and to the house of the God of Jacob; and he will teach us of his ways, and we will walk in his paths: for the law shall go forth of Zion, and the word of the LORD from Jerusalem.

Is. 2:2-3

[2]And it shall come to pass in the last days, *that* the mountain of the LORD'S house shall be established in the top of the mountains, and shall be exalted above the hills; and all nations shall flow unto it.

[3]And many people shall go and say, Come ye, and let us go up to the mountain of the LORD, to the house of the God of Jacob; and he will teach us of his ways, and we will walk in his paths: for out of Zion shall go forth the law, and the word of the LORD from Jerusalem.

The references above speak about the "house of the Lord" during the Millennial Reign of Christ on earth. We see that this temple will be greater than any of the temples built before and that many people will flock to it to worship and learn.

The Book of Ezekiel describes more about the Millennial Temple than does any other references in scripture. I will not provide all the scripture references found in Ezekiel, but encourage the reader to perform their own study of Ezekiel chapters 40-48 for a detailed description of the Millennial Temple. Some scholars believe that this is the Third Temple, or the Tribulation Temple, which will be re-consecrated and upgraded. Others believe that this is a description of a new Fourth Temple that will be constructed during the Millennium. Either camp could justifiably find supporting scripture for their arguments, so I will not pursue which is correct. There is no doubt that there will be a Millennial Temple whether new or an upgraded one and this will be the subject of our study.

Ezekiel gives detail measurements of this temple, description of what is contained in the temple, the priests that minister in the temple, the duties of these priests and the time period in which Ezekiel's temple exists. Let us show just a few references supporting the fact that this temple exists or is built during the Millennium.

Ez. 43:7

[7]And he said unto me, Son of man, the place of my throne, and the place of the soles of my feet, where I will dwell in the midst of the children of Israel for ever, and my holy name, shall the house of Israel no more defile, *neither* they, nor their kings, by their whoredom, nor by the carcases of their kings in their high places.

Here God states that the "place of my throne" will be where "the place of the soles of my feet" will be when He "dwells in the midst of the children of Israel for ever." Notice there will be no more defilement. This can only be during the Millennium.

Ez. 45:1

[1]Moreover, when ye shall divide by lot the land for inheritance, ye shall offer an oblation unto the LORD, an holy portion of the land: the length *shall be* the length of five and twenty thousand *reeds*, and the breadth *shall be* ten thousand. This *shall be* holy in all the borders thereof round about.

This temple will exist when the land is divided amongst the living Jews. This division will happen at the beginning of the Millennium.

Ez. 47:8

[8]Then said he unto me, These waters issue out toward the east country, and go down into the desert, and go into the sea: *which being* brought forth into the sea, the waters shall be healed.

Notice below the same description of these waters in Zechariah 14. When Jesus comes back to earth at the Second Coming and stands on the Mount of Olives, we are told it splits and a river is formed that stretches from the "former sea," the Mediterranean Sea, through the valley created at the Mount of Olives to the "hinder sea," the Dead Sea.

Zech. 14:4, 8-9

[4]And his feet shall stand in that day upon the mount of Olives, which *is* before Jerusalem on the east, and the mount of Olives shall cleave in the midst thereof toward the east and toward the west, *and there shall be* a very great valley; and half of the mountain shall remove toward the north, and half of it toward the south.

[8]And it shall be in that day, *that* living waters shall go out from Jerusalem; half of them toward the former sea, and half of them toward the hinder sea: in summer and in winter shall it be.

[9]And the LORD shall be king over all the earth: in that day shall there be one LORD, and his name one.

At this time I would like to include some unique features of the temple. I have quoted Dr. Harold Willmington several times in this book because he does such a fantastic job of describing events in an easy to understand fashion. Dr. Willmington states, as relates to the unique features of the Millennium Temple:

" Its unique features.

Several articles and objects present in the temples of Moses, Solomon, and Herod will be absent from the millennial temple.

1. There will be no veil. This was torn in two from top to bottom (Mt. 27:51) and will not reappear in this temple. Thus there will be no barrier to keep man from the glory of God.
2. There will be no table of shewbread. This will not be needed, for the Living Bread himself will be present.
3. There will be no lampstands. These will not be

needed either, since the Light of the World himself will personally shine forth.

4. There will be no Ark of the Covenant. This will also be unnecessary, since the Shekinah Glory himself will hover over all the world, as the glory cloud once did over the ark.

5. The east gate will be closed. Observe the words of Ezekiel: "This gate shall be shut, and no man shall enter in by it; because the Lord, the God of Israel, hath entered in by it; therefore, it shall be shut" (Ezek. 44:2).

This gate, it has been suggested, will remain closed for the following reasons:

> *a.* This will be the gate by which the Lord Jesus Christ enters the temple. As a mark of honor to an eastern king, no person could enter the gate by which he entered.
>
> *b.* It was from the eastern gate that the glory of God departed for the last time in the Old Testament (Ezek. 10:18,19). By sealing the gate, God reminds all those within that his glory will never again depart from his people." *(Willmington's Guide to the Bible, Tyndale House Publishers Inc., pages 222-223)*

The Teachings During the Millennium

The absolute truth will be taught during the Millennium Period. There will be no deceiving teachers during this time.

Ez. 36:25-27

[25]Then will I sprinkle clean water upon you, and ye shall be clean: from all your filthiness, and from all your idols, will I cleanse you.

[26]A new heart also will I give you, and a new spirit will I put within you: and I will take away the stony heart out of your flesh,

and I will give you an heart of flesh.
²⁷And I will put my spirit within you, and cause you to walk in my statutes, and ye shall keep my judgments, and do *them*.
Zech. 13:1-2
¹In that day there shall be a fountain opened to the house of David and to the inhabitants of Jerusalem for sin and for uncleanness.
²And it shall come to pass in that day, saith the LORD of hosts, *that* I will cut off the names of the idols out of the land, and they shall no more be remembered: and also I will cause the prophets and the unclean spirit to pass out of the land.

All those who lived through the Tribulation who were saved will be cleansed and their old nature will be changed to desire to walk in the laws and statutes of God. We are told that there will be no more idol worship during the Millennium and no need for prophets, nor will there be any unclean spirits. The Word of God is complete and there is no need for prophets to prophecy because it has all been written. All the demons have been cast into Hell and they will not be present to tempt mankind as they do today.

Mic. 4:2-5
²And many nations shall come, and say, Come, and let us go up to the mountain of the LORD, and to the house of the God of Jacob; and he will teach us of his ways, and we will walk in his paths: for the law shall go forth of Zion, and the word of the LORD from Jerusalem.
³And he shall judge among many people, and rebuke strong nations afar off; and they shall beat their swords into plowshares, and their spears into pruninghooks: nation shall not lift up a sword against nation, neither shall they learn war any more.
⁴But they shall sit every man under his vine and under his fig tree; and none shall make *them* afraid: for the mouth of the LORD of hosts hath spoken *it*.
⁵For all people will walk every one in the name of his god, and we will walk in the name of the LORD our God for ever and ever.

Micah tells us that Jesus will teach us His ways and His law during the Millennium. We will be taught not to raise our weapons against each other and that we will not be taught of war anymore. There will be no

history books depicting past wars, because God will
want all their attention toward Him and toward what
He has planned for them in the future. Old things will
truly be passed away when we come to this time in the
future.

Is. 12:4-6

⁴And in that day shall ye say, Praise the LORD, call upon his
name, declare his doings among the people, make mention that his
name is exalted.
⁵Sing unto the LORD; for he hath done excellent things: this *is*
known in all the earth.
⁶Cry out and shout, thou inhabitant of Zion: for great *is* the Holy
One of Israel in the midst of thee.

Jer. 50:5

⁵They shall ask the way to Zion with their faces thitherward,
saying, Come, and let us join ourselves to the LORD in a
perpetual covenant *that* shall not be forgotten.

Is. 26:1

¹In that day shall this song be sung in the land of Judah; We have
a strong city; salvation will *God* appoint *for* walls and bulwarks.

Is. 29: 18, 24

¹⁸And in that day shall the deaf hear the words of the book, and
the eyes of the blind shall see out of obscurity, and out of
darkness.
²⁴They also that erred in spirit shall come to understanding, and
they that murmured shall learn doctrine.

Is. 30:20-21

²⁰And *though* the Lord give you the bread of adversity, and the
water of affliction, yet shall not thy teachers be removed into a
corner any more, but thine eyes shall see thy teachers:
²¹And thine ears shall hear a word behind thee, saying, This *is* the
way, walk ye in it, when ye turn to the right hand, and when ye
turn to the left.

Is. 59:21

²¹As for me, this *is* my covenant with them, saith the LORD; My
spirit that *is* upon thee, and my words which I have put in thy
mouth, shall not depart out of thy mouth, nor out of the mouth of
thy seed, nor out of the mouth of thy seed's seed, saith the LORD,
from henceforth and for ever.

Is. 54:13-14

¹³And all thy children *shall be* taught of the LORD; and great
shall be the peace of thy children.

¹⁴In righteousness shalt thou be established: thou shalt be far from oppression; for thou shalt not fear: and from terror; for it shall not come near thee.

Zech. 8:16-17

¹⁶These *are* the things that ye shall do; Speak ye every man the truth to his neighbour; execute the judgment of truth and peace in your gates:

¹⁷And let none of you imagine evil in your hearts against his neighbour; and love no false oath: for all these *are things* that I hate, saith the LORD.

Ps. 85:8-13

⁸I will hear what God the LORD will speak: for he will speak peace unto his people, and to his saints: but let them not turn again to folly.

⁹Surely his salvation *is* nigh them that fear him; that glory may dwell in our land.

¹⁰Mercy and truth are met together; righteousness and peace have kissed *each other*.

¹¹Truth shall spring out of the earth; and righteousness shall look down from heaven.

¹²Yea, the LORD shall give *that which is* good; and our land shall yield her increase.

¹³Righteousness shall go before him; and shall set *us* in the way of his steps.

Ez. 44:23-24

²³And they shall teach my people *the difference* between the holy and profane, and cause them to discern between the unclean and the clean.

²⁴And in controversy they shall stand in judgment; *and* they shall judge it according to my judgments: and they shall keep my laws and my statutes in all mine assemblies; and they shall hallow my sabbaths.

I did not place a lot of commentary between the verses above, because I believe they speak for themselves without my input. However, as you can see we will learn all about God, His Word, the reasons for His laws and doctrines, right from wrong, true Godly love for our neighbor, the complete peace of God and the complete truth about God. This will be everyone's chance to ask questions and receive answers that are absolute truth. We will not have to guess at what God wants in our life during the Millennium, we will know exactly what He wants for us.

There will be a lot of singing. I personally believe that everyone will have the talent to sing praises to God during this time. There are many Christians today that cannot carry a tune, are tone deaf or cannot hear the music in their head. During the Millennium, you will be able to sing praises to the Lamb of God, Jesus Christ. Your voice will be sweet to hear and others will enjoy your talents. There will be no more deaf and blind and people who cannot speak.

I hope you have come to the conclusion that the Millennial Reign of Christ will be on earth and will be a time of joy and bliss that the world has never known. To those who do not believe in a Millennium Period on earth, you are missing out on some of the greatest blessings in scripture and excitement in your Christian life. Get excited about the future with Jesus on this earth and eternity forever. Study His Word and see how it does an excellent job of interpreting itself. When you do, I believe you will come to the same conclusions I have presented above.

16

The End of the Millennium
Satan Loosed
The Great White Throne of Judgment

The thousand years of bliss is over and we are about to see Satan loosed for the last time. During the thousand years of Christ's Reign on earth, many children were born and people lived for hundreds of years. There was no abortion during this time and very few people died because there was virtually no disease. Therefore, over this one thousand-year period billions occupy the earth. I hope the majority of them trusted Christ as their personal Savior, but as we have seen in the previous chapter, many will not accept Him. They have not felt liberty to expose their disbelief due to shame. All they needed was for someone or some being to show them the way of rebellion and they will jump on his bandwagon. The time has come for that individual and his name is Satan.

Satan Loosed and Unbelievers Rebel

Rev. 20:7
And when the thousand years are expired, Satan shall be loosed out of his prison,
Rev. 20:8
And shall go out to deceive the nations which are in the four quarters of the earth, Gog and Magog, to gather them together to battle: the number of whom *is* as the sand of the sea.

Is. 26:10
[10]Let favour be showed to the wicked, *yet* will he not learn righteousness: in the land of uprightness will he deal unjustly, and

will not behold the majesty of the LORD.

Many have asked the question, "Why did God loose Satan? Why did He not just do away with him after the Tribulation?" The answer is that God knew that many people would not trust His Son Jesus as personal Savior during the Millennium, even though they had ample opportunity. He also knew that eternity future was about to begin and He could not allow one unsaved, unholy soul to occupy eternity. He also wanted to show that mankind was inheritably sinful and needed a Savior. For centuries people have blamed society for the evil that people do, but this shows that even in a perfect society, man's evil nature causes him to rebel against God's authority, just like the Bible teaches.

Notice the verse in Isaiah 26 above, where God went out of His way, "Let favour be showed to the wicked," to have the unsaved learn about His Son Jesus, but to no avail. It states that even though the whole of the Millennium Period was to teach about the righteousness of Jesus Christ, they would still not trust Him.

Satan, the father of lies and rebellion, would be the one to expose the sin in these unsaved people. As we see in the scripture above, Satan is loosed after the Millennium from "his prison," the pit where he has been chained. He will deceive those from over the whole earth who are not saved. This is obviously an easy task for Satan, for those who are not saved are looking for an excuse to rebel against God. We are not told how long this took to deceive these people, but I suspect that it was fairly quick.

The "Gog, and Magog" is not the same group that we saw at the beginning of the Tribulation where Russia with its allies attacked Israel. The Gog and Magog mentioned here is a type of all who rebel against God. Their numbers are beyond numbering, which is sad, because of all the opportunities to trust Jesus. They will come from all the corners of the earth to gather for battle.

Rev. 20:9
And they went up on the breadth of the earth, and compassed the camp of the saints about, and the beloved city: and fire came down from God out of heaven, and devoured them.

Verse 9 tells us that they come from all over the earth to Jerusalem and encompass the city. It will not take God long to eradicate this group from the face of the earth. They are completely consumed with fire from heaven and the battle and rebellion is immediately over.

Is. 26:11

[11]LORD, *when* thy hand is lifted up, they will not see: *but* they shall see, and be ashamed for *their* envy at the people; yea, the fire of thine enemies shall devour them.

Isaiah 26:11 shows us that the LORD will destroy this unsaved group immediately. Notice that the reason for them not trusting Jesus is because of "envy" towards "the people." This could mean that they were jealous toward the nation of Israel or towards Godly people in general. It also shows that those who put their trust in Jesus will be blessed more than those who do not. These people could have the same blessings, but they decide in their hearts to let jealousy spring up and jealousy will turn to bitterness, bitterness to complete rebellion and rebellion to idol and cultic worship. Can you imagine someone being jealous of someone else in the Millennium? Everyone will have almost everything they could ask for. Remember that God will answer their prayers even before they pray them. He of course was speaking of those who are saved. The only prayer He will answer for an unsaved person is "God be merciful to me a sinner," or in other words, "God save me through your Son Jesus Christ." By the way, this is the same for all ages past, present and future. The only way to be saved is by trusting the finished work of Jesus on the cross, His burial and His resurrection. This group will not do this and therefore their lives will not be blessed in the same way as those who trust Christ during the Millennium. Therefore, they will become envious.

Satan Cast Into the Lake of Fire Forever

Rev. 20:10
And the devil that deceived them was cast into the lake of fire and brimstone, where the beast and the false prophet *are*, and shall be tormented day and night for ever and ever.

Satan is finally judged by God and cast into the Lake of Fire. This is a literal place, because the "beast" (the Antichrist), and the "false prophet" are still there. The Lake of Fire is the final place of judgment for all demons, Satan, the Antichrist, the False Prophet and as we will see shortly, all the unsaved dead throughout all the ages. It is not a place of annihilation, but a place of torment forever. They will feel pain and torment forever. It is not the same place we see in the Bible called "Hell," "Hades" or "Sheol." We will see the difference in the next few verses of Revelation.

Jude 1:6
[6]And the angels which kept not their first estate, but left their own habitation, he hath reserved in everlasting chains under darkness unto the judgment of the great day.

We are also told that there is a group of demon angels who will be chained like Satan and they will also be judged and cast into the Lake of Fire, which is the final judgment.

Is. 30:33
[33]For Tophet *is* ordained of old; yea, for the king it is prepared; he hath made *it* deep *and* large: the pile thereof *is* fire and much wood; the breath of the LORD, like a stream of brimstone, doth kindle it.

"Tophet" is the Old Testament name for the Lake of Fire. In the New Testament, the Greek word "Gehenna" is used to describe this same place. The earthly physical place of Tophet or Gehenna was probably located just south of Jerusalem. It was a garbage dump that was always burning. Back in the days of Ahaz, this was the place where he sacrificed children to the god Molech, whom he worshipped. It was to appease the "gods" and make them favorable towards Ahaz. However, the Lake of Fire is not on earth, but probably somewhere in the outer universe. We will see in the next few verses where the Lake of Fire is located. It is also called "outer darkness."

We also see that God is the one who "kindle it" or keeps it burning.

Great White Throne Judgment

Rev. 20:11
And I saw a great white throne, and him that sat on it, from whose face the earth and the heaven fled away; and there was found no place for them.

Jn. 5:22
[22]For the Father judgeth no man, but hath committed all judgment unto the Son:

It is very obvious that the one who sits on the "great white throne" is none other than Jesus Christ himself. As we see in John, Jesus will be the supreme judge of all creation, including the fallen angels.

I believe those who died during the Millennium Period that were saved are resurrected, along with those who are alive at this time and are given their glorified immortal bodies. This completes the "first resurrection."

Jn. 5:28-29
[28]Marvel not at this: for the hour is coming, in the which all that are in the graves shall hear his voice,
[29]And shall come forth; they that have done good, unto the resurrection of life; and they that have done evil, unto the resurrection of damnation.

As stated in John above, there will be another

resurrection of both saved and unsaved. The saved, or "done good," are those that died during the Millennium and the unsaved, or "done evil," will be those from all the ages. Remember previously our discussion about the resurrections? Those involved in the "first resurrection" will not see the "second death," the Lake of Fire. This is why those saved, who are living or who died during the Millennium, have to be resurrected before the final judgment of the unsaved.

I Cor. 15:50, 53-54

[50]Now this I say, brethren, that flesh and blood cannot inherit the kingdom of God; neither doth corruption inherit incorruption.

[53]For this corruptible must put on incorruption, and this mortal *must* put on immortality.

[54]So when this corruptible shall have put on incorruption, and this mortal shall have put on immortality, then shall be brought to pass the saying that is written, Death is swallowed up in victory.

The Millennium saints, both dead and alive at this time, cannot occupy eternity in their fleshly bodies, as we see in the scripture above. They have to be cleansed and transformed from corruptible to incorruptible. I also believe that the first resurrection has to be complete before the second resurrection can take place. The second resurrection is not what anyone would want to be a part.

Rev. 20:12

And I saw the dead, small and great, stand before God; and the books were opened: and another book was opened, which is *the book* of life: and the dead were judged out of those things which were written in the books, according to their works.

Rev. 20:13

And the sea gave up the dead which were in it; and death and hell delivered up the dead which were in them: and they were judged every man according to their works.

II Pet. 2:9

[9]The Lord knoweth how to deliver the godly out of temptations, and to reserve the unjust unto the day of judgment to be punished:

Here we see the "second resurrection" or the resurrection of all the unsaved dead from all the ages. As I mentioned previously, resurrection refers to the body. Therefore, all the souls of these people are reunited with their earthly bodies and stand before Jesus Christ to be judged. Colossians 1:17 states, "And he is before all things, and by him all things consist." The word "consist" means completely held together and refers to the even smallest particle. The smallest known particles in the universe are called "quarks and leptons" according to some scientists. Since Jesus controls all the particles of the universe and knows where each and every one is located, He is able to find every cell of each and everyone's body and bring it back together in its original form. These resurrected bodies will not be immortal like those who were a part of the first resurrection. These bodies will be like those that existed on earth, that will feel pain and suffering, yet will not be destroyed or consumed.

All those who were cast into Hell will be raised and reunited with their bodies. Notice it makes no difference if someone were buried at sea or on earth, cremated or any other way someone died. They will be raised to be judged by Jesus.

According to Verses 12-13, those who are judged at this Great White Throne Judgment, will be judged on their works. God has kept a record of everything someone does on earth, whether good or bad. These verses tend to suggest there will be degrees of punishment in the Lake of Fire. Some will suffer more than others, but all the unsaved will suffer forever.

Let us view some references to this judgment as relates to their works and degrees of punishment.

1.   Their Works.

Jude 1:15-16

[15]To execute judgment upon all, and to convince all that are ungodly among them of all their ungodly deeds which they have ungodly committed, and of all their hard *speeches* which ungodly sinners have spoken against him.
[16]These are murmurers, complainers, walking after their own lusts; and their mouth speaketh great swelling *words*, having men's persons in admiration because of

advantage.

Acts 17:31

[31]Because he hath appointed a day, in the which he will judge the world in righteousness by *that* man whom he hath ordained; *whereof* he hath given assurance unto all *men*, in that he hath raised him from the dead.

The fact is that there will be a judgment of those who are unsaved and it will be according to their deeds done on earth. Notice in Jude some of the characteristics that dominated those who are unsaved. Also in Acts we see that Jesus will be the judge and that all His judgments will be righteous. In other words, no one will have a chance to excuse or explain. Everyone will know they are guilty.

Heb. 4:13

[13]Neither is there any creature that is not manifest in his sight: but all things *are* naked and opened unto the eyes of him with whom we have to do.

Rom. 2:16

[16]In the day when God shall judge the secrets of men by Jesus Christ according to my gospel.

Mt. 7:21-23

[21]Not every one that saith unto me, Lord, Lord, shall enter into the kingdom of heaven; but he that doeth the will of my Father which is in heaven.
[22]Many will say to me in that day, Lord, Lord, have we not prophesied in thy name? and in thy name have cast out devils? and in thy name done many wonderful works?
[23]And then will I profess unto them, I never knew you: depart from me, ye that work iniquity.

Nothing will be hidden from Jesus. Everything will be brought to each individual's attention, including all their thoughts, even when they thought it was only known to themselves. Oh, the shame that will grip everyone as they stand one on one with Jesus and without excuse. They will now truly confess that Jesus is Lord, but it will be too late.

Notice that good works do not get you to heaven. It takes faith and trust in Jesus Christ as your personal Savior. Matthew tells us that there will be many "religious" people that fall into this category and realize too late that they trusted their religion, their church membership, their Jewish heritage, their leadership in the church, their giving to charities, etc., but they did not trust Christ.

2. The Degrees of Punishment.

Lk. 12:47-48

[47]And that servant, which knew his lord's will, and prepared not *himself*, neither did according to his will, shall be beaten with many *stripes*.
[48]But he that knew not, and did commit things worthy of stripes, shall be beaten with few *stripes*. For unto whomsoever much is given, of him shall be much required: and to whom men have committed much, of him they will ask the more.

Mt. 11:22-24

[22]But I say unto you, It shall be more tolerable for Tyre and Sidon at the day of judgment, than for you.
[23]And thou, Capernaum, which art exalted unto heaven, shalt be brought down to hell: for if the mighty works, which have been done in thee, had been done in Sodom, it would have remained until this day.
[24]But I say unto you, That it shall be more tolerable for the land of Sodom in the day of judgment, than for thee.

Rom. 2:5-6

[5]But after thy hardness and impenitent heart treasurest up unto thyself wrath against the day of wrath and revelation of the righteous judgment of God;
[6]Who will render to every man according to his deeds:

Mt. 23:14

[14]Woe unto you, scribes and Pharisees, hypocrites! for ye devour widows' houses, and for a pretence make long prayer: therefore ye shall receive the greater damnation.

The references above show that there will be

degrees of punishment in the Lake of Fire. However, regardless of the degree of punishment, whether it is less or more than someone else, the fact is that they will be tormented forever. If for no other reason, this is the reason we need to tell everyone about the saving power of Jesus Christ. Even though many will scoff and ridicule your witness for Jesus, you know that if they do not accept him, they will spend eternity in the Lake of Fire. As many people stand before Jesus and are judged, I am sure their thoughts will go back to the time when someone tried to tell them about Jesus and they would not listen. Their mocking and ridicule will now be turned to shame and torment.

Rev. 20:14
And death and hell were cast into the lake of fire. This is the second death.
Rev. 20:15
And whosoever was not found written in the book of life was cast into the lake of fire.

In these verses we see that "death and hell" are cast into the "lake of fire." We are also told that this is the "second death." This is not the death many believe today, where someone is buried and that is the end of it. This "second death" is separation from God forever in the Lake of Fire where unsaved mankind, Satan, the demons, the Antichrist and the False Prophet will be tormented forever. Neither Hell nor the Lake of Fire was prepared for man. It was prepared for Satan and his demons. However, because of man's sin and rejection of Jesus Christ as Savior, it became a place for unsaved mankind also.

We saw in Verses 12-13 that several books were opened for judgment purposes. Here we see "the book of life" is opened to see if their names are found written down. I believe that every person who was ever conceived, will have their name written in the book of life. The reason is that God is not willing that any should perish but have everlasting life, so He leaves their name in this book until they die. If they did not accept His Son Jesus while on earth, then I believe their name is blotted out of the book of life, sealing their doom to the Lake of Fire.

Someone might ask, what about babies, aborted babies and others that could never understand what sin was in their minds?

Ps. 139:13, 16

[13]For thou hast possessed my reins: thou hast covered me in my mother's womb.

[16]Thine eyes did see my substance, yet being unperfect; and in thy book all *my members* were written, *which* in continuance were fashioned, when *as yet there was* none of them.

For aborted babies, babies who die before or just after birth, very young children, many of the mentally handicap and anyone who dies that never came to the point in their life to know right from wrong, will also have their names in the book of life and their names will not be blotted out. Yes, the aborted babies have been named by God, even though they never had an earthly name.

Can someone's name be blotted out of this book of life?

Rev. 3:5

[5]He that overcometh, the same shall be clothed in white raiment; and I will not blot out his name out of the book of life, but I will confess his name before my Father, and before his angels.

Rev. 21:27

[27]And there shall in no wise enter into it any thing that defileth, neither *whatsoever* worketh abomination, or *maketh* a lie: but they which are written in the Lamb's book of life.

These verses talk about the book of life and that names can be blotted out of this book. Verse 27 states that only the saved will have their names left in the book of life. Unfortunately, God's pencil <u>does</u> have an eraser when it comes to the book of life. I hope your name is never erased. If someone trusts Jesus as their personal Savior, his name can never be erased, because God will never forsake His people. You cannot lose your salvation, because it is God who controls the eraser and not you and He has told us that He will never leave us nor forsake us. When you choose Jesus as Savior, God makes sure your name in the book of life is sealed in non-erasable ink. What God has sealed, no man or angel can remove.

Mt. 13:49-50

[49]So shall it be at the end of the world: the angels shall come forth, and sever the wicked from among the just,
[50]And shall cast them into the furnace of fire: there shall be wailing and gnashing of teeth.

Jude 1:7-8, 10-13

[7]Even as Sodom and Gomorrha, and the cities about them in like manner, giving themselves over to fornication, and going after strange flesh, are set forth for an example, suffering the vengeance of eternal fire.
[8]Likewise also these *filthy* dreamers defile the flesh, despise dominion, and speak evil of dignities.
[10]But these speak evil of those things which they know not: but what they know naturally, as brute beasts, in those things they corrupt themselves.
[11]Woe unto them! for they have gone in the way of Cain, and ran greedily after the error of Balaam for reward, and perished in the gainsaying of Core.
[12]These are spots in your feasts of charity, when they feast with you, feeding themselves without fear: clouds *they are* without water, carried about of winds; trees whose fruit withereth, without fruit, twice dead, plucked up by the roots;
[13]Raging waves of the sea, foaming out their own shame; wandering stars, to whom is reserved the blackness of darkness for ever.

We are told that this furnace of fire is an actual place of torment and that there will be blackness and darkness forever.

There will be awful suffering in this Lake of Fire for those who are condemned to this place.

Mt. 8:12
[12]But the children of the kingdom shall be cast out into outer darkness: there shall be weeping and gnashing of teeth.

Mt. 22:13
[13]Then said the king to the servants, Bind him hand and foot, and take him away, and cast *him* into outer darkness; there shall be weeping and gnashing of teeth.

Mt. 25:30
[30]And cast ye the unprofitable servant into outer darkness: there shall be weeping and gnashing of teeth.

Mk. 9:44
[44]Where their worm dieth not, and the fire is not quenched.

These verses tell of some of the awful suffering that will take place in the Lake of Fire. We are told that it is "outer darkness," which seems to suggest that it is somewhere out in the universe and not on earth. Hell is assumed to be in the center of the earth by most scholars, but the Lake of Fire will be somewhere beyond this universe. It sounds like the "black hole" that scientists say exists somewhere in the outer universe. Regardless of its location, it will be a place no one would dare choose to go. However, by not choosing Christ, they unknowingly choose the Lake of Fire. There will be weeping and gnashing of teeth because of the pain.

Is. 26:14
[14]*They are* dead, they shall not live; *they are* deceased, they shall not rise: therefore hast thou visited and destroyed them, and made all their memory to perish.

Isaiah tells us that these who are cast into the Lake of Fire will be remembered no more. When it states "their memory to perish," it does not mean that their individual memories will perish and that they will not remember what is happening to them. No, this means that the saved will no longer remember them anymore. We will see later where Jesus will wipe all the tears from the eyes of those who are saved. Their memories of these unsaved, will no longer be a part of their thoughts.

The word "destroyed" does not mean that their bodies are consumed as a result of the fire. It means that Jesus has overthrown, abandoned or made them to suffer in a desolate place.

As we saw in Revelation 21:14, Death and Hell are cast into the Lake of Fire. This means that those who died and were cast into Hell were a part of this judgment and that there will no longer be death and there will no longer be a place called Hell.

I Cor. 15:24-26

[24]Then *cometh* the end, when he shall have delivered up the kingdom to God, even the Father; when he shall have put down all rule and all authority and power.
[25]For he must reign, till he hath put all enemies under his feet.
[26]The last enemy *that* shall be destroyed *is* death.

As I Corinthians tells us, Jesus has now put down all rule and authority and power and has conquered all His enemies. Death was the last enemy to be destroyed. The earth, as we know it, is about to undergo a drastic change. Verse 24 also tells us that Jesus has taken His kingdom from off the earth to God the Father. The next chapter of this book will explain why this has happened.

17

New Heaven and New Earth
The New Jerusalem

New Heaven and New Earth

The first and second resurrections are now complete. Everyone who was part of the first resurrection, or the resurrection to life, has been given their immortal bodies and taken off the earth into heaven. Everyone who was a part of the second resurrection, or the second death, has been cast into the Lake of Fire. The earth as we know it at this point is no longer occupied by human beings.

I asked a question in the beginning of our study "Will this world, as we know it today, come to an end?" The answer is, Yes! This chapter will describe how this will happen. Note that the earth will not be consumed away to nothing, but will be reformed.

Rev. 21:1
And I saw a new heaven and a new earth: for the first heaven and the first earth were passed away; and there was no more sea.

There is now a new heaven and new earth. God has now refined the old earth with fire so that the old curse of sin would be removed. There will be no more sin since everyone has been judged for their sin. The unsaved were judged because of their unbelief. The sin judgment of those who were saved was placed on Jesus Christ at the cross, because they accepted His atonement for their sin when they believed and trusted in Jesus.

Verse 1 tells us "the first heaven and first earth were passed away." Heaven is the atmospheric heaven, not the heaven where the planets reside. The word "passed away" does not mean that it is annihilated, but that it is refined. When you take gold and refine it, it is purified, but not destroyed. The metal still exists, but all of the dross has been burned away from it. This is the same manner in which the new heaven and earth are refined.

Ps. 104:5

⁵*Who* laid the foundations of the earth, *that* it should not be removed for ever.

Psalms tells us that the foundations upon which this earth was built will never be removed. Therefore, the new heaven and new earth will be refined as I stated above and not annihilated.

Ps. 102:25-28

²⁵Of old hast thou laid the foundation of the earth: and the heavens *are* the work of thy hands.

²⁶They shall perish, but thou shalt endure: yea, all of them shall wax old like a garment; as a vesture shalt thou change them, and they shall be changed:

Heb. 1:10-12

¹⁰And, Thou, Lord, in the beginning hast laid the foundation of the earth; and the heavens are the works of thine hands:

¹¹They shall perish; but thou remainest; and they all shall wax old as doth a garment;

¹²And as a vesture shalt thou fold them up, and they shall be changed: but thou art the same, and thy years shall not fail.

In Psalms and Hebrews, we see that the foundations have been laid. The word "perish" once again does not mean to annihilate, but "to change." We see this in the last part of Psalms 102:26 and Hebrews 1:12, when it mentions that they shall be changed. Notice also in Hebrews verse 12, that God never changes and that He lives forever.

Another characteristic of the new earth is there will be no

more sea. The evolutionists scoff at this, because the sea to them is sacred because they believe "life evolved" from the sea. This proves even further that the sea is not the origin of life. God is the origin of life and He created Adam from the dust of the earth. He did not evolve him from the murk of the sea.

Is. 66:22

[22]For as the new heavens and the new earth, which I will make, shall remain before me, saith the LORD, so shall your seed and your name remain.

Mt. 5:18

[18]For verily I say unto you, Till heaven and earth pass, one jot or one tittle shall in no wise pass from the law, till all be fulfilled.

Lk. 21:33

[33]Heaven and earth shall pass away: but my words shall not pass away.

II Pet. 3:10-13

[10]But the day of the Lord will come as a thief in the night; in the which the heavens shall pass away with a great noise, and the elements shall melt with fervent heat, the earth also and the works that are therein shall be burned up.
[11]*Seeing* then *that* all these things shall be dissolved, what manner *of persons* ought ye to be in *all* holy conversation and godliness,
[12]Looking for and hasting unto the coming of the day of God, wherein the heavens being on fire shall be dissolved, and the elements shall melt with fervent heat?
[13]Nevertheless we, according to his promise, look for new heavens and a new earth, wherein dwelleth righteousness.

The references above support even further that the heavens and earth will be refined by fire and fervent heat. Sin has ruled the old earth since its beginning in the Garden of Eden. Because sin and death have been eradicated, God will purge this old earth to make it new.

The New Jerusalem

Since we now have a new heaven and new earth that is no longer affected by the curse of sin, God shows off His wonderful city that has been built for this specific time and purpose. We are about to see, literally, heaven on earth.

Jn. 14:1-3

[1]Let not your heart be troubled: ye believe in God, believe also in me.
[2]In my Father's house are many mansions: if *it were* not *so*, I would have told you. I go to prepare a place for you.
[3]And if I go and prepare a place for you, I will come again, and receive you unto myself; that where I am, *there* ye may be also.

The New Jerusalem is the place where Jesus stated in John, that He would go and prepare a place for us and will come again. We will see in the next several verses that beautiful city full of mansions, which Jesus specifically designed for all those who trusted Him as their personal Savior throughout all the ages.

Rev. 21:2

And I John saw the holy city, new Jerusalem, coming down from God out of heaven, prepared as a bride adorned for her husband.

John is as excited as anyone could be. Notice the emphasis, "And I John saw." There are only two places in the Bible where this is used. It is used in Verse 2 above and then again in Revelation 22:8. He is elated and excited to say the least. John was considered the most humble and loving of the Apostles. In his book, John, he never uses his name, so as not to call attention to anyone but Jesus Christ. He was also known as the beloved disciple. But here he is overwhelmed and excited about the fact that He is seeing the city that He wrote about in John 14. He was told by Jesus that Jesus was preparing a place full of mansions, but obviously he could never imagine the majesty. Now he sees it firsthand!

Ever notice at weddings in America, that everyone is looking at the bride? Even the homeliest of brides seem to glow in beauty at a wedding. By the way, beauty comes from the heart and not from the outward appearance. I have seen some Christian ladies that had no outward beauty, but were beautiful because of their sweet Christian spirit. I have also seen some of the most outwardly beautiful women that could be found on earth, yet their terrible countenance and bad attitude made their beauty of none affect.

I Cor. 2:9

⁹But as it is written, Eye hath not seen, nor ear heard, neither have entered into the heart of man, the things which God hath prepared for them that love him.

This New Jerusalem is gorgeous! We cannot comprehend what God has prepared for us. You have heard your friends come back from vacation and describe the scenery. And then they make the statement, "I wish you could have been there. You have to see it for yourself!" Well you can see this wonderful scene and live in one of these wonderful mansions if you have trusted Christ as your personal Savior. I have heard the old country preacher say, "Just give me a cabin on the hillside of heaven and that will be enough for me." We all know what he meant, but I am excited about this city filled with mansions, myself. Jesus has promised it and we are going to get it!

Rev. 21:3

And I heard a great voice out of heaven saying, Behold, the tabernacle of God *is* with men, and he will dwell with them, and they shall be his people, and God himself shall be with them, *and be* their God.

We are told that God will dwell with men and be their God forever. I happen to believe that this is the whole Godhead, including God the Father, God the Son and God the Holy Spirit. No one could see God the Father in their mortal bodies and live. Now all of the saved have their glorified immortal bodies and are able to look upon God the Father.

Rev. 7:16

They shall hunger no more, neither thirst any more; neither shall the sun light on them, nor any heat.

Rev. 7:17
For the Lamb which is in the midst of the throne shall feed them, and shall lead them unto living fountains of waters: and God shall wipe away all tears from their eyes.

I have also included these verses at this time because they depict the events of this time period.

Rev. 21:4
And God shall wipe away all tears from their eyes; and there shall be no more death, neither sorrow, nor crying, neither shall there be any more pain: for the former things are passed away.

Is. 65:19
[19]And I will rejoice in Jerusalem, and joy in my people: and the voice of weeping shall be no more heard in her, nor the voice of crying.

Is. 25:8
[8]He will swallow up death in victory; and the Lord GOD will wipe away tears from off all faces; and the rebuke of his people shall he take away from off all the earth: for the LORD hath spoken *it*.

These verses are what all of humanity has waited to hear. However, only the saved will hear that all their tears will be wiped away, there will be no more death, sorrow, crying or pain. All of these emotions were thrust upon man when Adam sinned in the garden and brought sin upon all mankind. The "former things" are talking about the sin cursed world.

Rev. 21:5
And he that sat upon the throne said, Behold, I make all things new. And he said unto me, Write: for these words are true and faithful.

Verse 5 tells us this is a new beginning, not the end, as most people have predicted. There is no question about what we are told in these verses, for God tells us that they are "true and faithful." We can trust everything God tells us.

Rev. 21:6
And he said unto me, It is done. I am Alpha and Omega, the

beginning and the end. I will give unto him that is athirst of the fountain of the water of life freely.

> Ps. 102:27-28
> [27]But thou *art* the same, and thy years shall have no end. [28]The children of thy servants shall continue, and their seed shall be established before thee.

"It is done," meaning that Jesus' plan for redemption of all creation is now complete. Salvation is finished and all the saved are with Him forever.

The words "Alpha and Omega" appear only in the Book of Revelation. Alpha is the first letter in the Greek alphabet and Omega is the last. In Revelation, this term is used four times. It specifically states that Jesus is God and that He is the beginning (the first) and He is the ending (the last). He is creator and He is eternity.

We also see in Verse 6 that anyone who "is athirst," He will give him the "water of life freely." This means that Jesus, who is the water of life, will satisfy the thirsty soul and make Himself known to everyone who desires to know Him. He told the Samaritan woman at the well that if she took of Him, the living water, she would never thirst again. He was talking about His salvation and eternity.

Rev. 21:7
He that overcometh shall inherit all things; and I will be his God, and he shall be my son.

Once again we are told that the saved "overcometh," and shall inherit "all things."

> Is. 60:21
> [21]Thy people also *shall be* all righteous: they shall inherit the land for ever, the branch of my planting, the work of my hands, that I may be glorified.

God tells Isaiah that all the righteous will inherit the land and all of God's blessings forever.

Rev. 21:8
But the fearful, and unbelieving, and the abominable, and

murderers, and whoremongers, and sorcerers, and idolaters, and all liars, shall have their part in the lake which burneth with fire and brimstone: which is the second death.

We are reminded that the unsaved will not be around anymore and that they, unfortunately, will continue to experience pain and suffering in the Lake of Fire. I left this verse in this spot because I believe that there is significance with it showing at this time again, in scripture. I believe that God wants us to know and understand that the Lake of Fire is a literal place and that even though He has made a new heaven and new earth and all things new, the Lake of Fire continues to torment its inhabitants throughout eternity.

Rev. 21:9
And there came unto me one of the seven angels which had the seven vials full of the seven last plagues, and talked with me, saying, Come hither, I will shew thee the bride, the Lamb's wife.

I believe that the New Jerusalem is the place that Jesus prepared for His bride, the Church. However, I believe that everyone will be invited to inherit this New Jerusalem, now as one family, God's family.

Ep. 1:10-11
[10]That in the dispensation of the fulness of times he might gather together in one all things in Christ, both which are in heaven, and which are on earth; *even* in him:
[11]In whom also we have obtained an inheritance, being predestinated according to the purpose of him who worketh all things after the counsel of his own will:

Ephesians tells us that every saved individual from all the ages, "fullness of times," along with everything in heaven will be brought together to be "one" family. The whole Bible was written to tell us about Jesus Christ our Savior and our personal relationship with Him.

Someone may have questioned earlier, "what happened to

all those who were on earth when it was refined with fire?" As I stated earlier, I believe that all the saved were taken off the earth just before the refining of the earth took place by God. In Revelation 21:9 and Ephesians 1, we see that all were taken to heaven just before the refining process occurred. Now we see them coming back from heaven in The New Jerusalem.

Rev. 21:10
And he carried me away in the spirit to a great and high mountain, and shewed me that great city, the holy Jerusalem, descending out of heaven from God,

The New Jerusalem is descending out of heaven and we are about to see the description of the foundation and materials that make up the New Jerusalem. As we will see later, this city will hover just above the earth and not actually rest on the earth.

Today when foundations are laid and walls built, builders use a variety of sand, dirt and gravel for the foundation and pour concrete on top. Walls are usually built with concrete, concrete block, steel, wood, brick, etc. In poorer countries, mud and straw are used. All of these materials are used to keep the cost down and provide support for the structure. God does not have a budget limitation. We will see in the following verses that our God inlays within these foundations of the New Jerusalem the most expensive precious stones known to man. He uses precious stones, which were part of His creation over 6000 years ago. He does not settle for three or four foundations, but this city will have twelve foundations with these stones inlaid within them. It will have twelve gates of pearl and the walls will be made out of precious stones also. Realize that there are different varieties of some stones as to the colors, but the fact remains that regardless of the color, the majestic beauty is beyond comprehension. We will never grow tired of "touring that city," as the old gospel song says. Now let us see the majesty of this city.

Rev. 21:11
Having the glory of God: and her light *was* like unto a stone most precious, even like a jasper stone, clear as crystal;

A jasper stone, clear as crystal, is known as a diamond. Have you ever gone to a jewelry store and seen the diamonds on display? Notice they have special lights beaming down on each of the diamonds, so you can see the glowing crystal clearness of each diamond. When the light shines through the diamond, the prisms create a rainbow effect. White light enters and rainbow colors exit. We are told in this verse that the "glory of God: and her light" is like this stone. I believe all of us will rejoice to see this sight, but I have to say, from the human standpoint, the ladies will enjoy this more than us men. Ladies seem to see beauty in things that most men seem to miss. However, no one will miss seeing the beauty at this time. With our glorified bodies, we will see this beauty as never before.

Rev. 21:12
And had a wall great and high, *and* had twelve gates, and at the gates twelve angels, and names written thereon, which are *the names* of the twelve tribes of the children of Israel:
Rev. 21:13
On the east three gates; on the north three gates; on the south three gates; and on the west three gates.

There are twelve gates in this city and each gate is named for each of the twelve tribes of Israel. Gates were used to allow access to the city. The twelve tribes of Israel were used by God to give us access to the scriptures and thereby give everyone opportunity to know Jesus Christ as Lord and Savior, since He is the Word. It was through the Jews that we were given the Word of God and it was through the Jews that our Savior Jesus Christ was born and walked among mankind. I have given the spiritual application to these verses, but these verses are a literal description of the gates of this literal city.

Rev. 21:14
And the wall of the city had twelve foundations, and in them the names of the twelve apostles of the Lamb.
Rev. 21:15
And he that talked with me had a golden reed to measure the city, and the gates thereof, and the wall thereof.
Rev. 21:16
And the city lieth foursquare, and the length is as large as the breadth: and he measured the city with the reed, twelve thousand furlongs. The length and the breadth and the height of it are equal.

As I stated earlier, in today's measurements, eight furlongs equates to approximately one mile. Therefore, this city would be 1500 miles wide, long and high. It is a city, as the gospel songs says, "that is built four square."

Rev. 21:17
And he measured the wall thereof, an hundred *and* forty *and* four cubits, *according to* the measure of a man, that is, of the angel.

A cubit is considered in today's measurements to be about 18 inches. Therefore, the walls will be about 216 feet high. These walls would not be considered very high when compared to the height of the city. It is obvious that they are not built for protection, for there would never be invaders. These walls were built for pure beauty!

Rev. 21:18
And the building of the wall of it was *of* jasper: and the city *was* pure gold, like unto clear glass.

Can you imagine walls built of solid "jasper?" What a beautiful sight to behold! Whether this jasper was the same clear jasper/diamond, as mentioned earlier, or the non-clear jasper, it will still be gorgeous.

Rev. 21:19
And the foundations of the wall of the city *were* garnished with all manner of precious stones. The first foundation *was* jasper; the

second, sapphire; the third, a chalcedony; the fourth, an emerald;

It is hard to visualize the beauty of these stone foundations. Remember in the verses above, that the city is 1500 miles square. That means that the foundations are at least 1500 miles wide and 1500 miles long. We are not given the depth of each foundation, nor what constitutes the makeup of the foundations themselves, but we do know that each foundation will be inlaid with these beautiful stones. All you will see are these stones. In most buildings, you never see the foundation. In this city, since it hovers slightly above the earth, all the foundations will be seen.

Rev. 21:20
The fifth, sardonyx; the sixth, sardius; the seventh, chrysolyte; the eighth, beryl; the ninth, a topaz; the tenth, a chrysoprasus; the eleventh, a jacinth; the twelfth, an amethyst.

Everyone of these twelve precious stones rank the highest in what is known as the Moh's Scale of Hardness. The diamond is the hardest stone by far and is used for cutting through other stones, minerals and products. Diamond tip drill bits, saws and other diamond tip tools are used to cut through hard materials that simply cannot be done with regular metal tips.

Rev. 21:21
And the twelve gates *were* twelve pearls; every several gate was of one pearl: and the street of the city *was* pure gold, as it were transparent glass.

Can you imagine each gate made out of one giant pearl? That would be one huge oyster! Of course, God does not need an oyster to make His pearls. Once again, we cannot comprehend this glowing beauty. We are also told the streets are "pure gold," so pure that they appear as "transparent glass."

Rev. 21:22
And I saw no temple therein: for the Lord God Almighty and the Lamb are the temple of it.
Rev. 21:23
And the city had no need of the sun, neither of the moon, to shine in it: for the glory of God did lighten it, and the Lamb *is* the light thereof.

Is. 60:19-20
[19]The sun shall be no more thy light by day; neither for brightness shall the moon give light unto thee: but the LORD shall be unto thee an everlasting light, and thy God thy glory.
[20]Thy sun shall no more go down; neither shall thy moon withdraw itself: for the LORD shall be thine everlasting light, and the days of thy mourning shall be ended.

We are told that eternity future will not have a temple, a sun or a moon. Jesus will be the temple and He will be the light.

Rev. 21:24
And the nations of them which are saved shall walk in the light of it: and the kings of the earth do bring their glory and honour into it.
Rev. 21:25
And the gates of it shall not be shut at all by day: for there shall be no night there.

There will be no night during eternity future, therefore I must conclude that there will only be daytime.

Rev. 21:26
And they shall bring the glory and honour of the nations into it.
Rev. 21:27
And there shall in no wise enter into it any thing that defileth, neither *whatsoever* worketh abomination, or *maketh* a lie: but they which are written in the Lamb's book of life.

Once again, we are told that only the saved will occupy this city. I also assume that there will be no more childbirth or new generations, since everyone will be in their glorified bodies.

Rev. 22:1
And he shewed me a pure river of water of life, clear as crystal, proceeding out of the throne of God and of the Lamb.

From the throne will proceed a river of crystal clear water. Have you ever visited the clear waters of Silver Springs, Florida and many other clear springs in Florida? The river mentioned above will be clearer than those waters found in Silver Springs. The water will not have to be filtered or contain additives, because it will be 100% pure.

Rev. 22:2
In the midst of the street of it, and on either side of the river, *was there* the tree of life, which bare twelve *manner of* fruits, *and* yielded her fruit every month: and the leaves of the tree *were* for the healing of the nations.

There will be the "tree of life" on both sides of this crystal clear river and this tree will produce twelve different kinds of fruit. This is the same type of tree that was in the original Garden of Eden. It seems as though we will still enjoy eating throughout eternity. Nothing will be forbidden. However, we will all be vegetarians, because there will be no more death of humans or animals. We will enjoy the fruits of the ground that God planted for us to enjoy originally, when He created Adam and placed him in the Garden of Eden.

Rev. 22:3
And there shall be no more curse: but the throne of God and of the Lamb shall be in it; and his servants shall serve him:
Rev. 22:4
And they shall see his face; and his name *shall be* in their foreheads.
Rev. 22:5
And there shall be no night there; and they need no candle, neither light of the sun; for the Lord God giveth them light: and they shall reign for ever and ever.

The curse on mankind and creation is finally lifted. The removal of the curse is what mankind has been waiting for since Adam sinned in the Garden of Eden.

Let us recap some of the characteristics of the new heavens and earth and The New Jerusalem, in no particular order.

1. No sun or moon, because Jesus will be the light.
2. No night, for it will always be daytime.
3. No temple, because Jesus will be the temple.
4. No sea.
5. No Satan or Demons.
6. No more curse, no more sin.
7. No death, crying, sorrow or pain.
8. All the redeemed of all the ages will be in their glorified immortal bodies.
9. We will see the Father face to face.
10. The New Jerusalem that Jesus prepared for everyone who trusted Him as Savior, will be our home.
11. The New Jerusalem will be 1500 miles square.
12. The New Jerusalem will hover above the earth.
13. It will have 12 foundations, inlaid with precious stones and named after the 12 Apostles.
14. It will have 12 gates, made of one pearl each, named after the 12 tribes of Israel.
15. It will have streets made of the purest gold that are so shiny that they are crystal clear.
16. The walls will be 216 feet high and made of jasper.
17. There will be the pure river of life flowing from God's throne and on each side of the river will be the tree of life.

I am sure this is just the beginning of the joys that we will experience during this time. This is certainly not the ending of the ages, but the true beginning when all the saints will rejoice forevermore.

18

Jesus' Closing Statements

We have just seen a glorious picture of what it will be like to live with Jesus throughout all eternity. However, as seen in the two scripture references below, what we have just studied about eternity future is only a smidgen of what actually will be prepared for all His saints. As seen in the verses below, we could not begin to imagine the glory that God has prepared, nor could we comprehend it with our human mind.

Is. 64:4

[4]For since the beginning of the world *men* have not heard, nor perceived by the ear, neither hath the eye seen, O God, beside thee, *what* he hath prepared for him that waiteth for him.

I Cor. 2:9

[9]But as it is written, Eye hath not seen, nor ear heard, neither have entered into the heart of man, the things which God hath prepared for them that love him.

Paul quotes Isaiah 64:4 in I Corinthians 2:9, but adds one more tidbit of information about what we do not know about what God has prepared for all His saints. Paul adds, "neither have entered into the heart of man," meaning not only our hearing and seeing senses, but all our senses have not known nor could comprehend the fabulous beauty that God has prepared for us. I do not know about you, but I cannot wait to experience eternity in my glorified immortal body.

As we leave the most exciting revelation that is known to man, we hear Jesus' admonition and closing remarks to John and to everyone.

Rev. 22:6
And he said unto me, These sayings *are* faithful and true: and the Lord God of the holy prophets sent his angel to show unto his servants the things which must shortly be done.

In His closing remarks, He assures us that what has just been said previously is "faithful and true" and that God through His holy prophets have given us His Word. I happen to believe that He is not only referring to the Book of Revelation, but to all the scriptures, for the Book of Revelation is the last of God's revealed Word to be penned into the canon of scripture. Let us see a few scripture references that tell us that God had all scripture penned by holy men of God as God himself directed them to write.

I Pet. 1:21
[21] For the prophecy came not in old time by the will of man: but holy men of God spake *as they were* moved by the Holy Ghost.

Heb. 1:1-2
[1] God, who at sundry times and in divers manners spake in time past unto the fathers by the prophets,
[2] Hath in these last days spoken unto us by *his* Son, whom he hath appointed heir of all things, by whom also he made the worlds;

II Tim. 3:16-17
[16] All scripture *is* given by inspiration of God, and *is* profitable for doctrine, for reproof, for correction, for instruction in righteousness:
[17] That the man of God may be perfect, thoroughly furnished unto all good works.

We see in the references above that the scripture of God was originally given to us through prophets. In the "last days," the New Testament was given to us through Jesus Christ, through His Apostles and Disciples who were used to pen the New Testament through the revelation of Jesus Christ. Obviously, all scripture is given by inspiration and Jesus is the Word. However, I do not believe that there are any more Prophets or Apostles living today or after John penned the last words of the Book of Revelation. See verses

18-19 below for further commentary on the canon of scripture.

Rev. 22:7
Behold, I come quickly: blessed *is* he that keepeth the sayings of the prophecy of this book.

Jesus is stating that He is coming again very soon. The word "keepeth" means "to take care of or attend to carefully." In other words, those who desire the prophecy in this book will be blessed because their desire is to study it carefully and with respect and reverence. Many people shy away from the study of the Book of Revelation and that is exactly why I wrote this book. I wanted to help those who truly desire to know the truths that are written herein, to receive this blessing that I have received as a result of careful study. I can tell you that I have truly written this book with care and prayer so that others could joy in the excitement contained herein. I truly hope you have been blessed with this study as much as I have been blessed presenting it. If so, pass your excitement on to others. Show them the way to salvation and show those who desire to know God's word how they can grow and look forward to Jesus' coming again.

Rev. 22:8
And I John saw these things, and heard *them*. And when I had heard and seen, I fell down to worship before the feet of the angel which showed me these things.
Rev. 22:9
Then saith he unto me, See *thou do it* not: for I am thy fellowservant, and of thy brethren the prophets, and of them which keep the sayings of this book: worship God.

As I stated earlier, John uses his name for the second time in all of his writings and it is because of his excitement of what he has just witnessed. We are told in the two verses above that John was told by the "angel" not to worship him for he was a "fellowservant" and "of thy brethren the prophets." I believe the better word to use here instead of "angel" is "messenger." I believe that this individual is none other than Daniel himself. John has been characterized by many scholars as the "New Testament Daniel" because of his style of writing and the visions being almost the same as Daniel's. I stated earlier in our study that in Daniel's visions he was the one who saw John and Jesus standing on the banks of the river. In the verses above, this individual tells John that he is a "fellowservant" and prophet. Angels are never considered to be a "fellowservant" or a prophet. Hebrews tells us that the angels would love to know what humans have experienced when it comes to the salvation by grace. Holy Angels cannot sin and Jesus did not die for the sins of angels, but for the sins of man. I believe this messenger/fellow servant/prophet is none other than Daniel himself.

Rev. 22:10
And he saith unto me, Seal not the sayings of the prophecy of this book: for the time is at hand.

Once again, this verse lends more credence to the theory that this "messenger" is Daniel the prophet. The messenger tells John to "Seal not the sayings of the prophecy of this book," but when Daniel saw some of the same visions, he was told to "seal the book" of his vision until the "time of the end."

Dan. 12:4, 9
[4]But thou, O Daniel, shut up the words, and seal the book, *even* to the time of the end: many shall run to and fro, and knowledge shall be increased.
[9]And he said, Go thy way, Daniel: for the words *are* closed up and sealed till the time of the end.

Is it not fitting that Jesus told Daniel to "seal the book, to the time of the end" and say no more, yet Daniel is the "messenger' to relate many of the "sayings" of this book to John? It is somewhat like a football game where the quarterback who has thrown the football many times from one end of the field to the other and is taken out for a rest. However, just before the team is about to score the touchdown, the coach sends the quarterback back in to call the play and pass the ball to the running back to make the score. I believe Daniel was the quarterback and John was the running back and together they scored the biggest prophecy of end times.

Rev. 22:11
He that is unjust, let him be unjust still: and he which is filthy, let him be filthy still: and he that is righteous, let him be righteous still: and he that is holy, let him be holy still.

There is no changing after the grave and God's judgments are true and just. Someone who dies and is not saved will always be unsaved, "unjust," and someone who is saved will always be saved forever, "righteous." Those evil angels who sided with Satan will always be evil, "filthy," and those holy angels will always be holy, "holy."

Rev. 22:12
And, behold, I come quickly; and my reward is with me, to give every man according as his work shall be.
Rev. 22:13
I am Alpha and Omega, the beginning and the end, the first and the last.

Jesus is the beginning and the end. He is coming again. He created all things and controls all things. Jesus has always been in control of everything and He will never allow anything to become out of control. There are those who state that Jesus never claimed to be God. I say to them, you have never read the Bible, for Jesus does claim this many times and the Bible is written about Him and the relationship a trusting individual can have with Him. What further proof does one need to see that the "first and the last" could be none other than God Himself?

Rev. 22:14
Blessed *are* they that do his commandments, that they may have right to the tree of life, and may enter in through the gates into the city.

Once again, those who have trusted Jesus as personal Savior will enter into the New Jerusalem and eternity with Christ. He is not teaching that one can be saved by just obeying His commandments, but those who are saved will want to obey His commandments because of their love and devotion to Him. Those who do not want to obey His commandments should double-check their hearts to see if they truly have trusted Him as Lord and Savior. To not want to obey His commandments means that a person is either backslidden or unsaved. To the human eye and mind, it is hard to tell the difference. However, the individual knows, if they will be true to themselves and God and examine their own self. True self-examination and repentance is the way to trusting Christ as Savior.

Rev. 22:15
For without *are* dogs, and sorcerers, and whoremongers, and murderers, and idolaters, and whosoever loveth and maketh a lie.

Outside of Christianity are all sorts of evil people. They are waiting to devour you and cause you to stumble. Stand on the truth of God's Word and flee the Devil and make a stand against evil every chance you have. Remember that you cannot fellowship with evil. An unequal yoke with evil will not cause evil to become righteous, but evil will cause you to stumble.

Rev. 22:16
I Jesus have sent mine angel to testify unto you these things in the churches. I am the root and the offspring of David, *and* the bright and morning star.
Rev. 22:17
And the Spirit and the bride say, Come. And let him that heareth say, Come. And let him that is athirst come. And whosoever will, let

him take the water of life freely.

Jesus affirms His signature on these prophecies that they are God-given. He is the "bright and morning star," the light that shines in a dark place, the star of David, the Star out of Jacob, the one and only true light. Without light, you cannot see the truth. This is why Jesus is referred to as the light, "the bright and morning star." Remember in Revelation 2:26-28, Jesus told those who trust Him as Lord and Savior "And I will give him the morning star." Jesus is the Morning Star!

The invitation is once again given to all who read and heed His call to salvation. It is the Holy Spirit who draws someone to Christ. It is the believers, "the bride," whose responsibility it is to spread the Word. Then those who heed His tug at their heart and accept Him, are invited to take of the "water of life freely." Jesus is the "water of life," the "living water."

Rev. 22:18
For I testify unto every man that heareth the words of the prophecy of this book, If any man shall add unto these things, God shall add unto him the plagues that are written in this book:
Rev. 22:19
And if any man shall take away from the words of the book of this prophecy, God shall take away his part out of the book of life, and out of the holy city, and *from* the things which are written in this book.

Verses 18-19 are stern warnings to anyone who adds to or takes away from the words of this book. The warning relates to anyone adding to or taking away from "this book," meaning the Book of Revelation. Even though this warning refers to the Book of Revelation, it certainly applies to any book of the Bible. We are never to add to nor take away from God's word. I believe we must be very careful in applying the interpretation also. The only way to interpret scripture is to allow scripture to interpret itself. In other words, you cannot set a doctrine based on one statement in scripture. I think the best statement about scripture interpretation that I have heard is "when the plain sense of scripture makes common sense, then seek no other sense, else it becomes nonsense."

God pronounces awful consequences to those who add to or take away from His Word. He will allow the plagues of this book to be pronounced upon the guilty party. It also states that His name will be removed from the book of life. Therefore, the only type of people who add to or take away from God's Word can be classified as "unsaved," since a truly saved person will never have their name blotted out of the book of life. Can I then state with all authority, based on scripture, that anyone who states they have received additional scripture from God, after the Book of Revelation, is unsaved? Absolutely! It is not I who would be making the pronouncement, it is Jesus Christ! Someone might believe that the Book of Revelation was not the last written book of the Bible. To them I suggest that the majority of Bible scholars from the early church and forward believed that this was truly the last inspired book that was written.

There is no need for new revelation because the Word of God is the final revelation or revealing to man. Some lay people and preachers today claim to have received new revelation from God and use the phrase(s) "thus saith the Lord" or "the Lord has prophesied through me" or "the Holy Spirit has given me new revelation." These statements stand on dangerous ground, for they are telling their hearers that God has given new revelation. All revelation is given in the existing Word of God and there is no new revelation. Today, Christians are illuminated as they read the word, meaning they have been enlightened into further meaning of a particular scripture that they may have never seen before, but they are not given new revelation. I would run from those who state they have been given extra revelation. Cults have been created by the same methods. Once and forever, all revelation ceased at the penning of the last verse of Revelation as stated in Verses 18-19.

Rev. 22:20
He which testifieth these things saith, Surely I come quickly. Amen.
Even so, come, Lord Jesus.
Rev. 22:21
The grace of our Lord Jesus Christ *be* with you all. Amen.

I hope you have enjoyed this study of Revelation and end-time events. I also hope you have become more excited about the Second Coming of Jesus Christ to earth and understand a little more about what the future will bring. If you have, may I invite you to tell others about this book and how it has been an encouragement to you. Also, please be about our Father's business of telling others about the saving knowledge of Jesus Christ, so they can share the joy of being a part of the New Jerusalem with us.

I encourage you to visit our website at revealpublishing.com and give us your comments.

May God richly bless the reader of this book. Come quickly Lord Jesus! Amen!

If you have come to know the Lord Jesus as your personal Savior and Lord as a direct or indirect result of this book, we would love for you to share this great news with us at our website.

Comments and book orders can also be made through our website:

www.revealpublishing.com

Appendix One

Chronology of Events

- Letters to the Seven Churches – Church history/prophecy
- Rapture of the Church
- Judgment Seat of Christ – Christians in heaven
- Jesus - Only one worthy to open the sealed book
- Antichrist arrives on the scene
- Seven-Year Tribulation period begins
- Two godly witnesses arrive on the scene
- Russia and her Muslim allies attack Israel
- Harlot religious system incorporated
- 1st Seal – White Horse – Antichrist conquers
- 2nd Seal – Red Horse - Peace taken from the earth
- 3rd Seal – Black Horse - Famine across the earth
- 4th Seal – Pale Horse - 1/4 of population killed
- 5th Seal – Saints in heaven ask about when God's vengeance will occur
- 6th Seal – Earthquake, sun darkened, moon turns like blood, stars fall from sky, atmospheric changes, mountains and hills moved out of their places
- 144,000 Evangelists sealed by God
- 7th Seal – Silence in heaven for 1/2 hour
- 1st Trumpet – 1/3 trees burned up and all green grass burned
- 2nd Trumpet – 1/3 sea becomes blood, 1/3 creatures in sea die, 1/3 shipping destroyed
- 3rd Trumpet – 1/3 fresh water undrinkable
- 4th Trumpet – 1/3 sun, moon and stars darkened
- 5th Trumpet – Locus/scorpion-like demons torment unsaved mankind for 5 months
- 6th Trumpet – 4 demons released from Euphrates River
- 3rd Temple is measured
- The middle of the Seven-Year Tribulation

- Last 3½ years of the Tribulation begin
- Temple defiled by the Antichrist
- Murder of the two godly witnesses
- 7th Trumpet – Christ's reign on earth predicted
- War in heaven - Satan and his demons kicked out of heaven
- Harlot Church and Rome destroyed
- Antichrist head wound and possessed by Satan
- False Prophet appears and 666 mark of the beast begins
- Jews persecuted
- Jewish remnant flee to Petra
- 144,000 Evangelists in heaven
- Gospel preached worldwide – Great commission fulfilled
- 1st Bowl – Sores on those who have the mark of the beast – 666
- 2nd Bowl – Sea becomes blood – Every soul in the sea dies
- 3rd Bowl – All fresh water becomes blood and cannot drink
- 4th Bowl – Sun scorches mankind
- 5th Bowl – Antichrist headquarters and kingdom thrust into complete darkness
- 6th Bowl – Euphrates River dried up
- 7th Bowl – Earth thrust into imbalance, earthquake, Jerusalem divided into 3 parts, 100-pound hailstones fall from the sky
- In one hour the new city of Babylon and its economic system are destroyed by God
- Wedding in heaven of Jesus and His Church
- Gathering of the birds and beast to the Battle of Armageddon
- Gathering of the Antichrist nations to the Battle of Armageddon
- 2nd Coming of Jesus and His holy angels and His saints from heaven to earth

- Battle of Armageddon and surrounding areas
- Jesus stands on Mount of Olives
- Antichrist armies destroyed with fire
- Antichrist and False Prophet cast into the Lake of Fire
- Judgment of Nations of those still alive on earth, unsaved cast into Hell, saved to remain on earth and replenish the earth
- Satan bound and chained in the bottomless pit for one thousand years
- Resurrection of Tribulation and Old Testament saints
- One thousand-year reign of Jesus Christ and His saints on earth
- Satan loosed, makes war with Christ and His saints again, Satan's armies destroyed
- Satan cast into the Lake of Fire
- Great White Throne of Judgment of unbelievers – unsaved taken from Hell and judged and cast into the Lake of Fire along with Death
- Old atmosphere and earth reformed by fire
- New atmosphere and earth formed for habitation of all the saints of all the ages and Christ
- New Jerusalem comes down from heaven to hover just above the earth
- All tears wiped away – No more death, pain, sorrow or crying
- New Jerusalem described
- Eternity Future

Printed in the United States
201321BV00004B/217-294/P